Hezbollah in International Law

Hezbollah in International Law

Mireille Rebeiz

EDINBURGH
University Press

Edinburgh University Press is one of the leading university presses in the UK. Publishing new research in the arts and humanities, EUP connects people and ideas to inspire creative thinking, open new perspectives and shape the world we live in. For more information, visit www.edinburghuniversitypress.com.

Edinburgh University Press Ltd
13 Infirmary Street, Edinburgh EH1 1LT

Typeset in 10.5/13 Adobe Sabon by
IDSUK (DataConnection) Ltd
Printed and bound in the UK using 100% renewable electricity by
CPI Group (UK) Ltd

A CIP record for this book is available from the British Library

ISBN 978 1 3995 5572 2 (hardback)
ISBN 978 1 3995 5574 6 (webready PDF)
ISBN 978 1 3995 5575 3 (epub)

EU Authorised Representative:
Easy Access System Europe
Mustamäe tee 50, 10621 Tallinn, Estonia
gpsr.requests@easproject.com

MIX
Paper | Supporting responsible forestry
FSC® C013604
www.fsc.org

This book is printed using paper from well-managed forests, recycling and other controlled sources

Contents

Acknowledgements

My interest in writing about Hezbollah as the State of Lebanon stems from my dismay about seeing my beloved home turn into something I no longer recognise, and nothing hurts more than witnessing its collapse. For years now, I have been helplessly watching Hezbollah's gradual takeover. There is nothing I can personally do except write, for writing is my form of resistance against the Iranisation of Lebanon.

This project would not have been possible without my crew's support: my husband, my child, my dog and my two cats. Thank you for all your sacrifices, for the space and time you gave me to focus on my writing, for your love and for believing in me.

I also want to thank my childhood friend, Dr Josiane Yazbeck, for the long legal discussions we had over Whatsapp; Professor of Law Sara Gerke for reading my work and for her insightful comments; all the librarians and Interlibrary Loan team at Dickinson College, without whom I would not have been able to do my work; my Mama, who taught me that it is our duty to stand up for what is right; my Baba, whose voice and spirit will always remain my guiding star.

To my Amareh, because without you, I am nothing.
You are my world,
Mireille

Abbreviations

ANF	Al Nusrah Front
AP I	Additional Protocol I to the Geneva Conventions of 12 August 1949 and relating to the Protection of Victims of International Armed Conflicts (Protocol I)
AP II	Additional Protocol II to the Geneva Conventions of 12 August 1949 and relating to the Protection of Victims of Non-International Armed Conflicts (Protocol II)
ARSIWA	Articles on Responsibility of States for Internationally Wrongful Acts
CAT	The Committee Against Torture
CRT	Critical Race Theory
CTC	Counter-Terrorism Committee
E. O.	Executive Order
EU	European Union
FPM	Free Patriotic Movement
GC I	Geneva Convention I for the Amelioration of the Condition of the Wounded and Sick in Armed Forces in the Field
GC II	Geneva Convention II for the Amelioration of the Condition of the Wounded, Sick and Shipwrecked Members of Armed Forces at Sea
GC III	Geneva Convention III Relative to the Treatment of Prisoners of War
GC IV	Geneva Convention IV Relative to the Protection of Civilian Persons in Time of War
GCC	Gulf Cooperation Council
ICCPR	International Covenant on Civil and Political Rights
ICESCR	International Covenant on Economic, Social and Cultural Rights
ICJ	International Court of Justice

ICRC	The International Committee of the Red Cross
ICTJ	The International Center for Transitional Justice
ICTR	The International Criminal Tribunal for Rwanda
ICTY	The International Criminal Tribunal for the former Yugoslavia
IDF	Israel Defence Forces
ISIS/ISIL	Islamic State of Iraq and Syria or Islamic State of Iraq and Levant
LAF	Lebanese Armed Forces
LF	Lebanese Forces
MP	Member of Parliament
NATO	The North Atlantic Treaty Organisation
NSA	Non-State Actor
OFAC	Office of Foreign Assets Control – US Department of Treasury
OHCHR	The Office of the United Nations High Commissioner for Human Rights
PLO	Palestine Liberation Organisation
PSP	Progressive Socialist Party
STL	Special Tribunal for Lebanon
UN	The United Nations
UNRWA	The United Nations Relief and Works Agency for Palestine Refugees in the Near East
WHO	World Health Organisation

Glossary

Amal	Lebanese Resistance Regiments
Al-Muqawamah al-Islamiyyah	The Islamic Resistance (which implies Hezbollah)
Dar al-Harb	Territory of War
Dar al-Islam	Territory of Peace
Dawla	Local Government or State
Jihad	War or Struggle
Jizyah	Tax
Kataeb	Right Wing Christian Group (also known as Phalanges)
La Ghaleb wala Maghloub	No Victor and No Vanquished
Majlis al-Shura	The Council
Al-Mithaq al-Watani	National Pact
Umma	Communities of Muslims regardless of ethnicities, borders and governments
Wilayat al-faqih	Guardianship of the Islamic jurist

Chapter 1

General Introduction

This book examines the legal status of Hezbollah as a State or armed non-State actor in Lebanon. The legal classification of armed entities as State or non-State actor is of great importance and has become particularly relevant after the Hamas terrorist attack on Israel on 7 October 2023 and Hezbollah's intervention in the conflict the following day. In fact, as war rages in Gaza, Israel and Lebanon, international lawyers are confronted with serious legal questions: some are related to allegations of war crimes and genocide, others are relevant to the legal classification of Hamas as State or armed non-State actor on the Palestine-Israel front as well as the legal classification of Hezbollah on the Lebanon-Israel front.

The distinction between the two categories of State and non-State actor carries consequences in the international legal system. First, it regulates the qualification of the conflict itself as international or non-international armed conflict or internal disturbance or tensions, which impacts the rules for war or its prevention (or *jus ad bellum*) and determines the applicability of international humanitarian law (or *jus in bello*) and international human rights law. For instance, the distinction between State and non-State actors as well as the qualification of the conflict have an immediate effect on the rules relevant to the use of force and its proportionality, detention and parties' conduct during hostilities. Second, the legal classification of an armed entity and the conflict in which it is engaged affect criminal law, for accountability in international criminal law is different from that in domestic criminal law.

For some scholars, Hamas is a non-State actor. Violence between Israel and Hamas does not call for the application of international humanitarian law, as it amounts to terrorism. Therefore, only Israeli domestic law applies. For others, Hamas is representative of the occupied State of Palestine, and the war is thus international armed conflict. For John Balouziyeh, the North American Regional Forum Liaison Officer for the International Bar Association's War Crimes Committee in New York, the answer is not evident:

> . . . if Hamas is deemed to be a State actor, its fighters could be granted combatant immunity and prisoner of war status if captured, but if Hamas is deemed to be an armed group under the law of non-international armed conflict, combatant immunity would not apply, and its fighters could be tried under Israeli criminal law if captured.[1]

It is true that the conflict between Israel and Hamas is more complex than the one between Israel and Hezbollah, for various reasons including the fact that Palestine's statehood is up for discussion; Lebanon's statehood is not.

Despite this complexity and the differences in the scenarios, the question of the legal classification of Hezbollah as a State or non-State actor remains significant and even urgent because, at the time of writing this book, violence is quickly escalating between Hezbollah and Israel.[2] Understanding the legal classification of Hezbollah as a State or non-State actor will generate legal consequences related to the applicability of international humanitarian law, international human rights law, international criminal law and State responsibility. Therefore, considering past events, it is necessary to propose a detailed examination of the legal status of Hezbollah in times of both war and peace. This book asks the following questions: what is the legal status of Hezbollah under international law? Is it a subject of international law with legal capacity? Is Hezbollah the State of Lebanon? How would this legal classification impact *jus ad bellum* and *jus in bello*, and what would the State's responsibility be?

Promptly answering that Hezbollah is a terrorist organisation does not explain the nature of its relationship with the Lebanese State, nor the consequences of this relationship for international humanitarian law and international human rights law. It certainly does not answer the question of the State's responsibility for the wrong-doing of another State or an armed non-State actor.

Rationale

It is easy to proclaim Hezbollah to be a terrorist non-State entity. However, the situation is not so simple when one considers Hezbollah's relations with the Lebanese State: there are times when Hezbollah collaborates with Lebanon. Then there are times where Hezbollah acts against the Lebanese State; other times, Hezbollah acts as an Iranian

State agent operating from Lebanese soil. Depending on the context, these varying scenarios generate different legal consequences. Hezbollah's legal status was seriously considered during the 2006 armed conflict with Israel; its classification as a State or non-State entity determined the nature of the armed conflict (international or non-international), the applicable international humanitarian law, the right to self-defence and State responsibility.

The question was once again raised in the context of the Syrian armed conflict. Hezbollah has been present in Syria since 2011. The legal classification of Hezbollah as State or non-State actor plays an important role when deciding on State responsibility and when prosecuting war crimes and crimes against humanity. Today, the question remains relevant as violence has been escalating between Hezbollah and Israel since 8 October 2023. Israel already announced that it will hold the State of Lebanon responsible for Hezbollah's attacks and therefore target the entire Lebanese territory.[3] It is true that a relationship between two entities does not necessarily mean understanding the classification of each entity on its own. One may understand the relationship between points A and B without fully understanding the nature of A and B.

This statement does not hold true in the case of international law and the question of statehood. In fact, international law has prerequisites for an entity to be considered a State. However, it does not have a clear definition for non-State entities which are only defined by negation and in relation to State entities. For this reason, it is essential to examine Hezbollah in relation to the State of Lebanon. Understanding this relation in a specific context allows for a better understanding of State responsibility.

Research Questions

This book answers the following main questions:

1. What is the legal status of Hezbollah under international law? Is it a subject of international law, or does it possess an international legal personality?
2. Is Hezbollah a State? Is Hezbollah the State of Lebanon?
3. Is Hezbollah a non-State actor? If so, what kind?
4. Is Hezbollah an international organisation?
5. Is it a national liberation movement or a terrorist organisation?
6. What are the legal consequences of all these categories in international law?

7. Shifting the discussion from the legal status of Hezbollah to its responsibility, to what extent do Hezbollah's acts engage Lebanon's responsibility?
8. Can Lebanon be responsible for the wrong-doing of a non-State actor operating from its territory?
9. Can Lebanon be responsible for the wrong-doing of Iran's wrongful acts both domestically and internationally?

Theoretical Frame

There are subjects and objects of international law. A subject of international law 'is an entity that bears international legal rights or duties'.[4] Also known as an 'international legal person', a subject of international law can fully participate in the international legal system, exercise rights and observe duties under international law. It is an actor, or player, on the international stage,[5] an entity that 'is not subordinate to another authority; in other words, it must have the ability to recognise any entity as a superior'.[6] By contrast, objects of international law are 'the who, what, and where the subjects act upon [. . .] the legitimate topics of international legal regulation'.[7]

Traditionally, States are the 'original, primary and universal subjects of international law'.[8] In this conservative view, non-State actors are not subjects of international law:[9] 'They have no inherent authority to create international conventional or customary law; they are incapable of public accountability which is necessary in order to exercise the authority to create international laws'.[10] They depend on States, which are the gatekeepers of international law. Another theory argues that States are not the only subjects of international law and do not have the monopoly over creating international law. Social actors and non-State entities can also be subjects of international law – for example, the Holy See of the Vatican, belligerent or insurgent groups and international organisations.

The Holy See, where the Pontiff rules as the leader of the Catholic Church, has a territory, people and government. The Holy See acts as a State, holds rights and duties and has signed multiple treaties.[11] Belligerents and insurgents, who may potentially develop into States, could also be attributed rights and duties usually reserved for States. To give an example, during the Spanish Civil War, the Republican and legally elected Spanish Government was replaced by the Nationalist Government led by General Franco. The international community viewed the Republican Government and the Nationalist Government as belligerents and therefore subjects of international law with rights and duties. They treated them as equal, as if they both had been the one and true representative of Spain.[12]

The Confederacy in the United States can serve as another example of a non-State entity given rights and duties as if it were a subject of international law. In fact, the Confederacy, which was created by states who wanted to secede from the United States in 1861, was recognised by France, Great Britain and Mexico as a belligerent in the civil war. The Confederacy even signed international agreements with these countries. Unlike Spain, where a belligerent party managed to take over the State's control, the insurgents of the Confederacy failed to create a new State. However, despite this failure, they were still treated as subjects of international law.[13] These examples reflect the following:

> Throughout the history of modern international relations, the main feature of subjects of international law has been their ability to assert they are not subordinates to other authorities; in other words, subjects of international were those entities *superiorem non recognoscentes*, able not to recognise any superior within the international community.[14]

This concept of 'no higher authority' stems from the principle that there is no hierarchy within the international community; it is only composed of peers. This principle is easy to apply in the context of States, since all States are equal in the eyes of international law.[15] As seen in the previous two examples of Spain and the Confederacy, this principle applies to insurgents and belligerents as well when these threaten the existence of the already formed government. In other words, the belligerent group might become so powerful that the international community has no other choice but to recognise the existence of two subjects of international law: the legally formed government and representative of the State, and the belligerent group.

Intergovernmental organisations such as the European Union or the African Union are also subjects of international law. They form independent entities with rights and duties separate from those attributed to their State-members. In 1980, the International Court of Justice (ICJ) rendered an Advisory Opinion on the interpretation of the Agreement of 25 March 1951 between the World Health Organisation (WHO) and Egypt. The case was introduced by the Director-General of the WHO, and the ICJ had to determine whether an international organisation was a subject of international law. In its Advisory Opinion, the ICJ stated that the 'term public international organisations [. . .] include only international organisations the membership of which consists of States or Governments, and understands that it has been used in this sense in a number of recent international instruments, including the Statute of the International Court of Justice'.[16] The ICJ added that '[i]nternational organisations are subjects of international law and, as such, are bound by any obligations incumbent upon them under general rules of international law, under their constitutions or under international agreements to which they are parties'.[17]

This is not the first time that the ICJ examines the status of an international organisation as a subject of international law. In 1949, the court held that the functionality of the United Nations meant that the organisation possessed an international personality and had the capacity to operate on an international level: 'It can bring an international claim against the responsible *de jure* or *de facto* government with a view to obtaining the reparation due in respect of the damage causes the United Nations'.[18] Thus, international organisations are subjects of international law. They must abide by the instruments that created them and by the treaties that they conclude. They have rights and duties in the international community.

This book agrees that the qualification of 'subject of international law' is no longer exclusive to States and extends to non-State entities such as intergovernmental organisations, international organisations, belligerents and insurgents. While these non-State entities lack sovereignty, they remain important actors in the international community, ones that do not have a higher authority. However, it would be reckless to extend the label of 'subject of international law' to every non-State entity. Clearly, one must proceed on a case-by-case basis and examine the authority within the entity itself, its relations to others to determine its level of independence and whether it really operates as higher authority.

If these two tests are inconclusive, it is possible to shift the focus from legal personality to legal responsibility.[19] In other words, instead of checking an entity's rights and duties in international law, one can turn to determine its responsibilities in a specific context. This approach is particularly useful, especially for international criminal law. Acquaviva has stated:

> The necessary condition for an entity to be considered a 'power', a subject of international law, seems to be the fact that the entity is able to establish itself as *superiom non recognoscens*, as an entity that engages in relations as a peer with other subjects and that, therefore is held responsible when it causes damage. The best way to understand if an entity is really *superiom non recognoscens* and if it is indeed a subject of international law (whether the international agrees to calling it 'state' or not) is the fact that breaches emanating from its 'organs' – considered in the broadest terms – are imputed to that entity, and not to others. Thus,

> although from a logical standpoint personality comes before responsibility, the latter is a mean to carry out the complex empirical analysis needed to establish whether an entity is sovereign.[20]

Considering the above and in order to fully understand Hezbollah's status, it is important to define key terms such as 'State' and 'non-State actor'. To do so, this book will rely on the Peace Treaty of Westphalia of 1648, which laid the foundations of the modern concept of statehood. It will also examine the 1933 Montevideo Convention on the Rights and Duties of States which have codified the definition of statehood. Article 1 stipulates: 'The State as a person of international law should possess the following qualifications: (a) a permanent population; (b) a defined territory; (c) government; and (d) capacity to enter into relations with the other States'.[21]

James Crawford and Rowan Nicholson have adopted this definition of statehood. James Crawford (1948–2021) – an outstanding public international lawyer, member of the International Law Commission and judge at the International Court of Justice – shaped the field particularly with his work on the issue of statehood. He is best known for his book *The Creation of States in International Law*,[22] which in 2007 has appeared in its second edition with Oxford University Press and to this day remains a foundational text. Crawford's *The Creation of States of International Law* and Nicholson's *Statehood and the State-Like in International Law*[23] have argued that, for an entity to exist as a State, it must have legal personality, and it must exist as a fact with rights and duties on the international stage. In other words, it must exist as a subject of international law.

Moreover, for an entity to exist as a State, it must be recognised as such. Crawford and Nicholson have advanced two theories: effectiveness theory (which Crawford has called declaratory theory) and recognition theory (which Crawford has termed constitutive theory). As for effectiveness theory, an entity can only be a State when it has some non-negotiable criteria such as territory, people, government and the capacity to enter into relations with other States. Here, Crawford has added the criterion of independence. As for recognition theory, a State is a State when recognised or declared as such by other States. For Crawford, historically, statehood recognition has depended on domestic laws and not on the will of other States. Today, however, we live in the era of positive laws, and this form of recognition is no longer valid. Therefore, statehood recognition depends on State actors and the international community.

Crawford, Nicholson and other scholars such as Yaël Ronen[24] have recognised that the traditional definition of statehood is out-dated and that the two theories of effectiveness and recognition cannot necessarily explain some political realities. Furthermore, international law does not offer a solid definition of non-State actors. This legal conundrum becomes even more complicated when (1) an entity acts like a State but is not recognised as such; and (2) an entity uses force, which is traditionally an exclusive State right. To solve this puzzle, Nicholson has advanced the theory of 'State-like' actors (which Ronen has called 'quasi-State'). This expression refers to entities that are in-between State and non-State actors. They have rights and duties on the international stage, yet they are not recognised as a State.

To understand Hezbollah's legal status in international law, this book relies on Crawford and Nicholson's approaches to statehood and subject of international law; it agrees that the traditional definition of statehood is out-dated and that the two theories of statehood recognition cannot capture Hezbollah's reality. Consequently, this book proposes to examine Hezbollah's status as a quasi-State (or State-like entity) with some rights and duties and asks whether a quasi-State is a subject of international law. Since the quasi-State approach is new and has only existed in the theoretical realm, this book will move forward to examine Hezbollah's status as a non-State actor. To do so, it relies on the work of several scholars, particularly in the field of international criminal law. Furthermore, this book will shifts the discussion to State responsibility and examine Lebanon's responsibilities for Hezbollah and Iran's wrong-doings.

The Structure of this Study

This book is divided into a general introduction (Chapter 1), three parts with seven chapters and a general conclusion (Chapter 9.).

Part I includes two chapters: Chapter 2 will examine the history of the Lebanese Civil War, the birth and rise of Hezbollah, its ideology, structure, warfare techniques and involvement in Lebanese political life as of 1992. It will also study the demographic shift in Lebanon since the 1970s and its impact on Hezbollah. The sectarian nature of the civil war forced many Lebanese to migrate. The size of the once-thriving Christian community and the educated middle class has decreased drastically. Furthermore, the armed presence of Palestinian refugees and the recent influx of Syrian refugees have compounded the crisis and played a great role in empowering Hezbollah. Chapter 3 will focus on Hezbollah's legal classification according to Lebanese law. It will examine the 1909 Law on Associations, the Taif Agreement of 1989 and the General Amnesty Law of 1991, arguing that domestic laws and State practice indicate that Hezbollah exists as a political party, national and international non-profit organisation and legal armed force in Lebanon. The two questions that follow are relevant to the legal classification of Hezbollah in international law and whether it is a State, quasi-State, or non-State actor.

Part II will examine whether Hezbollah is a State by distinguishing between State, quasi-State and non-State entity. Chapter 4 will discuss the legal definition of statehood and two of the theories of statehood recognition. It will answer two questions: what is a State, and how can a State be recognised? Chapter 5 will take up the theory outlined in Chapter 4 and apply it to Hezbollah; it will conclude that the definition of statehood therein does not apply to Hezbollah. Chapter 5 will then turn to two alternative theories: the definition of statehood in Islamic law and the new theory of quasi-State. Chapter 5 will argue that Hezbollah operates outside the traditional realm of international law, for Islamic law has a different approach to authority and a different definition of statehood. In this scenario, Hezbollah's statehood in the traditional sense becomes irrelevant.

Another possibility is the theory of the quasi-State, according to which Hezbollah acts like a State but lacks the international recognition of statehood. Many international lawyers have urged the acceptance of the theory of the State-like or quasi-State entity, especially in the context of the Global South and of weak or failing States. While this theory certainly has some merits, it is not yet State practice. Consequently, Hezbollah is not a State. Although it acts as a State, it is a non-State entity.

Part III will study the multiple types of non-State actors, and whether Hezbollah qualifies as a national liberation movement, insurgency, rebellion or terrorist organisation. Also, it will examine Lebanon's responsibility for Hezbollah's wrong-doings. Chapter 6 will offer general comments on the growth of non-State actors, their role in society and their status in the case of use of force. Chapter 7 will distinguish between the categories of national liberation movement, insurgency, rebellion and terrorist organisation, examining international and regional instruments, various domestic laws and the position of the Special Tribunal for Lebanon (STL) to determine Hezbollah's legal status as an armed non-State actor and potentially subject of international law. Chapter 8 will address the question of Lebanon's legal responsibility for Hezbollah activities. It will consider Lebanon's responsibility by attribution or for complicity and differentiate between State responsibility for the wrong-doing of a non-State actor and State responsibility for the wrong-doing of another State. Can Hezbollah's acts be fully attributed to Lebanon? Is Lebanon complicit in Hezbollah's unlawful acts? Since Iran funds Hezbollah as per the acknowledgement of its Secretary General, can Iran be held responsible for Hezbollah's unlawful acts in and outside of Lebanon? The question of legal responsibility is important as it allows us to understand the nature of the Hezbollah-Iran relationship and therefore decide whether Hezbollah is a subject of international law, one that acts independently with no higher authority.

Methodology and Challenges

Some challenges are related to the topic itself; others are related to the research method. Non-State armed actors present a legal challenge to the international community. Answers regarding their status and responsibilities vary, depending on the setting in which they operate. They may function in domestic and/or international contexts; they may be legal domestically and illegal in the eyes of international law; they may be involved in non-international or international armed conflicts. They exist in what Katharine Fortin and Ezequiel Heffes have called the 'shadowland', for they operate in multi-layered, overlapping, complementing but also sometimes conflicting legal frameworks. Therefore, 'it is not outside the imagination of international law for an individual to be an armed group member, terrorist, criminal, law-abiding citizen, fighter, military leader, lawmaker and law enforcer at the same moment in time'.[25] As we will see, Hezbollah exists in this 'shadowland', in a complex eco-system where legality and illegality co-exist.

Furthermore, armed groups impact international humanitarian law and are bound by some of its provisions. Yet, international law is hesitant to recognise their role and status as subjects of international law. Consequently, armed groups are only examined from the States' position and through the States' lens. They are almost never examined from their own positions and, therefore, may always be operating from outside the law.[26] This would be the case with Hezbollah, Hamas and other similar entities. One does not stop to examine their motivation or how they define themselves. For this reason, armed groups can exist in 'a web of prohibitions and permissions that sometimes contradict each other'.[27] It is important to recognise that it is hard to find the right balance in how to deal with these entities, for legalising them may threaten a State's existence.

There exists one more challenge related to the topic itself – that is, the fluidity of the current situation in the Middle East. At the time of writing this book, Israel is still bombing Gaza and Lebanon. On 1 October 2024, nearly a year after the attacks of 7 October on Israeli civilians, Israel launched an intense air campaign and ground invasion of southern Lebanon. A cease-fire was implemented on 26 November 2024. In February 2025, Israel announced that its forces would remain in five strategic points inside Lebanon, in violation of the terms of the cease-fire which had set a deadline for Israel's full withdrawal.[28] This serious escalation will not be addressed in this book, which considers Israel-Hezbollah relations only up to 2023.

As to the research method, this book is a library-based project with theoretical and doctrinal approaches. Comparative analysis is also employed. The benefit of these methods lies in that they attempt to organise the disorganised world of State and non-State actors. The materials examined here consist mainly of books, articles, court cases, domestic and international legislation, newspaper articles and reports by international organisations. This book focuses primarily on scholarly work published in English, with the occasional reference to work published in French or Arabic. For these, formal translation will be provided when available. This is the case for the Lebanese Constitution of 1926 and the Lebanese Criminal Code, which were translated for the Special Tribunal for Lebanon. In the absence of any official translation, the author of this book provides her own translation.

Transliteration and some terminologies may also present challenges. For instance, Hezbollah is known under other names and spellings, such as Hizbullah, Hezballah, the Party of God, the Islamic Jihad, the Islamic Resistance for the Liberation of Palestine and *al-Muqawamah al-Islamiyyah* (The Islamic Resistance), among others. To avoid potential confusion, this book adopts the spelling 'Hezbollah'.

This book lacks references to Lebanese court decisions, and there is a specific reason for this absence: in 1991, the Lebanese Parliament adopted a General Amnesty Law that forgave all crimes committed during the Lebanese Civil War (1975–91). Thereafter, numerous unlawful acts were committed by Hezbollah members; yet there exists not a single domestic court decision on the matter. Clearly, Lebanon has an accountability issue. To fill this gap, this book will turn to international adjudication and rely on decisions from the Permanent Court of International Justice, the International Court of Justice, the International Criminal Tribunal for the Former Yugoslavia, the International Criminal Tribunal for Rwanda and the Special Tribunal for Lebanon. These courts have examined issues of statehood and State responsibility, including attribution and complicity. Their cases are relevant to this book.

The present book will utilise the outside approach, which addresses the relationship between Hezbollah and external stakeholders such as the Lebanese State and international entities. It will briefly examine

Hezbollah's internal approach to law (with a concise discussion of Islamic Law). However, it will focus on how Lebanese law and international law look at Hezbollah and assess its status as an armed group.

Sources

This book will scrutinise Lebanese laws, regional and international instruments. In terms of domestic law, it relies primarily on Lebanese laws: the 1909 Law on Associations, the Lebanese Constitution of 1926, the Lebanese Criminal Code, the Taif Agreement of 1989 that amended the constitution and put an end to the civil war, and the General Amnesty Law of 1991. It will reference domestic legislations (especially criminal law) from other countries, among them the United States of America, Australia, the United Kingdom, France, Israel, Germany and Singapore. The approach is a general overview of different domestic laws for their definitions of statehood and terrorism. These countries were selected because of their strong relationship with Lebanon or their respective position on Hezbollah and terrorism.

Lebanon is an Arab State and member of the Arab League. Thus, the book will reference instruments and decisions adopted by the Arab League and neighbouring Arab States when appropriate. It also uses documents of the European Union and the African Union. Since the main issue is statehood (State/quasi-State/non-State actor), this study will heavily rely on State practice as evidence of international law: it will be based on newspaper articles in Arabic, French and English and offer a legal interpretation of facts. The intent here is not to provide a political analysis or journalistic position, but rather an analysis of the legal implications of the events described. Furthermore, this book will rely on international instruments adopted by different States, the United Nations, or the International Committee of the Red Cross.

Scope and Limits

In political science, scholars often refer to Hezbollah's statehood or terrorism. However, there exists no comprehensive analysis of Hezbollah's legal classification, which has been taken for granted by many. The originality of this book resides in its detailed legal analysis of Hezbollah's status, one that goes beyond superficial political statements. Furthermore, to my knowledge, there has been no complete examination of Hezbollah as a State/non-State actor in international law. Therefore, this book fills a serious gap in international law and terrorism studies. However, it is beyond the present scope to examine all of Hezbollah's unlawful acts. The book primarily focuses on Hezbollah's status according to domestic laws, the 2006 armed conflict with Israel, the 2008 conflict in Lebanon, Hezbollah's involvement in the Syrian conflict and the attack of 14 February 2005, killing former Prime Minister Rafic Hariri and twenty-one others and injured at least 226 persons. It does not investigate Lebanon's current crisis, nor crimes committed during the Lebanese Civil War.

Although Lebanon is predominantly a Muslim country, Islamic law is not the main source of law. In fact, Islamic law only applies to those who practice Islam and to family matters (marriage, divorce, inheritance, custody and so on). Since Hezbollah is a conservative Shiite Islamic group, this book will briefly outline Islamic law and Hezbollah's approach to it. However, it does not reference international Islamic law: 'Islamic international law may be of great historical interest, and a source of inspiration for Islamic militants, but it has no relevance whatsoever for contemporary international law'.[29] In fact, early Islamic international law was about peace, war, conquest, rules of engagement and relationship between Muslim and non-Muslim States.

With the disintegration of the Islamic Empire in the eleventh century, the application of Islamic international law disappeared:

> From the nineteenth century onwards, we see the emergence of modern nation states in the Muslim world. Their modernity is reflected, from a legal perspective, in the adoption of Western legal systems ad laws, the introduction of the concepts of citizenship and nationality [. . .] and participation as members of the international community in international relations as conducted and developed on a worldwide scale.[30]

Even the most conservative Muslim countries, such as Saudi Arabia and Pakistan, where Islamic law is applied to domestic affairs such as family law and penal code, agree on international transactions and other State relations according to international law.

It is true that many countries from the Global South, including Muslim countries, tend to see international law as a space of western hegemony. Nevertheless, they indicate their dissatisfaction in making reservations to treaties and conventions. In other words, they continue to participate in the order created by public international law, but they make sure to share their grievances. Therefore, the 'relevance of Islamic international law to the contemporary Muslim world is, at best, scant'.[31] Furthermore, Islamic international law and public international law have different foundations: the first emanates from religious leaders, while the second relies primarily on States, State practices and institutions.[32]

For this reason, this book will focus on public international law and only briefly mention Islamic law. It will reference the position of major Islamic institutions such as the Arab League, the Organisation of Islamic Cooperation and others. As we will see, their position on Hezbollah does not differ from the one adopted by the international community.

Part I
Hezbollah in Domestic Law

Introduction to Part I

Hezbollah emerged in the early 1980s, after the Israeli occupation of Lebanon. It claimed to fight for a noble cause: to represent the Shiite community who had thus far been abandoned by the Lebanese State and to resist against the Israeli occupation and American hegemony in the region. Since then, Hezbollah's agenda has evolved to include national political aspirations. In 1992, Hezbollah members won seats in parliament. In 2005, they entered the Lebanese Government. Furthermore, Hezbollah's reach has outgrown the borders of Lebanon with a rapidly developing international footprint.

This part aims to examine Hezbollah's legal classification according to domestic law. It seeks to answer the following questions: what is the legal status of Hezbollah inside Lebanon? Is it a legally recognised political party? Is it a national and international non-profit organisation? Is it a lawful armed group? To understand Hezbollah's legal status, this part includes two chapters: Chapter 2 will offer a brief history of the conflict, the birth of Hezbollah, its ideology, structure and involvement in political life after 1992. Furthermore, it will examine the shift in Lebanon's population during and after the war as well as its impact on Hezbollah in the region. Chapter 3 will discuss Hezbollah's legal status according to the 1909 Law on Associations, the Taif Agreement of 1989 and the General Amnesty Law of 1991.

It is important to note that there exists a certain level of ambiguity surrounding Hezbollah's legal status inside Lebanon. This is a complex question, and this complexity is the result of numerous factors: (1) Hezbollah emerged during the Lebanese Civil War, when lawlessness was rampant. After the General Amnesty Law of 1991, the legal status of many unlawful activities that started during the civil war was never questioned. Many continued to exist unchallenged. (2) Hezbollah's legal status will be examined in relation to the 1909 Law on Associations, which is out-dated and inadequate in today's context. (3) The Lebanese State remains a weak State. In many cases, it cannot enforce the law, nor put an end to certain practices. Consequently, the State's silence, inaction, or ineffectiveness complicates the legal interpretation of Hezbollah's acts and practices.

Despite this ambiguity, this part will argue that Hezbollah exists in Lebanon as a political party and as an armed force, as an entity that is legally accepted by the State of Lebanon.

Chapter 2

The History of Lebanon and the Rise of Hezbollah

Hezbollah, or the party of God, emerged as Islamic religious resistance during the Lebanese Civil War and after the Israeli invasion of Lebanon in 1982. Its goals have shifted over time. At first, it aimed to give a voice to the destitute Shiite community in Lebanon, to fight American and Israeli imperialism in the Middle East and to free the occupied Palestinian territories. Today, Hezbollah has a wider and more ambitious political agenda, as it seeks to control the Lebanese State, foster strong relations with Syria and Iran and develop an international presence in other countries.[1] This chapter will examine the history of the Lebanese Civil War and discuss the birth of Hezbollah, its ideology, structure, leadership, warfare and involvement in political life after 1992.

A History of the Lebanese Civil War

Before World War I, Lebanon was part of the Ottoman Empire. In 1916, the Sykes-Picot agreement divided the region between France and Great Britain.[2] After World War I and the Treaty of Versailles of 1919, Lebanon was placed under French mandate, which lasted from 1 September 1920 to 22 November 1943.

Lebanon is a multi-religious society. The Lebanese Constitution, which was promulgated on 23 May 1926, stipulates in its Article 9:

> There shall be absolute freedom of conscience. The state in rendering homage to the God Almighty shall respect all religions and creeds and shall guarantee under its protection the free exercise of all religious rites provided that public order is not disturbed. It shall also guarantee that the personal status and religious interests of the population, to whatever religious sect they belong, shall be respected.[3]

The National Pact of 1943 or *al-Mithaq al-Watani* distributed political power between the dominant religions: the president of the republic should be a Christian Maronite, the prime minister should be a Sunni Muslim and the speaker of parliament should be a Shiite Muslim. The parliament is composed of 128 seats, divided equally between Muslims and Christians, knowing that Lebanon recognises eighteen religious communities distributed as follows: five Muslim groups (Sunni, Shiite, Druze, Alawite and Ismaili), twelve Christian groups (Maronites, Greek Orthodox, Greek Catholics [also called Melkites], Armenian Orthodox, Armenian Catholics, Syriac Orthodox, Syriac Catholics, Assyrians, Chaldean Catholics, Copts, Protestants and Roman Catholics) and the Jewish community.[4] Lebanon's last census dates to 1932.[5] According to the State Department's 2019 Report on international religious freedom, 67.6 per cent of the citizens are estimated to be Muslims, 32.4 per cent Christians and 4.52 per cent Druze. There also is a small number of Jews, Baha'is, Buddhists and Hindus.[6]

Great Britain had colonial ambitions in the region and wanted to guarantee Palestine's allegiance to the West against Türkiye[7] and the Ottoman Empire.[8] In 1917, the Balfour Declaration announced support to a Jewish homeland, provided that 'nothing shall be done which may prejudice the civil and religious rights of existing non-Jewish communities in Palestine or the rights and political status enjoyed by Jews in any other country'.[9] The proclamation of the State of Israel in 1948, the Suez Canal crisis of 1956[10] and the Six Day War in 1967 resulted in a mass exodus of Palestinians to Lebanon.[11] In the early 1970s, an estimated number of 20,000 Palestinians fighters entered the country and used Lebanon as a front line to launch attacks against Israel.[12] Clashes erupted between the Lebanese and Palestinians. Some Lebanese supported the Palestinian cause, while others feared the quick increase in the Muslim population in Lebanon since most Palestinians entering Lebanon were Muslim. Some wanted to sign peace with Israel. In short, the Palestinian–Israeli conflict was exported to Lebanon.

In 1969, General Emile Bustani of the Lebanese army and Yasser Arafat, Chairman of the Palestine Liberation Organisation (PLO), signed an agreement in Egypt, 'whereby control over the 16 Palestine refugee camps in Lebanon passes from the Lebanese Armed Forces to the Palestinian Armed Struggle Command'.[13] On 21 May 1987, this agreement, known as the 'Cairo Agreement', was nullified by the Lebanese Parliament. However, the damage was already done as it effectively weakened the State of Lebanon and undermined its authority. The State of Lebanon no longer held the monopoly over the armed forces on its own territory and shared these powers with a non-State actor.[14] Violence escalated between Palestinians and Lebanese, and civil war erupted with the infamous bus incident on 13 April 1975. Gunmen belonging to the

Christian right-wing militia opened fire on a bus full of Palestinian fighters; twenty-two were killed. The Christian right-wing militia reported that this had been in response to the Palestinians' attacks on and harassment of Christian communities.[15]

In 1976, Syrian Armed Forces entered Lebanon to end the war and support the Lebanese State and Maronite community. Initially, this intervention was meant to be brief, but the Syrian Armed Forces ended up staying until 30 April 2005.The assassination of Prime Minister Rafic Hariri sparked the Cedar Revolution, which demanded their imminent departure from Lebanon.[16] Some scholars have argued that the Syrian presence in Lebanon was an occupation as it reflected Syria's intentions to re-annex Lebanon. In 1982, Israel launched 'Operation Peace for Galilee' and entered Lebanon with the objective to eliminate the PLO from Lebanon and Syria. Abandoned by the State of Lebanon, living in poverty and experiencing a high rate of illiteracy, the Shiites suffered from the Palestinian–Israeli conflict. Following years of abuse, the Shiite residents briefly welcomed the 1982 Israeli invasion, until they realised that Israeli tactics did not distinguish between them and the Palestinian fighters.[17]

The civil war lasted nearly seventeen years and ended with the signing of the Taif Agreement in 1989 in Saudi Arabia, followed by the General Amnesty Law of 1991.[18] During these years of sectarian violence, serious violations of Lebanese law and of international human rights law and humanitarian law occurred. The International Centre for Transition Justice (ICTJ) clearly recorded them in its September 2013 report titled 'Lebanon's Legacy of Political Violence: A Mapping of Serious Violations of International Human Rights and Humanitarian Law in Lebanon, 1975–2008'. In addition to the bus incident that triggered the civil war, the report provides details on other major crimes and violations. It is beyond the scope of this chapter to examine all the serious violations that took place during the Lebanese Civil War, nor is it possible to enumerate every single one of them. However, it is important to mention those that sparked international and national outcry as they depict a gloomy picture of what happened during these bloody years.

After the infamous bus incident, there occurred several clashes, notably in suburban areas. One of them was the 'Black Saturday' on 5 December 1975. Four young Christian men were kidnapped and killed. Their mutilated bodies were found in the Metn area. Other Christians met with a similar fate. In response, a Christian militia – known as Kataeb – proceeded to kidnap and murder Lebanese and Palestinian Muslims: between fifty-six and seventy were killed.[19]

Sectarian killing and forced displacement became the norm. In January 1976, Christian militias imposed a siege on the Tel al-Zaatar refugee camp and the neighbouring shanty-towns that were predominantly inhabited by Muslims. The siege was followed by a civilian massacre. In retaliation, Palestinian militias and their Lebanese Muslim allies assaulted and killed Christian civilians from the villages of Damour and Jiyeh.[20] Some were forced into displacement. Sectarian killing spread to the mountains as well, and clashes erupted between Christians and Druze.[21]

After the assassination of the Druze leader and founder of the Progressive Socialist Party (PSP) Kamal Jumblatt on 16 March 1977, violence erupted in the mountains, particularly in the Shouf area where Druze and Maronite Christians lived side by side. Many Christian civilians were kidnapped and executed, women were raped, and massacres were reported in places such as Mazraat al-Shouf (fifty-two killed), Maasser al-Shouf (twenty-one dead), al-Barouk (twenty-eight dead), Botmeh (nine victims), Kfarnabrakh (six killed) and Fraydis (six victims), among others.[22] 'Between the summer of 1975 and 1977, as a result of successive attacks that terrorized the population, around 260,000 people (more than 60 percent of the region's Christians) left'.[23] In the south, several attacks and counter-attacks took place between Israelis and their allies, the PLO fighters and Lebanese militias. During the Israeli invasion, 176 Lebanese civilians were slaughtered at a mosque. An estimated number of 700 to 1,000 Lebanese and Palestinians were killed, and about 250,000 were displaced towards the northern areas. The Christian militias that had allied themselves with the Israeli forces killed Shiite civilians, including women and children.[24]

The north was not spared either, and violence erupted between different Christian militias and the Syrian forces. In the Beqaa Valley, Christian militias – namely, the Lebanese Forces (LF) – launched attacks against the Syrian forces which retaliated in what is today known as the Battle of Zahleh. In April 1981, the Syrian Armed Forces fired hundreds of bombs on Zahleh, a predominantly Catholic village in the Beqaa Valley, killing 200 civilians and injuring over 2,000. The Syrian forces also targeted hospitals, schools and residential areas and placed Zahleh under siege.[25] Beirut and its suburbs were the stage of all kinds of serious human rights violations, from car bombs over abductions and assassinations to sectarian killing.

In September 1983, the Israeli forces withdrew from Mount Lebanon and retreated southwards. Lebanese Druze and Christian militias (that is, PSP and the LF) fought to take control over the area. The 'War of the Mountain', as it was dubbed, resulted in massive killings of civilians, the siege of the Deir-al-Qamar area from September to December 1983 and the forced departure of thousands of Christians.[26] Other battles erupted in Tripoli in 1983, between the Syrian Armed Forces and their Palestinian allies, as well as the PLO fighters and their Lebanese allies. In March 1985 and after the Israeli withdrawal, clashes erupted between the LF and the LAF.[27] Israel did not entirely withdraw from the Lebanese soil but kept the south of Lebanon under occupation, which sparked waves of violence between the Israeli forces and different Lebanese and Palestinian fighters. The Israeli occupation lasted until 24 May 2000.[28]

In September 1988, President Amine Gemayel's mandate expired. Since the parliament could not agree on a new president, Gemayel appointed the Army Commander in Chief Michel Aoun as prime minister for a military council. However, Prime Minister Salim Hoss still held his civilian cabinet and considered Gemayel's appointment a violation of the constitution. The Lebanese were divided once more. Some supported the military council and saw Aoun as a man of law and order, willing to end the Syrian occupation and to confront all militias. Others supported the civilian government.

On 14 March 1989, Aoun announced the War of Liberation against the Syrian forces, which led to a Syrian siege of the east and northeast of Beirut, massive bombardments, the killing of civilians (850 dead, 3,000 wounded) and the displacement of people of all religions from the Greater Beirut areas.[29] This assault was followed by intersectarian wars among the Shiites and the Christians themselves. On 13 October 1990, Syria launched a full-fledged assault on Aoun and his army, resulting in the latter's defeat.[30] Aoun managed to flee to the French embassy where he hid for a couple of months. Eventually, he left Lebanon to live in exile in France.[31] Many of the Lebanese officers loyal to Aoun were either executed or illegally detained by the Syrian forces in unknown locations.[32]

Violence spared no one and spread across all of Lebanon; it impacted all civilians and all religions. In its 2014 report 'Lebanon, Failing to Deal with the Past: What Cost to Lebanon?', the ICTJ stated:

> It is estimated that some 2.7 percent of the population was killed as a result of violence. 4 percent wounded (the overwhelming majority being civilians), 30 percent displaced, and about 33 percent have emigrated. Further, 0.36 percent of the population was permanently disabled, and 0.75 percent forcibly disappeared. Serious human rights violations have included systematic and mass displacement, wide-scale killing, rape, torture, arbitrary detention, and enforced disappearance.[33]

The civil war ended with the signing of the Taif Agreement in Saudi Arabi in October 1989 and its approval by the Lebanese Parliament on 4 November 1989.[34] Clashes between Hezbollah fighters and other resistance movements continued to erupt in south Lebanon as they fought against the Israeli occupation.

Hezbollah's Birth

The year 1982 marked the beginning of the Shiite resistance in Lebanon. On 6 June 1982, Israel invaded Lebanon and arrived in Beirut. Israel claimed that PLO fighters had violated the terms of the eleven-month cease-fire with their attempt to assassinate the Israeli ambassador to the United Kingdom, Shlomo Argov. The invasion led to the gradual mobilisation of the Shiite community.[35] The former Israeli Prime Minister Ehud Barak noted in an interview that, 'when we entered Lebanon, there was no Hizballah. We were accepted by perfumed rice and flowers by the Shi'a in the south. It was our presence there that created Hizballah'.[36]

Historically, the Shiite community has been marginalised in Lebanon, with the Maronites and Sunni Muslims holding most of the political power. Concentrated in the south of Lebanon and living in poor rural conditions, the Shiites in the 1950s joined different leftist and pan-Arab political parties and militias, such as the Lebanese communist party, the Syrian Social Nationalist and the Baath party.[37] From these poor living conditions emerged a political and religious Iranian-Lebanese leader: the founder of the Movement of the Deprived, Imam Musa as-Sadr, gave a voice to the Shiite community. He was a reformer who called on the Lebanese Government to take up its duties in the south, to build schools and medical facilities and to allocate a bigger share of the national budget to the neglected Shiite villages.[38]

In 1958, Lebanon witnessed its first crisis which led to sectarian killing between Sunnis, Druze and Christians. Opposition to Maronite elitism and hegemony was at the heart of the conflict, and the conflict ended with the arrival of US Marines and the election of President Fouad Chehab who promised reforms.[39] In the late 1960s, as-Sadr called for a general strike which eventually led to the creation of the Council of the South, *Majlis al-Janub*. The council's mission was to help improve the quality of life in the south and to address the concerns of the Shiite community. However, the Council of the South was highly ineffective and became a hub for corruption.[40]

Despite this small effort, the Lebanese Government continued to ignore the Shiite community, which led Imam as-Sadr to push its people to organise, and the first paramilitary group known as Amal (an acronym for Lebanese Resistance Regiments, with 'amal' also meaning hope in Arabic) was born under the leadership of Nabih Berri. As-Sadr's position towards the Palestinians was complex. He sympathised with the Palestinian cause. However, he acknowledged the Shiites' suffering at the hands of the PLO and repeatedly warned Palestinian leaders against violating Lebanon's sovereignty.[41] As-Sadr 'was hardly a man of war. His weapons were words, and in a country where the force of arms increasingly held sway, his political efforts were eventually short-circuited'.[42] In August 1978, as-Sadr flew from Beirut to Libya to celebrate the Libyan leader Muammar Gaddafi's arrival to power in 1969. He never arrived at his destination. Some said that he left for Italy, but as-Sadr's supporters claimed that his baggage was found in a hotel in Tripoli. There exists no hard evidence that he did in fact fly to Italy or Libya. He simply disappeared, and his case remains unsolved to this date.[43]

When Israel invaded Lebanon, the relationships within the Shiite community were deteriorating. Some viewed the PLO as a foreign force in the south of Lebanon and welcomed the Israelis, while others aligned themselves with the Palestinian cause and its fighters. After 1983, many Amal fighters ignored their leader's call not to resist the occupier. Some joined the PLO, while others moved to create their own Shiite military group, and Hezbollah was born in the mid-1980s. Shiite religious leaders appealed to Iran for help; Iran obliged and sent fighters, advisors and weapons to the Beqaa Valley where Iranian Revolutionary Guards Corps trained Hezbollah fighters. Iranian money and the Iranian Islamic Revolution drew many Shiites who wanted to join this growing resistance movement. Among the recruits were Abbas al-Musawi and Hassan Nasrallah: Musawi, who would be assassinated by Israel in 1992, became Hezbollah's Secretary General. Nasrallah succeeded him.

Some Shiites did not want to swear allegiance to Iran and its Supreme Leader Sayyid Ruhollah Musavi Khomeini, preferring Arab clerics such as Sayyid Muhammad Hussein Fadlallah instead. Pledging allegiance to Iran, a non-Arab country, divided the Shiite community. Clashes erupted between Amal and Hezbollah, particularly in the 'war of the camps' between 1985 and 1988.[44] Upon the withdrawal of the Israeli forces from Beirut, Amal, the emerging resistance group of Hezbollah, and PLO fighters fought fiercely to establish their dominance over the Palestinian camps and the void left behind by the Israeli forces. Amal had a larger group of fighters and was heavily armed, but 'Hezbollah compensated for its numerical inferiority with superior discipline and small unit tactics'.[45] Hezbollah fighters clashed also with the Syrian troops who came to aid Amal fighters. In fact, these clashes jeopardised the Syrian–Iranian relationship, since Syria supported Amal and Iran supported Hezbollah.[46] To avoid an escalation of tensions, Syria and Iran called for negotiations between the two fighting parties.

In many ways, Hezbollah is Iran's creation in Lebanon, as 'Iran's political and financial support proved vital for Hezbollah's early expansion'.[47] Today, Hezbollah's effectiveness greatly depends on Iran's support. Iran trains Hezbollah fighters, pays their salaries and offers them welfare benefits such as healthcare, education and pensions. Iran also provides weapons to Hezbollah and sanctuary to its fighters, and it puts political pressure on Lebanon and the region.

Ideology, Structure and Leadership

The Sunni-Shiite split occurred in the seventh century. The conflict leading to this split arose between the Caliph Muawiya and Ali, the Prophet's son-in-law, about who should succeed the Prophet Mohammad in leading Islam:

> Even after the death of Ali, they [the Shiites] clung to this cause; their breach with the Sunnis was widened and made permanent by the Battle of Kerbela (681) in which Ali's son Husain was killed after the defeat of his army by that of the Umayyads. The Shi'is regard the succession to the Prophet as having passed, not to the orthodox line of Caliphs whom the Sunnis recognise, but to a hereditary line of Imams who were both the spiritual and the temporal heads of Islam, and of whom the first was Ali. The majority of Shi'is recognise twelve such Imams, the last of whom disappeared during the ninth century but will, it is believed, some day reappear.[48]

Hezbollah's religious ideology is founded on three pillars: the principle of the 'guardianship of the Islamic jurist' or *wilayat al-faqih*, which was developed by Iran's Supreme Leader R. Khomeini, Shiite ideology and the doctrine of jihad or Islamic resistance.[49] Hezbollah sees itself as an Islamic Shiite resistance tasked to protect Lebanon.

On 16 February 1985, Hezbollah's founders issued an 'open letter addressed to the oppressed in Lebanon and the world'. Known as the 1985 Manifesto, the letter defined Hezbollah as an Islamic group that aims to follow the guidelines of the Islamic Revolution in Iran and its Supreme Leader. It considers jihad as the duty of every Muslim. The manifesto identifies America as the source of all catastrophes and rejects its support to the State of Israel:

> The US, its NATO allies, and the Zionist entity in the holy land of Palestine [Israel] attacked us and continues to do so without respite. Their aim is to continuously humiliate us. This is why we are, more and more, in a state of permanent alert in order to repel aggression and defend our religion, our existence, and our dignity.[50]

In addition to the United States and Israel, the manifesto also labels France and the LF right-wing Christian militia as enemies; it considers the United Nations (UN), the Security Council and other international organisations as an ineffective, insufficient and fake 'podium for the oppressed'.[51]

The manifesto clearly states Hezbollah's objectives: to expel foreign forces from Lebanon, including Israelis, Americans and French troops; to submit the LF members to a just trial for the crimes they committed against Muslims and Christians in Lebanon; and to promote the right to self-determination with a clear preference for the establishment of an Islamic State.[52] The manifesto calls on Lebanese Christians to adhere to Islam as God's religion. However, it specifically states that Hezbollah will not coerce Christians to convert if they do not engage in aggression against Muslims.[53] Also, the manifesto shames the Arab regimes that signed peace treaties with Israel: 'These regimes cannot think of confronting the Zionist entity that raped Palestine because they were founded under colonial guardianship, which had a great role in the shaping of these rusty regimes . . .'[54] Finally, the manifesto calls on all Muslims and on the 'noble oppressed' to join their cause, no matter where they are in the world.

On 30 November 2009, Hezbollah issued a New Manifesto in which it re-affirmed its commitment to the Islamic resistance and the Shiite credo; it renewed its opposition to the United States and Israel for their continuous oppression in the region and in the world. Also, it detailed its vision for Lebanon and its people:

> We want Lebanon to be one and united – land, people, government and institutions. We refuse any form of division or federation, whether camouflaged or blatantly declared. We want Lebanon to be free, sovereign and independent, generous, impregnably strong and able, a presence within the equations of the region, and a main contributor shaping the present and the future as it has always contributed to the configuration of history.[55]

This announcement came to oppose the call to amend Lebanon's form of governance and to create a federation that would guarantee minority rights. It is interesting to note that the New Manifesto rejects political sectarianism, Lebanon's then current form of governance. However, it acknowledges that it would be hard to change this form of governance since it had been established by the Taif Agreement of 1989. Consequently, Hezbollah found a compromise and instead called for a consensual democracy.[56]

This call outraged several legislators and politicians, as it was interpreted as a rejection of parliamentary elections. Additionally, many wondered about Hezbollah's continued allegiance to Iran and its Supreme Leader. The Secretary General's Deputy Naim Qassem put an end to this debate and told the Lebanese newspaper *Daily Star* that Hezbollah remained committed to their 1985 principles.[57] In other words, he re-affirmed Hezbollah's commitment to Iran and its Supreme Leader.

As for its structure, a religious council with seven members was created in the 1980s; it has branches and committees that govern different aspects, including finances, social, political and military issues. The Council or *Majlis al-Shura* has regional offices in Beirut, the Beqaa Valley and the south of Lebanon. At the end of the war, two more bodies were added: an executive council and a politburo. The religious council was chaired by Sayyid Muhammad Hussein Fadlallah who offered religious guidance to the Shiite community and was often described as Hezbollah's spiritual leader.[58] Both the council and Hezbollah swear allegiance to Iran's Supreme Leader. The council is also tasked to select Hezbollah's Secretary General. After Israel's assassination of Hezbollah's co-founder Abbas al-Musawi in 1992,[59] Hassan Nasrallah assumed this role and has remained Secretary General to this day.

Hezbollah turned into a political party in 1992, when its members decided to participate in the Lebanese elections. Hezbollah's ideology shifted from fighting the Israeli occupation to participating in Lebanese political life; eight of its members were elected to parliament. In 2005, Hezbollah members entered the government with two cabinet positions. In the most recent elections of May 2022, Hezbollah still held some parliamentarian positions. However, it has lost the parliamentarian majority.[60]

Hezbollah's Warfare in the Civil War and Post-War Era

As of 1982, Hezbollah perpetrated attacks, and 'most observers agree that the recent wave of suicide terrorism began in the early 1980s and in Lebanon'.[61] Other militias used car bombs as means to eliminate their enemies. However, Hezbollah's originality was in inserting a driver wishing to be a martyr.[62] This warfare technique was developed by Imad Mughniyeh,[63] who played an important role during the civil war and later occupied an essential position in Hezbollah.

The Beirut barracks bombing was one of the largest suicide bomb attacks taking place in Lebanon during the Civil War. On 6 June 1982, on the orders of the Defence Minister Ariel Sharon, Israel Defence Forces launched 'Operation Peace for Galilee' and invaded Lebanon to eliminate the PLO members and to stop the rocket attacks on its soil. A multi-national peace-keeping mission was deployed in Lebanon, at Lebanon's request, to oversee the departure of PLO members and to aid the Lebanese Armed Forces (LAF) in restoring peace and order.[64] On 23

October 1983, witnesses reported seeing a yellow Mercedes speeding towards the barracks. Loaded with explosives, the Mercedes flattened the concrete building which housed the American troops. Minutes later, an identical attack occurred at the French barracks. These attacks killed 241 American servicemen and fifty-eight French paratroopers. To this day, the Beirut barracks bombing remains the deadliest single-day attack on the United States Marine Corps since the Battle of Iwo Jima in 1945. The Islamic Jihad, a pro-Iranian Shiite group, claimed responsibility for the attacks. The group was allegedly linked to Hezbollah.[65]

Other techniques included kidnapping and hostage-taking. Lebanese citizens were kidnapped and held hostage in exchange for ransom. However, Westerners were the real target. Hezbollah and its allies kidnapped around eighty-seven European and American hostages. These kidnappings were intended to put financial and diplomatic pressure on the West. They also benefited Iran.[66] On 16 June 1976, US Ambassador Francis Melloy and his advisor Robert Waring were kidnapped in Beirut, along with the embassy driver. They were all shot to death by unidentified assailants.[67] On 19 January 1984, Islamic Jihad assassinated Professor Malcom Kerr, president of the American University of Beirut, on campus.[68]

David Dodge and Terry Anderson were also among the kidnapping victims. David Dodge, president of the American University of Beirut, was kidnapped on 19 July 1982. With the help of the Syrian government, Dodge was released on 19 July 1983.[69] Terry Anderson, a professional journalist, was kidnapped on 16 March 1985 and remained in captivity for seven years. He was released on 4 December 1991.[70] CIA Station Chief William Buckley was not as fortunate, as he was held and tortured for fourteen months. He died in terrorist custody.[71] On 14 June 1985, Hezbollah's fighter Imad Mughniyeh planned the sky-jacking of TWA flight 847 to Beirut and demanded the release of 766 Lebanese prisoners held in Israel, 'many of whom languished in extremely difficult conditions, with no recourse to the protections of international law. Some of the captives had participated in resistance operations, but others were merely suspects that Israel held hostage'.[72] There is no evidence that Iran was directly involved in the kidnappings, but still there is no doubt that its ideology influenced the kidnappers, and that these criminal acts benefited the Iranian regime.[73] This wave of kidnappings pushed many Westerners to flee Lebanon. The United States imposed travel restrictions on Lebanon. In 1987, Secretary of State George Schultz declared US passports invalid for travel to Lebanon. This restriction was lifted in 1996.[74] In October 1997, the United States listed Hezbollah as a foreign terrorist organisation.[75]

At the end of the hostage era and the Lebanese Civil War, Hezbollah had attracted the attention of the international community on three occasions: in 1992, 1994 and 2012. On 17 March 1992, a bomb exploded in the building of the Israeli Embassy in Buenos Aires (Argentina), killing twenty-nine and injuring more than 200 persons. Four Israeli diplomats were killed. With the approval of the Argentinian authorities, the Israeli Government sent its own investigators and accused Iran and Hezbollah of being behind the attack.[76] Two years later, on 18 July 1994, another attack targeted the Argentine Israelite Mutual Association in Buenos Aires, killing eighty-five and wounding more than 300 persons. Several states immediately pointed the finger at Iran and Hezbollah. On 18 July 2012, a bus carrying Israeli tourists in Bulgaria was subject to a suicide attack. Five Israeli tourists were killed, and the Bulgarian driver and more than thirty were wounded.[77] Israel and the United States immediately accused Iran and Hezbollah of being behind the attack.

Hezbollah after 1992

At its inception in 1985, Hezbollah was not interested in political life. However, as pointed out by Imad Mansour in 'The State of Hezbollah? Sovereignty as a Potentiality in Global South Contexts', the political environment and the 1992 parliamentary elections forced Hezbollah to face two realities:

> . . . the domestic consensus among Lebanon's actors was that the political process was the only viable option through which they should continue to interact, and that the use of military force should be avoided in domestic political competition. Second [. . .] alliances were valuable strategies, which could serve important functions for actors, such as pooling capacities and preventing monopolies.[78]

The year 1992 marked the beginning of Hezbollah's participation in political life. Its members ran for elections and won twelve (out of 128) seats in parliament.[79] Under Syrian pressure, the Lebanese Parliament amended the constitution in August 2004 and extended the presidential mandate for three years, thus prolonging the mandate of the pro-Syrian President Emile Lahoud.[80] This was met with general protests in the streets.

On 2 September 2004, the UN Security Council adopted Resolution 1559 which re-affirmed . . .

> . . . its call for the strict respect of the sovereignty, territorial integrity, unity, and political independence of Lebanon under the sole and exclusive

> authority of the Government of Lebanon throughout Lebanon; 2. Call[ed] upon all remaining foreign forces to withdraw from Lebanon; 3. Call[ed] for the disbanding and disarmament of all Lebanese and non-Lebanese militias; 4. Support[ed] the extension of the control of the Government of Lebanon over all Lebanese territory;5. Declar[ed] its support for a free and fair electoral process in Lebanon's upcoming presidential election conducted according.[81]

On 28 January 2005, the Security Council adopted Resolution 1583; it called on the Lebanese Government . . .

> . . . to fully extend and exercise its sole and effective authority throughout the south, including through the deployment of sufficient numbers of Lebanese armed and security forces, to ensure a calm environment throughout the area, including along the Blue Line, and to exert control over the use of force on its territory and from it.[82]

In 2005, the circumstances changed with the assassination of Prime Minister Rafic Hariri.[83] As per the Taif Agreement of 1989, Syrian forces were supposed to help the Lebanese authorities regain control over the entirety of the territory and to leave Lebanon within the maximum period of two years after the ratification of the agreement. Sixteen years later, they were still in Lebanon. Anti-Syrian sentiment was growing inside and outside of Lebanon, and international pressure was mounting against the pro-Syrian Lebanese government. Amid massive anti-government and anti-Syrian protests, Prime Minister Omar Karami resigned.[84] As a counter-narrative, Hezbollah and its political allies on 8 March organised a demonstration to thank Syria for supporting Lebanon during the civil war and post-war periods.[85] This coalition was labelled 8 March.

Prime Minister Rafic Hariri was assassinated on 14 February 2005. One month later, Lebanon witnessed the Cedar Revolution, which led to the departure of the Syrian troops.[86] The politicians and lawmakers who participated in this national movement were dubbed 14 March. The year 2005 witnessed the assassination of other prominent anti-Syrian figures. For instance, a blast killed the anti-Syrian journalist Samir Kassir.[87] The former Communist party leader George Hawi[88] and the journalist and lawmaker Gibran Tueni[89] were also killed in car bombs. There were also assassination attempts on Defence Minister Elias Murr[90] and journalist May Chidiac;[91] the latter was severely injured by a car bomb.

Tensions grew between the 14 March and 8 March groups, and while 14 March reinforced its relations with Western political powers and Saudi Arabia, 8 March grew closer to Syria and Iran. In May 2005, Lebanon held its first legislative elections without the physical presence of Syrian forces, and 14 March won the majority in parliament. In June 2005, Prime Minister Fouad Siniora formed a cabinet of twenty-three ministers. Hezbollah, who had been in parliament since 1992, gained representation in the government with two ministers.[92] Hezbollah continued to gain popularity by providing different social and healthcare services to its constituents. Its political activities and participation in both parliament and government were celebrated. In July 2006, Hezbollah kidnapped two Israeli soldiers, and Israel responded with a full-blown war on Lebanon, which lasted thirty-four days. After the 2006 war, UN peace-keeping forces were deployed along the southern border; these were followed by the LAF, which was a first, since Hezbollah had maintained control of this border since Israel's withdrawal in 2000.[93]

In 2007, Lebanon witnessed terrorist activities on its norther borders where Jihadists infiltrated the Nahr al-Bared Palestinian refugee camp and launched deadly attacks against the LAF.[94] This event carries importance as it marked the beginning of a collaboration between the LAF and Hezbollah members in fighting domestic terrorism. In 2008, deadly clashes broke out between Lebanese Sunnis and Shiites. Controlled by 14 March, the government ordered to monitor Hezbollah's communication network. Hezbollah argued that this move would jeopardise its operations. Consequently, Hezbollah deployed its arms internally in areas that were not traditionally under its control. While Hezbollah did not act against the LAF, its members carried out deadly attacks against civilians and members of other political parties and armed groups.[95] The Secretary General of Hezbollah, Hassan Nasrallah, considered the government's move 'a declaration of war'.[96] Fear about another civil war was on the rise, and many politicians, lawmakers and activists called for peace and reconciliation. In May 2008, a meeting was held in Qatar where Lebanese political leaders affirmed their rejection of war and their commitment to the constitution and the Taif Agreement of 1989.

The Doha Agreement called for national dialogue. After months of presidential vacuum, the participants agreed that the Lebanese parliament would convene to elect the former General Michel Suleiman as president. The participants also agreed to form a government of national unity, which would include thirty ministers 'allocated as follows: 16 to the majority, 11 to the opposition and three to the President. All parties pledge[d] by virtue of this Agreement not to resign or obstruct the work of the Government'. Additionally, they decided to hold parliamentarian elections according to the 1960 electoral law and to refrain from using weapons for political gain. More importantly, they agreed to the following:

- Resort to the use of weapons or violence to resolve differences of any kind under any circumstances is prohibited, in order to ensure that there is no violation of the national contract of partnership based on the determination of the Lebanese to co-exist within a democratic system. Security and military authority over Lebanese nationals and residents is reserved to the State, to guarantee continued communal existence and civil peace for all Lebanese. The parties pledge to this.
- The law is to be applied and the sovereignty of the State honoured in all Lebanese regions. There will be no regions in which fugitives from justice may take refuge, out of respect for the rule of law, and anyone who commits crimes or violations will be brought before the Lebanese justice system.[97]

In July 2008, Prime Minister Fouad Siniora formed a government of national unity. Composed of thirty members, it allowed Hezbollah and its allies to enjoy veto powers. In the summer of 2009, 14 March and the anti-Syrian bloc won the legislative elections again. Saad Hariri, Rafic Hariri's son, was appointed prime minister. However, he was unable to form a government due to Hezbollah's opposition. After months of executive void, a government was formed, but it did not last long. It collapsed again in January 2011 with Hezbollah's resignation. Prime Minister Najib Mikati formed a new Hezbollah-dominated cabinet.[98]

In March 2011, the Syrian Civil War broke out, which fuelled tensions on the Lebanese-Syrian border. The big influx of Syrian refugees aggravated the political situation in Lebanon, and clashes erupted in Lebanon between anti-Syrian and pro-Syrian supporters. In 2013, Hezbollah publicly recognised its participation in the Syrian war and support for the Syrian regime, resulting in clashes between Syrian refugees, anti-Syrian regime supporters and Hezbollah members on Lebanese soil. This led the European Union (EU) to list Hezbollah's military wing as a terrorist organisation.[99] Unlike the United States and the United Kingdom, the EU distinguishes between Hezbollah's military and political branches.

In November 2013, double-suicide bombs exploded outside the Iranian embassy in Beirut. Hezbollah openly accused Saudi Arabia, and this led to more hostility between Sunnis and Shiites in Lebanon and in the region.[100] In 2014, despite the large opposition, the parliament, citing concerns over the Syrian crisis and threats of war in Lebanon, extended its own mandate to 2017. In May 2014, President Michel Suleiman ended his term, and Lebanon entered another long presidential vacuum. After nearly three years, former General Michel Aoun, who had returned to Lebanon in May 2005 after fourteen years of exile in France, was elected president. Ali Akbar Velayati, a senior adviser to Ali Khamenei, Leader of the Islamic Revolution, congratulated Lebanon for electing President Aoun, 'describing the choice as a victory for the Islamic Resistance movement in Lebanon'.[101] Backed by Hezbollah, President Michel Aoun and his political party, the Free Patriotic Movement, pushed to amend the electoral law. In 2017, a new electoral law was approved by parliament, under political pressure. Its gerrymandering allowed for Hezbollah and the Free Patriotic Movement to gain the majority in parliament.

On 17 October 2019, mass protests erupted in Lebanon against the taxation of internet and Whatsapp services. These evolved into a revolt against the government and its corruption, which led to the resignation of Prime Minister Saad Hariri on 29 October. The demands were not unified. Some called for the resignation of the president, the government and the parliament, as well as the nomination of an independent technocratic government without political affiliation with any political party. Others called for early parliamentarian elections, the amendment of the constitution and the implementation of civil rather than sectarian laws. Others called for legal actions against corrupt politicians and the safe return of Syrian refugees back to Syria. However, two demands were in common: the first was the rejection of all political parties. The protests' motto was 'All Means All', implying a rejection of all corrupt politicians and political parties. The second demand was the disarmament of Hezbollah.[102]

Although peaceful, the protests were met with violence from the Lebanese State as well as Hezbollah and Amal supporters. Amnesty International reported that the Lebanese authorities used excessive force (beating, tear gas and live ammunition) to disperse peaceful protesters. They blocked roads and failed to protect protesters from pro-Hezbollah thugs. They forcibly dispersed protesters and illegally arrested and detained several. Many protesters reported being either tortured or ill-treated while under arrest. Others reported being harassed and intimidated by the Lebanese authorities and Hezbollah members for their participation in the protests. The pandemic gave Lebanese authorities the perfect excuse to put an end to this peaceful movement. They announced a lockdown in March 2020, which remained in effect for over a year.[103] On 4 August 2020, Beirut witnessed a massive explosion that killed at least 200. The OHCHR called for an international investigation of this powerful blast 'in which a stockpile of ammonium nitrate stored in a port warehouse exploded on 4 August 2020 – [it] destroyed 77,000 apartments, wounded 7,000 people, displaced over 300,000 more and left at least 80,000 children homeless'.[104] At the time of writing this book, there still is no justice. Investigative journalism has revealed the possible involvement of many corrupt Lebanese leaders, including Hezbollah members in parliament and in the government.[105]

Today, the shift in Lebanon's demographics provides Hezbollah with a larger recruiting ground and popularity. The destabilisation of the country, the widespread corruption and dysfunctional government has forced many Lebanese Christians to leave.[106] New World Bank Data indicate that more than 44 per cent of Lebanese live in multi-dimensional poverty.[107] Lebanon has the largest number of refugees per capita per square kilometre in the world, with an estimated 1.5 million Syrian refugees and more than 11,238 refugees of other nationalities.[108] According to former Minister Charbel Nahas, 'among children between the ages of one and four years, the number of Syrian children is more than double that of the Lebanese',[109] and by 2038 the Syrians could represent between 72 and 52 per cent of Lebanon's total population. The erosion of the middle-class and of religious diversity, poverty, limited access to proper education and the high number of pro-Hezbollah refugees are all factors that play to Hezbollah's favour.

Hezbollah's history is deeply linked to the history of the Lebanese Civil War, the Israeli occupation and the Islamic Revolution in Iran. Now, it has infiltrated all Lebanese institutions and possesses a global footprint as well as a wide network of organised crime and unlawful activities. This leaves us with an important question: what is the legal status of Hezbollah in domestic law?

Chapter 3

Hezbollah's Legal Classification in Domestic Law

Having examined the history of Hezbollah, its structure and ideology, it is essential to analyse Hezbollah's legal classification according to domestic law. First, this chapter will study the 1909 Law on Associations and consider whether Hezbollah exists as an association or political party inside Lebanon. Second, it will scrutinise the Taif Agreement of 1989, which put an end to the Lebanese Civil War and the General Amnesty Law of 1991. This chapter will argue that these legal texts, along with Lebanese State practice, have legalised Hezbollah and recognised it as a political party, non-profit organisation and armed actor inside Lebanon.

The 1909 Law on Associations

Overview of the 1909 Law on Associations

Associations or non-governmental organisations (NGOs) are important for the life of a democracy: they can defend human rights, create spaces to discuss ideas and push for reforms. There are clear international, regional and domestic protections for the right to peaceful assembly. Article 20, paragraph 1 of the Universal Declaration of Human Rights stipulates: 'Everyone has the right to freedom of peaceful assembly and association'.[1] The International Covenant on Civil and Political Rights of 1967, which Lebanon ratified in 1972, stipulates in its Article 21:

> The right of peaceful assembly shall be recognised. No restrictions may be placed on the exercise of this right other than those imposed in conformity with the law and which are necessary in a democratic society in the interests of national security or public safety, public order (ordre public), the protection of public health or morals or the protection of the rights and freedoms of others.[2]

Article 22 continues:

1. Everyone shall have the right to freedom of association with others, including the right to form and join trade unions for the protection of his interests.
2. No restrictions may be placed on the exercise of this right other than those which are prescribed by law and which are necessary in a democratic society in the interests of national security or public safety, public order (ordre public), the protection of public health or morals or the protection of the rights and freedoms of others. This article shall not prevent the imposition of lawful restrictions on members of the armed forces and of the police in their exercise of this right.
3. Nothing in this article shall authorize States Parties to the International Labour Organisation Convention of 1948 concerning Freedom of Association and Protection of the Right to Organize to take legislative measures which would prejudice, or to apply the law in such a manner as to prejudice, the guarantees provided for in that Convention.[3]

In *Sidiropoulous* v. *Greece*, the European Court of Human Rights has emphasised the value of freedom of association, stating that 'the way in which national legislation enshrines this freedom and its practical application by the authorities reveal the state of democracy in the country concerned'.[4]

Paragraphs 5 and 6 of Article 24 of the Arab Charter of Human Rights state that every citizen has the right '(5) to freely form and join association with others. (6) to freedom of association and peaceful assembly'.[5] In Lebanon, this right is protected by the constitution and the 1909 Law on Associations. The 1909 Law on Associations precedes the constitution of 1926.[6] Adopted under the Ottoman Empire and before Lebanon's independence, this law was inspired by the French Law on Associations of 1 July 1901;[7] it requires a simple declaration or notification about the formation of an association.

Article 13 of the Lebanese Constitution of 1926 stipulates that 'the freedom of opinion, expression through speech and writing, the freedom of the press, the freedom of assembly, and the freedom of association, are all guaranteed within the scope of the law'.[8] The Lebanese Constitution of 1926 does not provide details on the right to peacefully assemble or create an association. It merely proclaims it to be a constitutional right. Article 2 of the 1909 Law on Associations states that 'establishing an association requires no prior permit, but by virtue of Article 6, notifying the government of its establishment is a prerequisite'.[9] Prior authorisation is required for some groups, such as foreign associations, youth and sports associations, syndicates and trade unions. Otherwise, the 1909 Law's system of notification seems liberal with minimal administrative intervention. Article 6 of the 1909 Law stipulates that the founders of the association . . .

> . . . must submit a signed and sealed statement containing its address, goals, objectives, main office, and the names, capacity, and position of those entrusted with its governance. The statement is submitted to the Department of Interior (Ministry of Interior) if the association's headquarters is in the capital (Dar el Sa'ada) or to the senior royal commissioner if it is based outside the capital. Two certified copies of the association's statutes, sealed by the association's official stamp, must be attached to this statement. In return, the association is granted a notification. Then, the founders may declare the establishment of the association and how it was set up. All associations are obliged to immediately inform the government of any amendment or alteration to their statutes, administrative board, or location. This amendment or alteration shall be implemented on a third party as of the date of informing the government, and shall be registered in the register created for this purpose. This register must be available whenever the judicial or royal governments request to review it.[10]

It is noteworthy that the 1909 Law does not dictate a specific deadline for the founders to declare their association, nor for the Lebanese authorities to provide receipts. The absence of firm deadlines opens the door to interpretation and possible abuse. For Marc Makary, it puts in doubt the association's legal capacity: is the legal capacity available at the time of the declaration of the association, or when the receipt is issued?

As Makary has reminded us, the State Council affirmed in its decision of 25 September 1946 that an association enjoys legal capacity from its declaration as intended in Articles 2 and 6 and if the association abides by these stipulations.[11] This decision was re-affirmed in the State Council's decision of 18 November 2003.[12] Once the association has legal capacity, it has several rights and obligations. According to Article 8 of the 1909 Law, the association . . .

> . . . may stand before the courts as plaintiff or defendant by means of a mediator [. . .] It may not govern or dispose of State grants and aid that are bindings, but may dispose of the following:
>
> – monetary contributions paid by members, on the condition that the contribution does not exceed twenty-four gold coins a year;

- The location designated for governing the association and the meeting places.
- The fixed assets needed to reach the set objectives in accordance with its bylaws.

These associations are prohibited from disposing of the other fixed assets.[13]

As such, an association formed according to the 1909 Law has a legal personality that allows it to open a bank account, among other things. This is confirmed by Article 166 of the Law of Finances and Credits, which authorises associations to open bank accounts. It stipulates: 'A bank may receive deposits from a natural person or non-profit organisations'.[14] According to Mazhar El-Haraka in 'The Legal Framework of Associations in Lebanon', any official documentation can be submitted to the bank to prove the legality of the association. Since the 1909 Law does not require publication of the association's establishment in the Official Gazette, members of the association can provide documents such as the association's statutes or by-laws with founders' signatures, and the bank account can be opened.[15]

Clandestine associations or malevolent associations created with the intention to commit crimes are strictly prohibited under Section III of the Penal Code, Articles 335 to 339.[16] Finally, it is worth mentioning that the 1909 Law on Associations prohibits political assemblies. In fact, Article 3 of the 1909 Law on Associations, which was amended by virtue of the Law of 26 May 1928, stipulates:

> It is prohibited to establish associations on illegitimate grounds that contradict the provisions of laws and public mores, that disturb the peace of the Empire, that aim to change the standing form of government, or that aim to politically separate the different Ottoman entities. They are not to be granted a notification, and they are to be dissolved and banned by a decree issued by the Council of Ministers.[17]

Article 4 adds: 'The establishment of political associations of a nationalistic nature or dictum is strictly forbidden'.[18]

The 1909 Law on Associations was established under the authoritarian regime of the Ottoman Empire. As such, it was interpreted narrowly to imply a banning of all forms of political parties or associations aimed to discuss or change the political system in place. After Lebanon's independence, this narrow interpretation was lifted. The formation of political parties was allowed, and political parties were considered part of public life and in compliance with public laws. While a modern interpretation allows for political parties to legally exist, it deserves note that they are considered associations. In other words, Lebanon does not have special laws or regulations for political parties. They fall under the 1909 Law on Associations. Hence, they are legally bound by the same rights and obligations as non-governmental organisations.

Hezbollah and the 1909 Law on Associations

In Lebanon and on the ground, Hezbollah exists in two forms: as an armed group and as a political party. Hezbollah's military form will be examined in the section below on the Taif Agreement of 1989 and the General Amnesty Law of 1991. As to its political attributes, there is no doubt that Hezbollah operates as a political party: its members participate in Lebanon's political life and elections. However, to this day Hezbollah has not declared itself a political party, nor notified public authorities of its existence as dictated by the 1909 Law on Associations.

Moreover, Article 7 of the 1909 Law on Associations clearly stipulates that an association must have headquarters, books and accounts. It states:

> The headquarters of any association must contain an administrative board of at least two individuals. If the association has branches, each branch is to have an administrative board affiliated to the central administrative board. These boards must keep three books/accounts: all information related to the members of the association and when each joined the association must be recorded in the first; decisions, correspondences, and notifications must be recorded in the second; and revenues, income, the type and amount of operations or transactions must be recorded in the third. These three books/accounts shall be presented to the judicial or royal governments upon request.[19]

Article 11 adds: 'All associations are prohibited from entering and keeping firearms and weapons in their meeting places. Clubs offering hunting and fencing activities are allowed to keep and store as many weapons as needed on condition of informing the police'.[20] Furthermore, Article 18 stipulates:

> The police are entitled to inspect associations and clubs; therefore, the latter must keep their meeting places and offices open for police inspection at all times. Yet, the police must present a search warrant to prove that their inspection is conducted for due reasons. The search warrant can be issued by the police commissioner if in the capital (Dar el Sa'ada) and by the local senior royal commissioners, or their deputies, if in the districts.[21]

To this date, Hezbollah has not publicly shared information about its headquarters, offices, branches, administrative board, or budget. Moreover, it is a well-known fact that Hezbollah members are heavily armed, and that the Lebanese national police cannot enter areas under Hezbollah's control. This is particularly the case in the southern suburbs of Beirut and South Lebanon where Hezbollah has security control over buildings and streets.

Hezbollah oversees numerous non-governmental organisations that provide services in Lebanon. Empirical evidence indicates that Hezbollah has three main units of services: the Social Unit, the Education Unit and the Islamic Health Unit. Together, these associations create a network servicing almost exclusively Lebanon's Shiites.[22] The Social Unit has four associations: the Jihad Construction Foundation (or *Jihad al-Binaa)*, the Martyrs' Foundation, the Foundation for the Wounded and the Khomeini Support Committee. The Jihad Construction Foundation played a key role after the 2006 armed conflict with Israel. It assessed damage to the infrastructure in Beirut's southern suburbs and southern Lebanon, paid residents for reconstruction and provided other services such as water and food. The Martyr's Foundation is exclusive to the families of fighters killed in combat. It primarily offers financial aid to widows and children.

The Health Unit has at least three hospitals, twelve health centres, twenty infirmaries, twenty dental clinics and ten defence departments. All of these facilities are in areas with high a concentration of Lebanese Shiites, mainly in Beirut's southern suburbs, the Bekaa Valley and southern Lebanon. This unit offers services at low to no cost to Shiites. It proposes its own health, dental, vision and prescription coverages. As to the Education Unit, Lebanon's public school system is of low quality, and Lebanese tend to send their children to private schools and universities. Hezbollah offers an alternative system for families who cannot afford to pay for private schools. It funds multiple private Islamic schools that serve at least 14,000 students per year. The Education Unit also offers scholarships and financial aid to pay for books and other school-related supplies.[23]

In the absence of state services, these non-profit organisations have flourished. Many of them operate within the bounds of the law. They often meet the regulatory requirements of the 1909 Law on Associations. Some of these non-profit organisations have a religious identity and operate as charity. As such, they evade the 1909 Law on Associations entirely. In fact, on 13 March 1936, the Decision of French Colonial Powers No. 60, published in the Official Gazette number 3273 on 29 April 1936, allowed for associations with charity, cultural or education objectives to operate exclusively under the umbrella of religious authorities. Thus, these charity or religious non-profit organisations do not declare or pay taxes.[24] They do not have to declare the national or international donations that they receive. Article 7 of the decision states that these non-profit organisations have legal capacity with all the rights and obligations that result from such status.[25] Consequently, these non-profit associations operate legally, can sign contracts, open bank accounts, receive donations and offer services. They exist independently from the 1909 Law on Associations, as they are managed by religious authorities.[26]

Overall, there are two important takeaways:

1. As an entity, Hezbollah exists in violation of the 1909 Law on Associations: although it operates as a political party, it has not declared itself as an association, nor as a political group to the State of Lebanon; it is heavily armed; its headquarters, budget, structures and administrative offices are not public information.
2. Hezbollah supports numerous non-profit organisations that have a legal personality and exist according to the rules and regulations of 1909 Law on Associations or Decision number 60/1936.

One may argue that Hezbollah's 'open letter addressed to the oppressed in Lebanon and the world' of 16 February 1985 is a form of declaration. Known as the 1985 Manifesto, the document defines Hezbollah as an Islamic group that follows the guidelines of the Islamic Revolution and its Supreme Leader in Iran.[27] There are numerous legal consequences to this interpretation:

1. If the 1985 Manifesto is to be interpretated as declaration, it can be argued that Hezbollah has the status of a legal association (or political party), as dictated by the 1909 Law on Association. While the Lebanese authorities have not necessarily responded in writing to this declaration as required by the 1909 Law on Association, it is possible to say that the subsequent interaction between public offices, State representatives and the private sector with Hezbollah members indicate implicit recognition of legal status as an association or political party.
2. Despite the potential existence of a declaration, there is no doubt that Hezbollah does not fulfil all the legal requirements of the 1909 Law on Associations.
3. In the 1985 Manifesto, Hezbollah proclaimed its agenda and allegiance to a legal system that is foreign to the Lebanese legal system: the Islamic Law of the Republic of Iran.

This approach to Hezbollah's legal status in Lebanon seems to be the dominant one. Hezbollah exists *ipso facto*. The State of Lebanon is not strong enough to enforce the 1909 Law on Associations and to make Hezbollah abide by all its requirements. It is interesting to note here that some international players do recognise Hezbollah as a political party in Lebanon. For instance, the European Union distinguishes between Hezbollah's political and military branches. While it recognises the legal existence of the first, it considers the second a terrorist organisation. On 12 July 2023, for the first time the European Parliament adopted Resolution 2742 which called the European Union to end this distinction and to add Hezbollah in its two branches to its list of banned terrorist organisations.[28]

Assuming that Hezbollah's political branch can be domestically classified as a political party under the 1909 Law on Associations, how does domestic law classify Hezbollah's military branch? As we will see in the following section, the State of Lebanon has legalised Hezbollah's armed branch as legal resistance.

The Taif Agreement of 1989, the General Amnesty Law of 1991 and Hezbollah

Hezbollah and the Taif Agreement of 1989

In October 1989, the Taif Agreement was signed in Saudi Arabia to end the Lebanese Civil War.[29] It was approved by the Lebanese Parliament on 4 November 1989. The peace agreement itself did not include amnesty provisions. An amnesty law was adopted later by the Government of President Elias Hrawi on 26 August 1991[30] and published in the Official Gazette on 27 August 1991.

Despite the end of the armed conflict, Lebanon remained under the control of two neighbouring countries: Israel and Syria. Israel withdrew from Lebanon on 16 June 2020 (but the status of the Shebaa Farms remains unresolved). Syria withdrew on 5 March 2005. The Taif Agreement of 1989 only introduced political reforms. It re-affirmed the political power-sharing based on sectarian affiliations and allowed for Syria to maintain its control over Lebanon under the disguise of peace-keeping. Article 2, paragraph D, of the Taif Agreement of 1989 stipulates:

> Syrian forces shall thankfully assist the forces of the legitimate Lebanese government to spread the authority of the State of Lebanon within a set period of no more than 2 years, beginning with ratification of the national accord charter, election of the president of the republic, formation of the national accord cabinet, and approval of the political reforms constitutionally.[31]

It deserves mention that the Syrian Arab Army entered Lebanon 1 May 1976 and did not leave until 30 April 2005. Also, the Taif Agreement of 1989 called for the dismantling of all militias. It stipulates in its Second Section on Lebanon's sovereignty that '[a] disbanding of all Lebanese and non-Lebanese militias shall be announced. The militias' weapons shall be delivered to the State of Lebanon within a period of 6 months, beginning with the approval of the national accord charter'.[32]

The Taif Agreement of 1989 called for the strengthening of the armed forces so that they could defend the homeland and maintain security. Second Section, paragraph C, states:

> 1. The fundamental task of the armed forces is to defend the homeland, and if necessary, protect public order when the danger exceeds the capability of the internal security forces to deal with such a danger on their own. 2. The armed forces shall be used to support the internal security forces in preserving security under conditions determined by the cabinet. 3. The armed forces shall be unified, prepared, and trained in order that they may be able to shoulder their national responsibilities in confronting Israeli aggression. 4. When the internal security forces become ready to assume their security tasks, the armed forces shall return to their barracks. 5. The armed forces intelligence shall be reorganized to serve military objectives exclusively.[33]

Finally, the Taif Agreement of 1989 affirmed Lebanon's right to fight against the Israeli occupation, so that Lebanon could regain control over its entire territory along the borders recognised by the international community. The Third Section on 'Liberating Lebanon from the Israeli Occupation' stipulates in its paragraph C:

> Taking all the steps necessary to liberate all Lebanese territories from the Israeli occupation, to spread state sovereignty over all the territories, and to deploy the Lebanese army in the border area adjacent to Israel; and making efforts to reinforce the presence of the UN forces in South Lebanon to insure the Israeli withdrawal and to provide the opportunity for the return of security and stability to the border area.[34]

On 19 January 1991, Prime Minister Omar Karami issued a Ministerial Statement re-affirming Lebanon's commitment to the principles of the Taif Agreement of 1989, especially the dismantling of militias and Lebanon's right to fight the Israeli occupation. The Taif Agreement of 1989 and the 1991 Ministerial Statement did not refer to Hezbollah *per se*. They used general terms that conveyed the meanings of resistance against occupation and self-defence. Despite the absence of explicit language, both documents were interpreted in Hezbollah's favour: Hezbollah was not considered a militia as defined by domestic law and, therefore, it was exempted from the obligation to disarm.

Consequently, it can be argued that the domestic legal practice that followed the Taif Agreement of 1989 legalised Hezbollah as an 'armed force' engaged in the constitutionally recognised right to resist occupying forces. The reasons for this interpretation are that (1) Hezbollah was excluded from the militia status attributed to all other armed groups and, therefore, also excluded from the requirement to disarm. (2) The Second Section, paragraph C, on 'Strengthening Armed Forces' of the Taif Agreement of 1989 defines the role of the armed forces inside Lebanon. However, it does not specify that the State has the monopoly of force, and it does not make the distinction between State and non-State actors. The category of 'armed forces' is thus left open to interpretation, which potentially allows the legal inclusion of Hezbollah.[35]

The General Amnesty Law of 1991

On 26 August 1991, Law number 84 on General Amnesty was adopted by parliament. Article 53, clause 9, of the Lebanese Constitution of 1926 allows the President of the Republic to 'grant particular pardons by Decree, but a general amnesty cannot be granted except by a law'.[36] The constitution identifies the authorities that have the power to grant a pardon or amnesty. However, it does not include any precise terms of the content of these immunity tools, nor the conditions of their applications.

Composed of ten articles, the law was published as official law on 27 August 1991. Article 1 of the General Lebanese Amnesty Law of 1991 grants amnesty to all crimes committed before 28 March 1991. Article 2 defines the crimes included in the amnesty, notably crimes labelled as such in Articles 196–69 and Article 569, paragraphs 1 to 4, of the Lebanese Penal Code, Articles 107–71 of the Lebanese Military Penal Code and Articles 72, 73, 75, 76, 77 and 78 of the Law on Munitions and Explosives, as well as the subsequent amendments of these laws.[37] Article 2 of the General Amnesty Law of 1991 adds in its last paragraph several conditions to the amnesty: amnesty will no longer apply in case of continuous crimes, crimes perpetrated after the implementation of the amnesty law and recidivism.[38] Article 3 excludes some crimes from this amnesty, such as 'crimes of the assassination or attempted assassination of religious figures, political leaders, and foreign or Arab diplomats'.[39] Articles 4 and 5 address the issue of punishments for crimes not covered by the General Amnesty Law of 1991. Article 6 covers the statutory limitations, and Article 7 concerns the right to civil action suits. Article 8 extends the jurisdiction of the Justice Council[40] to crimes committed prior to 28 March 1991, of assassination or attempted assassination of religious and political leaders. Article 9 affords the Council of Ministers exceptional powers for the period of six months to grant special amnesty to any person charged with any of the exceptions to the amnesty listed in the General Amnesty Law of 1991. Finally, Article 10 proclaims the law immediately applicable as of its publication in the Official Gazette.

Despite the few conditions, the General Amnesty Law of 1991 is closer to a blanket amnesty law as it covers a wide range of offences such as political crimes, homicide, torture and kidnapping. It is a self-serving amnesty, enacted to benefit the governing elites since it criminalises assassination and assassination attempts against religious and political leaders close to the people who fought the war, warlords and militia members.[41] In contrast, it does not criminalise these same offences against civilians.

Furthermore, it does not exclude serious crimes such as genocide, war crimes, crimes against humanity, torture and enforced disappearance. Although it recognises the survivor's right to remedy (Article 9) in compliance with international law,[42] it does not organise programmes to aid survivors, either financially or legally, in seeking their right.[43] Additionally, some have argued that Article 9 of the General Amnesty Law of 1991 creates a constitutional crisis since it provides the Council of Ministers with more powers than those stipulated by the constitution. It equates the Council of Ministers with the President of the Republic who has the right to issue pardons.[44] Others have noted that the law empowers the executive branch over the judicial branch, which violates the constitution.[45]

Many have hailed the General Amnesty Law of 1991 since it was drafted under urgent circumstances and allowed the return to peace. However, many have also opposed it and even decried its validity.[46] The last parliamentary elections were held in 1972. Between 1972 and 1991, the parliament lost several members for various reasons, including natural causes. On 6 June 1991, the Lebanese Government appointed members to fill these seats to maintain an equal representation of Christians and Muslims, as dictated by the Taif Agreement of 1989.[47] The General Amnesty Law of 1991 was enacted by a parliament that had been partially elected in 1972 and partially nominated by the government in 1991.

Hezbollah and the General Amnesty Law of 1991

The General Amnesty Law of 1991 does not necessarily impact the domestic legal classification of Hezbollah. However, it creates an environment of amnesia and impunity which benefits Hezbollah and allows it to continue asserting itself as an authority inside Lebanon. In fact, the General Amnesty Law of 1991 did not include a preamble acknowledging the war and its impact on the Lebanese people, nor did it recognise any of the crimes committed during the civil war, nor name any of the perpetrators, whether Lebanese or not. It had 'a silencing effect rather than an atoning one'.[48]

The civil society and local and international non-governmental agencies tried to fill the gaps created by the General Amnesty Law of 1991, by shedding light on the serious crimes that occurred during the Lebanese Civil War. Some of their efforts included recording witnesses' testimonies about the crimes committed during the war, producing documentaries and reports on grave human rights violations,[49] mapping gendered crimes such as rape, sexual assault and the forced displacement of women and children,[50] the digging of mass graves,[51] fighting for the right to know the truth about those who were kidnapped and those who were illegally detained and tortured in Syrian prisons[52] and, finally, encouraging reconciliatory measures in different war-torn villages. These public efforts forced the Lebanese authorities to at least recognise the right to know the truth about those who were forcibly disappeared. However, this right generated much tension between those who wanted to acknowledge this right and those who wanted, for political reasons, to let go of the past.

Moreover, the General Amnesty Law of 1991 contributed to creating a culture of impunity. Retributive justice dictates that, when a law is violated, a punishment should follow. In a way, justice is reactionary, as it 'reacts to restore any law that has been breached'.[53] When justice does not react, the offender walks away from the punishment, and the victim is in fact the one who is punished. 'The victim, therefore, becomes twice victimised',[54] by the offence itself and then by the lack of justice.

After the dismantling of the militias, many warlords and militia members entered political life, converted their militias into political parties and ran for elections. The warlords of yesterday became today's elected officials. None of them faced any legal repercussions for their acts during the civil war. In this culture of impunity, the Lebanese people felt powerless and distrustful of the legal and judiciary systems. This explains the almost complete absence of legal cases against warlords and militia members.[55] Very few cases were examined by the Justice Council, and these often were dismissed for lack of evidence, due to political pressure, or to comply with the General Amnesty Law of 1991. For instance, the Justice Council could not reach any verdict regarding the well-documented massacres of Bmaryam and Kfarmatta that took place in Mount Lebanon between the Christians and the Druze.[56] On an international level, Geahchan has argued that the almost non-existent jurisprudence against

Lebanon is perhaps due to the 'lack of legal awareness of the Lebanese citizen of their international rights'.[57] The amnesia and impunity culture created by the General Amnesty Law of 1991 allowed Hezbollah to continue acting as an implicitly legalised armed force inside Lebanon. In other words, it permitted Hezbollah's legal status to go unchallenged and unchecked.

To conclude this chapter, it is important that Hezbollah may be classified as a political party within Lebanon. While Hezbollah may fulfil the bare requirement of declaration as required by the 1909 Law on Associations, it certainly does not fulfil the remaining obligations. Nevertheless, it exists *ipso facto*, and State practice suggests the acceptance of Hezbollah as political party for its apparent and visible participation in political and public life. As to Hezbollah's military branch, State practice indicates that it has recognised it as a legal armed group. This is particularly true following the Taif Agreement of 1989, the General Amnesty Law of 1991 and all the Ministerial Statements that followed.

Conclusion to Part I

This part has examined the history of the Lebanese Civil War, Hezbollah's rise to power, as well as its ideology, structure and legal classification according to domestic laws. Hezbollah is legally recognised as political party, non-profit organisation and armed actor inside Lebanon. Several questions arise from this State practice: what is the legal status of Hezbollah in international law? Is it a subject of international law? Considering its legal status in Lebanon, is it a State or a non-State Actor? Is it a representative of the State of Lebanon? The answers to these questions and the legal consequences that they generate vary, depending on the context and whether Hezbollah is acting in times of peace or times of armed conflict.

Part II
The Statehood of Hezbollah

Introduction to Part II

Hezbollah is a legally recognised entity inside Lebanon. Politically speaking, Hezbollah appears to be the dominant entity on Lebanese territory. It holds tremendous power in all three branches of government. It has significant representation and allies in both the executive and the legislative. It is a well-known but hard-to-prove fact that Hezbollah puts political pressure on some judges and pays others. Furthermore, Hezbollah has strongholds in the south of Beirut, in the east of Lebanon (particularly in the Beqaa Valley and Baalbek) and the south of Lebanon. Hezbollah offers various services to the Shiites residing in these areas, who in return offer their allegiance.

What is the legal classification of Hezbollah in international law? Is it a subject of international law? Considering its domestic status and role on the ground, is it a State or a non-State actor? Are its members representatives of the State of Lebanon? Is Hezbollah the State of Lebanon?

To answer these questions and identify Hezbollah's status in international law, this part will begin with an examination of the definition of statehood. Chapter 4 will answer the following questions: how does international law define a State? How can an entity acquire statehood, and how can a State recognise an entity as a State? How can one distinguish between a State and Non-State actors? These questions are important as they allow us to determine the legal status of Hezbollah. Chapter 5 will address the following questions: is Hezbollah a State or a non-State actor? Does its status vary, depending on the context in which it operates and in times of peace or armed conflict? This last question carries particular significance, since the legal status of Hezbollah came under scrutiny in the 2006 armed conflict with Israel. The international community had to decide whether Hezbollah acted as the State of Lebanon and therefore to determine the *jus ad bellum* and *jus in bello* to apply.

At the time of writing this book, this question has once again become relevant. After the 7 October attack on Israeli civilians, violence erupted between Hezbollah and Israel. Today, violence is reaching a dangerous level, and both parties to the conflict have announced that they will not abide by the rules of war. Israel specifically has mentioned that it will target all of Lebanese territories and infrastructure, and that it will not limit its attacks to Hezbollah territory. This statement once more raises the question of Hezbollah's legal status and its classification as the State of Lebanon.

Chapter 4

What is a State?[1]

As Duncan French has pointed out, the State 'is the most fundamental unit of the international legal order'.[2] To understand what a State is, one must assess different facts through the lens of the law. It is interesting, if not ironic, that scholars wish to examine statehood in legal terms when statehood is often born out of an unlawful event such as a revolution or a coup. Furthermore, scholars wish to leave political considerations out of the legal analysis, when in fact they are an important part of the process. Despite these two minor critiques, statehood remains unquestioned when there is a symmetry between law and facts – in other words, when there is no dispute. However, the question is of value when reality does not match the law. This is the case with Lebanon and Hezbollah. On a superficial level, Lebanon's statehood is maintained. However, reality might differ from the State criteria set by international law.[3]

This chapter will begin with the definition of statehood based on the Peace Treaty of Westphalia; then, it will proceed to study the legal definition of personality as defined by Rowan Nicholson in *Statehood and the State-Like in International Law*. For a State to exist, it must have personality; it must exist as a fact with rights and duties on an international level. Also, it must be recognised as a State, but how can an entity claim statehood and be recognised as a State by other States? To answer this question, this chapter will examine the two opposing theories of effectiveness and recognition. Effectiveness theory dictates that some criteria must be fulfilled for a State to exist and to obtain international legal recognition. Territory, people, government and the capacity to enter into relations with other States count among these criteria. For recognition theory, a State is a State when recognised or declared as such by other States. The last section will examine the distinction between State and non-State actors. The loose definition of a State is problematic as it raises a serious legal question: how can one distinguish between State and non-State actor, especially if scholars of international law cannot agree on one?

Origins of Statehood: The Westphalian Definition

The two notions of State and international law are intertwined. If international law is defined as treaties and customary law created by States that have agreed to bind themselves by these rules, then the next question would be: what is a State in the eyes of international law? For Michel Miaille, the State is not an eternal category that was rationally created to ensure order; it was a historical phenomenon that appeared at a given time in history to resolve the contradictions that appeared within civil society: 'L'État n'est pas, comme l'affirment implicitement les juristes, une catégorie éternelle, découlant logiquement de la nécéssité d'assurer un ordre; il est un phénomène historique apparu à un moment donné de l'histoire pour résourdre les contradictions apparues dans la société civile'.[4] Similarly, Vaughan Lowe has noted that a State is an entity that was created at some point in time by people who decided to organise themselves to live in this specific context:[5] 'Whatever the nature of the State, whether it is a democracy or a theocracy, liberal or repressive, egalitarian or elitist or whatever, it is the State which stands as the most prominent social unit within which the rules and values that are the main external constraints on individual action are articulated'.[6]

The definition of statehood as we know it today emerged after the Peace Treaty of Westphalia, which was signed and sealed in Münster on 24 October 1648 to end the Thirty Year's War within the Holy Roman Empire and the Eight Year's War between Spain and the Netherlands. Two peace treaties were negotiated in Münster and Osnabrück.[7] For Eric David, these Treaties are important in the history of international law: the negotiations that led to the adoption of these treaties immobilised multiple representatives from different European entities. For the first time in history, many delegates of sovereign entities met in one place to discuss norms and a peace agreement. In a way, it was the first international diplomatic meeting in history. These treaties had four legal consequences: they announced the principle of equal sovereignty among parties,[8] the supremacy of international law over the domestic law of the contracting parties and the supremacy of international law over previous agreements.[9] The treaties also instated the rule of peaceful resolution of conflict,[10] as well as the right for foreign troops to peacefully cross over the territory of the contracting parties.[11]

Therefore, for some, the Peace Treaty of Westphalia laid solid foundations for the creation of the modern concept of a sovereign State in public international law. This State, no matter its size or its power, is equal to other sovereign States and has domestic law applicable on its own territory.[12] For James Crawford in *The Creation of States in International Law* . . .

> The effect of the Peace of Westphalia was to consolidate the existing States and principalities (including those whose existence or autonomy it recognised or established) at the expense of the Empire, and ultimately at the expense of the notion of the *civitas gentium maxima* – the universal community of mankind transcending the authority of States.[13]

Statehood as an Entity with Personality

In *Statehood and the State-Like in International Law*, Rowan Nicholson has argued that, for a State to exist, it must have legal personality. In other words, it must be a subject of international law. There is no one definition of personality, at least not one that is universally accepted.[14] Hence, Nicholson has offered the following: personality is 'an entity that is constructed as a fact by norms of international law and to which such norms give at least one right or duty'.[15] A norm is what dictates either a conduct or an omission and allows the distinction between lawfulness and unlawfulness. For instance, a State should not use force against another State. In case of the use of force, this action is unlawful. In sum, 'conduct norms are traditionally understood as ought-statements but can also be thought about in another way: as conditional statements that apply an irreducible binary distinction – the distinction between lawfulness and unlawfulness – to conduct'.[16]

The second component in Nicholson's definition of personality is right and duty. Following Hohfeld's writings on legal conceptions, Nicholson has argued that entities have a synallagmatic relationship where each party is bound to provide something or to perform a certain conduct towards the other party. While one has a duty to perform, the other has the right to receive this performance. Therefore, the relationship is correlative. Nicholson has added that 'a freedom is just the absence of a duty',[17] and that the absence of freedom implies a no-right. In addition to these four correlative relations of right, duty, freedom and no freedom, Nicholson has examined one more relation between entities with personality: the relation of power, which Hohfeld has defined as ability to 'effect [a] particular change to legal relations, which might involve creating or terminating relations we well as modifying existing ones'.[18] A State's decision to deploy its military on another's State's soil would be an example of relation of power.[19] This power relation must be mutual, otherwise it would be a form of 'disability',[20] an unbalanced relationship where one entity has more rights than another entity. This distortion may generate immunities and possibly unlawful conduct. This is, for instance, true when a State controls another State, and the controlling State can get away with certain unlawful conduct in the dominated State.

The last element in Nicholson's definition of personality which is required for a State to exist is facts: 'In order to be a person, something must exist in some sense as a matter of fact'.[21] Does this mean that the entity must have a physical presence? Nicholson has answered that it is not required for the entity to exist physically, but its existence should be legally constructed as a reality. As Crawford has pointed out, '[a] State is not a fact in the sense that a chair is a fact: it is a fact in the sense in which it may be said a treaty is a fact: that is, a legal status attaching to a certain state of affairs by virtue of certain rules or practices'.[22] Therefore, a State must be constructed as a fact, as an entity with personality that performs acts or omissions according to norms.[23]

In the nineteenth century, Western European countries with expansionist agendas denied some non-Western entities personality and therefore statehood. They justified this exclusion by claiming that these entities were uncivilised. As Nicholson has noted, the argument of 'civilisation' belongs to the political realm rather than to international law. Nevertheless, it had important legal repercussions. First, it introduced a racist legal ranking of different entities and made a distinction between European and non-European entities. Second, it falsely considered international law as only applicable among 'civilised' European countries. Despite the division of the world between civilised and uncivilised, Muslim and non-Muslim entities, there were still treaties signed between European entities and the Ottoman Empire.[24] The wave of decolonisation that followed World War I and World War II led to the emergence of a new world order and new independent States, undeniable facts with rights and duties recognised as such by international law.

State Recognition: Effectiveness *versus* Recognition Theories

A State must have personality; it must exist as a fact with rights and duties. The next question to ponder is how one can recognise an entity as a State. At the birth of the United Nations, there was a discussion on whether statehood recognition should depend on the discretion of individual States or on a collective body deciding for the international community.[25] The second idea was quickly abandoned in the name of State sovereignty. To this day, there is no specific international mechanism or procedure to recognise a State. Yet, these procedures would be helpful in case of statehood disputes.[26] This became very apparent in the recent discussion of Palestine's statehood. On 18 April 2024, the Security Council blocked Palestine's request to become a full member of the United Nations; it failed to recognise Palestine's statehood following a United States veto on a draft resolution that would have amended its status.[27] On 10 May 2024, in an Emergency Special Session, the General Assembly overwhelmingly backed Palestine's membership in the United Nations. It urged the Security Council to support its resolution.[28] Despite the wide endorsement, Palestine remains a non-State entity.

In *Democratic Statehood in International Law: The Emergence of New States in Post-Cold War Practice*, Jure Vidmar has argued that 'the emergence of a new state is not a factual occurrence but a law-governed political process which leads to a change in the legal status of certain territory'.[29] In fact, for Vidmar, a State does not necessarily exist as soon as it fulfils the requirements of the Montevideo Convention or following international acceptance. It exists through several democratic procedures, procedures that guarantee the right to vote, the right to run for elections and access to free media (among other rights): 'States cannot emerge automatically as a matter of object fact: they can only emerge in the legal circumstances where the claim to territorial integrity is either overcome or becomes inapplicable'.[30] The conundrum here is that the recognition of statehood might be a legal concept, but the process by which an entity acquires statehood is not always legal. As Anthony Carty has argued, '[l]aw governs neither the coming into existence nor the disappearance of states, although both may appear to have legal aspects'.[31] In other words, the question cannot be exclusively examined through the lens of Kelsen's Pure Theory of Law, for there are other factors to consider, such as politics, cultures, national identity and so on.

For Duncan French, the assessment of statehood has not been examined within the context of compliance or breach of law. Instead, it depends on various facts that are considered through the lens of the law: '[S]tatehood is the assessment of a conglomeration of facts through manifold legal prisms, which can either be focused and narrow or broad and all-encompassing, such variations dependent upon whether statehood is viewed – usually *a priori* – as acceptable or impermissible in any given situation'.[32] Similarly, in 'Statehood and Recognition in World Politics: Towards a Critical Research Agenda', Gëzim Visoka has advocated for an interdisciplinary approach to statehood recognition. He has argued that we should move away from the traditional 'power-driven, conservative, positivist, and legal interpretations'[33] of statehood. This approach is . . .

> . . . dominated by particular and narrow epistemological frameworks for thinking and acting on world politics that directly impact on how

> the recognition of state is (re)produced both in theory and practice. The mainstream knowledge on state recognition seeks to preserve the interests of existing powers at the expense of the rights and freedoms of subjugated peoples who see creation of a new state as a sanctuary for collective emancipation and escape from human rights abuses by the base state.[34]

Math Noortman has held a very similar position by calling for an interdisciplinary approach to identifying State and non-State actors. In 'Towards an Interdisciplinary Approach to Non-State Participation in the Formation of Global Law and Order', Noortmann has openly criticised international law for its narrow definition of statehood and its lack of inclusivity. He has argued that international law must revise its approach to statehood to include political transnational events and other important participants, such as non-State actors.[35]

In fact, the current theories of statehood do not account for the political, economic, social and other multiple identities that play a role in self-determination and the rise of a State, and it is not surprising to see the already existing international order attempting to preserve the status quo. Clearly, the question of statehood recognition generated a long legal debate that remains unsettled to this date. Despite the numerous publications on the subject, scholars of international law continue to be divided between two theories: constitutive theory and declaratory theory.

Constitutive theory, as defined by Crawford, posits that a competent organ determines whether an entity is functioning properly within a system. In international law, this assessment can only be performed by other States who examine the entity in question and decide whether it is functioning as a subject of their legal system.[36] This occurs when an entity is recognised as a State by other States. Nicholson has called it theory of recognition, where 'recognition is sufficient and necessary for statehood and [. . .] effectiveness is irrelevant'.[37] Declaratory theory, which Nicholson has called effectiveness theory, requires an entity to comply with 'criteria of effectiveness (including at least territory, people, and government)'.[38] In this theory, recognition of a new State is not a legal act but merely 'a political act, which is, in principle, independent of the existence of the new State as subject of international law'.[39]

This study recognises the importance of new legal theories and analysis and will adopt an interdisciplinary approach to the two theories of statehood. It will examine the traditional framework of effectiveness theory and recognition theory while paying close attention to non-legal elements such as international politics and diplomatic relations.

Effectiveness Theory

According to effectiveness theory (as Nicholson has called it), for a State to exist and be considered as such, it must have three attributes: the State must exist as a fact that meets the effectiveness criteria; the State must have rights and duties as per customary law; and, finally, the State must contribute to the formation of customary law.

The State as a Fact

The Peace Treaty of Westphalia and the 1933 Montevideo Convention on the Rights and Duties of States established several criteria that today remain widely used to define a State. Article I of the Montevideo Convention stipulates: 'The state as a person of international law should possess the following qualifications: a. a permanent population; b. a defined territory; c. government; and d. capacity to enter into relations with the other states'.[40]

As for territory, a State must have one on which to exercise domestic jurisdiction. Despite this requirement, 'there appears to be no rule prescribing the minimum area of that territory'.[41] The area can be small or large, and it does not have to include the entirety of the territory. Nicholson has given the example of 1918 Poland, when the Polish National Committee proclaimed itself as a national government. While Germany recognised Poland's statehood, Russia refused to cede territory that should have been under Polish control. A German-Polish Arbitral Tribunal examined the case and proclaimed that Germany's recognition and Russia's non-recognition had no effect on Poland's existence as a State and its right to control its territory. What matters are 'the conditions of possessing a territory, a people inhabiting the territory, and a public power which is exercised over the people and the territory'.[42] Furthermore, the Tribunal continued to say that, '[i]n order to say that a State exists and can be recognised as such [. . .] it is enough that this territory has a sufficient consistency, even though its boundaries have not yet been accurately delimited, and that the State actually exercises public authority over that territory'.[43] According to Crawford, two possible disputes can arise from the territory criterion: one regarding the entire territory of a new State and one regarding its boundaries. In some cases, these two disputes co-exist; this is the case with Israel, Kuwait, Mauritania and Belize, among others.[44]

As for people, a State must also have a permanent population occupying its territory. In its 2020 report, the World Bank shows the number of populations living in small States, and this number varies from approximately 11,000 in Nauru to 3,000,000 in Qatar.[45] This goes to show that 'no minimum is apparently prescribed'.[46] However, for Karen Knop in 'Statehood: Territory, People, Government', the formula of State-territory-people is not always clear, for 'there is not necessary correspondence between a state and a people'.[47] The criteria of territory and people can be expanded, thus expanding the limits of statehood. This would be the case with nationals residing in foreign States with voting rights in their home States or diplomatic immunity – a legal cover from their home State in their State of residency. In these examples, a State 'exercise[s] jurisdiction outside its territory on the basis of nationality, thereby producing a jurisdiction that overlaps or sometimes even replaces that of the territorial state'.[48] This also applies to migrant workers with rights and duties engaging both their States of origin and their hosting States.

Therefore, the formula territory-people is not always limited to universally recognised State borders and its residents, and statehood rights and duties can expand beyond a State's identified borders and its residents. The formula of territory-people in a State is also questioned within the contexts of colonisation and occupation, where 'the people and territory governed are not part of the state [. . .] Under the law of occupation, the occupying state governs, but does not acquire the occupied territory'.[49] Knop has given the example of Israel who governs the Palestinian people and territories that are not part of the State of Israel.[50]

The right to self-determination as guaranteed by the 1945 UN Charter[51] and the 1966 International Covenant on Economic, Social and Cultural rights (ICESCR) also illustrates this misalliance of State-territory-people. Some scholars have argued that colonisation created artificial States, since the determination of territory-people-government did not come from within but was often imposed by the colonial powers. This theory not only questions the Westphalian model of territory-people-government but has the potential of jeopardising the legal existence of many States today. To respond to this threat, some scholars have stated that these States have 'earned sovereignty', which implies that the current statehood has internalised the elements of territory-people-government as introduced by the international administration.[52] Despite its historical attribute as it is often tied to decolonisation, the right to self-determination today remains of an important legal value. Knop has presented the example of Quebec; in 1998, it requested to secede from Canada. The invasion of Iraq in 2003 serves as another example; it raised the questions of the Iraqis' right to self-determination and the effectiveness of war in state-building.[53]

As for government, a State must also have an effective one where powers are centralised. Crawford has made the point that international law does not define territory in a real estate sense but rather considers it in the context of governmental power in its three branches of legislative, executive and judicial: 'Territorial sovereignty is not ownership of but governing power with respect to territory. There is thus a good case for regarding government as the most important single criterion of statehood, since all the others depend upon it'.[54] As such, there is an overlap between statehood and government.

Contrary to Crawford, Nicholson does not seem to favour this overlapping view. Early international lawyers did not make the distinction between State and government. When a State recognised the new government of another State, it assumed that the conditions of statehood remained intact, and that the State in question continued to have control over its territory and people. Yet, for Nicholson, the two categories of State/government should be separated. The category of State is tied to the existence of an entity with all its rights and duties, and the category of government is related to the identities of individuals who may act lawfully or unlawfully.[55]

Although it seems easy to recognise a government, it is much harder to identify an effective government. Crawford has provided the example of the former Belgian Congo which today is the Democratic Republic of Congo. The issue of its effectiveness concerns multiple factors: there was no preparation for its independence in 1960; there were several violent secession movements; the central government was divided into two fractions; and the Belgian troops returned to the Congo after independence, for the purpose of rendering humanitarian aid, followed by the UN forces which entered the Congo to maintain peace.[56] For Crawford, it is difficult to interpret the criterion of effective government. To understand the example of the Democratic Republic of Congo, he has advanced different theories:

1. Congo was not a State when it was recognised as such since it did not meet the criterion of effective government. In other words, its recognition was premature.
2. It may also be that the recognition of its statehood was an unclear case of constitutive theory.
3. Finally, it is possible that the criteria of effective government were interpreted very loosely.

Crawford has concluded that '[t]his third view is to be preferred. The point about "government" is that it has two aspects: the actual exercise of authority, and the right or title to exercise that authority'.[57]

Consequently, for an entity to have statehood, it must have a government and general control over a population and a territory. If this statehood is disputed, the criteria of effective government and territory will be examined more strictly by the international community. Furthermore, there is a distinction to be made between the creation of a new State and the survival of an already existing State. Crawford has argued that, '[i]n the former situation, the criterion of effective government may be applied more strictly'.[58] In addition to the criteria of territory, people and government, Crawford has added other requirements for statehood recognition: the capacity to enter into relations with other States and independence.

As for the capacity to enter into relations with other States, there exists a debate on whether this capacity is a consequence of statehood rather than a criterion as to its recognition. In other words, the debate is whether legal capacity presents a consequence of a State's legal personality and status as a subject of international law. Chronologically speaking, it would make sense to say that legal personality is the prerequisite for an entity's legal capacity to sign treaties or enter into agreements with other entities. Irrespective of this time issue, the capacity to enter into relations remains tied to independence and effective governance. In order words, legal capacity cannot exist if an entity is not independent (or recognised as such) and equipped with a functioning government.

For instance, in 1988, the PLO and the Southwest Africa People's Organisation requested to have observer status at the United Nations under the 1975 Vienna Convention on the Representation of States in their Relations with International Organisations of Universal Character.[59] The United Kingdom voted against the proposed General Assembly Resolution, stating the following:

> [T]he Convention of 1975 applies only to States. It does not apply to national liberation movements and its scope cannot be widened by resolution so as to extend to them [. . .] there is no justification for the resolution to call upon States to accord to certain national liberation movements, functional privileges and immunities. An entity other than a State cannot be regarded as the same as the government of a State. A national liberal movement does not have the same ability as a government to provide the guarantee of good conduct and behaviour which a host country is entitled to require.[60]

As for independence, it is simultaneously 'a central criterion for statehood'[61] and a State right. Article 3 of the 1933 Montevideo Convention on the Rights and Duties of States stipulates that a State has the right to protect its integrity and independence.[62] Without independence, an entity may not be considered a State but only part of another dominant State; unilateral declarations of independence violate the territorial integrity of the host State.[63] In this context, if statehood is granted, it might trigger several legal consequences, including the legal responsibility of the grantor.[64]

To define independence, Crawford has referred to the frequently cited 1931 case of the Austro-German Customs Union where the Court was asked to examine whether the proposed customs union between Germany and Austria complied with the Austrian obligations as dictated by the Treaty of Saint-Germain and the Protocol of Geneva. The court held that the proposed customs were unlawful. The majority opinion held that it had the potential of threatening Austria's economic independence. Judge Anzilotti's definition of independence has become a well-cited paragraph:

> The independence of Austria within the meaning of Article 88 is nothing else but the existence of Austria, within the frontiers laid down by the Treaty of Saint-Germain, as a separate State and not subject to the authority of any other State of group of States. Independence as thus understood is really no more than the normal condition of States according to international law; it may also be described as sovereignty *(suprema potestas)*, or external sovereignty, by which is meant that the State has over it no other authority than that of international law [. . .] It follows that the legal conception of independence has nothing to do with a State's subordination to international law or with the numerous and constantly increasing states of *de facto* dependence which characterize the relation of one country to other countries. It also follows that the restrictions upon a State's liberty, whether arising out of ordinary international law or contractual agreement do not as such in the least affect its independence. As long as those restrictions do not place the State under the legal authority of another State, the former remains an independent State however extensive and burdensome those obligations may be.[65]

Crawford has concluded that independence requires two elements: the existence of an entity within identifiable borders, and its separation from the authority of another State or States. In other words, independence is guaranteed when a State is subject to international law with no other authority above it.[66]

Furthermore, Crawford has made a distinction between formal and actual independence. Formal independence demonstrates the absence of real independence, and 'the entity should be regarded as not independent'.[67] By contrast, real or actual independence is 'the minimum degree of real governmental power at the disposal of the authorities of the putative State'.[68] Crawford has investigated multiple situations, including three that derogate from actual independence: the first case concerns an instance 'when an entity comes into existence in violation of certain basic rules of international law, its title to be a "State" is in issue'.[69] The second case concerns the creation of a State or government in an occupied territory under belligerent conditions, and the third case a State being under substantial control of another State.

The third scenario is of interest to this chapter, and Crawford has described it as follows: 'an entity, even one possessing formal marks of independence, which is subject to foreign domination and control on a permanent or long-term basis is not "independent" for the purposes of statehood in international law'.[70] Two potential conflicts arise from this definition: first, how to determine whether the substantial external domination is indeed foreign and not domestic? Second, how can one determine whether the external domination is, in fact, domination and not just influence?[71]

To answer the first question, Crawford has argued that it is important to observe the facts and understand the capacity in which the different entities are acting.[72] As to the second question, it arises in three situations: this is relevant in case of protectorates that depend on other States.[73] It is also relevant in case of puppet States and governments which Crawford has defined as 'nominal sovereigns under effective foreign control, especially in cases where the establishment of the puppet State is intended as a cloak for illegality'.[74] Finally, it exists in the context of partial independence.

To a certain extent, protectorates are easy to determine since they are often related to colonial history and colonial powers. The relation of a puppet State or government is more complex to identify. Belligerent occupation, illegal intervention and the threat or use of force are situations that are assumed to lead to a puppet State or government. If the puppet entity was established unlawfully, . . .

> . . . that it was imposed on, and rejected by the vast majority of the population it claimed to govern; that in important matters it was subject to foreign direction or control, that it was staffed, especially in more important positions, by nationals of the dominant State. It was not regarded as relevant that certain individuals or groups (including minority groups) in the territory concerned carried out normal administrative functions, or constituted the formal government, if the elements mentioned above were present.[75]

Crawford has added that acts imposed by the puppet State or government must be considered void, unless we are in the context of a belligerent occupation, in which case the laws of occupation apply.

Finally, the question of how to determine whether an external domination is, in fact, actual control and not just influence arises in the context of partial independence, or what Crawford has called 'purported grants of colonial independence [. . .] where there is evidence that real control has not been transferred'.[76] Crawford has used the examples of Syria and Lebanon in 1942–46. After World War I and the collapse of the Ottoman Empire, these two entities were placed under French mandate until 1943 in Lebanon and until 1946 in Syria, respectively. In 1941, the French Delegate-General approved a limited independence for Syria only for the purposes of war requirements. Although the United Kingdom recognised Syria and Lebanon, the United States refused to do so. It was only after the full transfer of rights, prerogatives and duties that the United States recognised these two States of Syria and Lebanon. The French troops remained in the Levant after the proclamation of independence, yet their presence was not considered an obstacle to the recognition of Lebanon's and Syria's statehood. According to Crawford, the examples of Syria and Lebanon are important as they demonstrate two facts: first, independence is important for statehood recognition; second, statehood can be maintained even with foreign troops on the ground if the local government exercises the local control.[77]

It is important to add that, in all the above cases on independence, one must prove that actual independence is lacking and that a foreign entity is systematically and permanently controlling all the decision-making, which is not a small task; it would be difficult to prove in the absence of a foreign occupation or unlawful military intervention.

To conclude the analysis of the State as a fact, while some scholars have limited the theory to the three components of territory-people-government, others – such as Crawford – have expanded the formula and added the capacity to sign treaties and independence. Regardless of how narrow or large the definition of the State as a fact is, many scholars have criticised it as inadequate for the twenty-first century. As pointed out earlier in the discussion on effectiveness theory, scholars such as Vidmar, French, Visoka and Noortmann have considered the Westphalian model outdated, calling for its revision and for the adoption of other approaches to statehood recognition. Nicholson has criticised the chronological conundrum that it creates: how can one require from an entity (1) to have exclusive jurisdiction over its territory, people and government, (2) to be recognised as an independent State and (3) to be able to have international relations, when all these items come after the State proclamation?

The State Must Have Rights and Duties as per Customary Law

In addition to territory, people, government, the capacity to enter into relations with other States and independence, an entity must proclaim its statehood by either claiming independence from another State or claiming to have rights and duties as a State. Nicholson has given the example of Australia and other British dominions. Although they satisfied the criteria of territory, people and government, they were not considered as States until 1919 and after they had formally claimed their statehood and independence.[78]

Independence and sovereignty[79] can be considered fundamental rights to statehood. Article 3 of the 1933 Montevideo Convention stipulates:

> The political existence of the State is independent of recognition by the other States. Even before recognition the State has the right to defend its integrity and independence, to provide for its conservation and prosperity, and consequently to organise itself as it sees fit, to legislate upon its interests, administer its services, and to define the jurisdiction and competence of its courts. The exercise of these rights has no other limitation than the exercise of the rights of other States according to international law.[80]

However, what if an entity refuses to make the statehood claim yet benefits from some State attributes? Providing the example of the Islamic State, Nicholson has argued that this lacuna would allow an entity to evade international law and all of the State's responsibilities. Although Nicholson has not elaborated on this hypothetical question since it is rather exceptional, it certainly merits our attention, particularly in the context of Hezbollah-Lebanon relations.

What if Hezbollah is not a State in the Westphalian sense of 'territory, people, government', especially in that it has not claimed its statehood, and yet it still benefits from non-State attributes such as the evasion of international law and State responsibility? This interesting question will be examined in the next chapter on Hezbollah's statehood.

The State Must Contribute to the Formation of Customary Law[81]

Finally, the third element of effectiveness theory dictates that a State must contribute to the formation of customary law. Once again, one can note the chronological paradox of such a statement where a State creates norms and norms create a State. Nicholson has asked the following question: 'If states are defined by a customary norm, how can that customary norm derive its validity from states?'[82] To answer, he has advanced five possible answers:

1. One must suspend judgment and accept the statement as is.
2. The second possible answer argues that some customary laws are not ordinary, such as natural laws.

3. Sextus Empiricus's skepticism is the third answer: one is asked to suspend judgment to avoid error for issues that cannot be resolved. Nicholson has called this relativism.
4. The fourth solution proposes that some rules generate great social pressure beyond which one does not need to investigate or look.
5. Finally, the fifth solution is circularity; it suggests that some customary norms define certain entities as States. Once established and functional, these States create customary norms: 'Custom creates states; states create custom'.[83]

Although having advanced these theories, Nicholson has also recognised that they are not conclusive. Contrary to points 1 and 3, it is not easy for one to suspend judgment (especially for inquisitive souls). Points 2 and 4 generate more questions than answers: if one agrees that some laws are not ordinary, who determines the validity of these laws? Who identifies rules created under great social pressure? As to point 5, like the others, it 'is not intuitively satisfactory'.[84] In fact, 'logical circularity is deprecated [. . .] and involves a suspension of judgment'.[85]

Nicholson has asked whether the theory of effectiveness is sufficient or necessary, noting that it is hard to find evidence in favour or against this theory since almost all States are well-established. However, he has argued that effectiveness is necessary for statehood. In fact, the statehood status is kept even if the terms of effectiveness theory are barely maintained. This would be the case with Somalia.[86] Despite its general absence from international law, the statehood of Somalia continues to be recognised since Somalia maintains territory-people-government. Albeit unsuccessful, it also continues to have rights and duties and to participate in creating customary laws. One can conclude that, once a State is recognised as such, it is hard to fall out of this recognition.

Recognition Theory

Some scholars of international law have favoured the theory of recognition over that of effectiveness. Some have gone even further and argued that recognition of an entity as a State is enough, and that effectiveness is irrelevant. For instance, on 9 July 2011, 'Japan recognised the Republic of South Sudan as a new state'[87] The United States of America also announced 'South Sudan as a sovereign, independent state on July 9, 2011, following its secession from Sudan'.[88] Historically, this approach was due to dynastic legitimacy, when monarchs inherited their powers, governed over land and people and were recognised by other entities as the one source of authority. As such, 'although some entities are strong or important enough that others have little practical choice but to recognise them, it is still by recognition that they are constituted as states'.[89]

Nicholson has raised the question whether the theory of recognition is enough to establish statehood. On the one hand, sovereign States have the right to recognise or not to recognise the statehood of another entity. On the other hand, their recognition might be based on facts interpreted differently by each State. For instance, this is the case with Palestine, where international lawyers and scholars have analysed facts differently. On 15 November 1988, Yasser Arafat, the Chairman of the Palestine Liberation Organisation, proclaimed the independence of the Palestinian State. Although the proclamation recognised the State of Israel, it did not precisely define the borders of the Palestinian territories. In his speech, Mr Arafat proclaimed that '[t]he Palestine National Council announces in the name of God, in the name of the people, of the Arab Palestinian people, the establishment of the state of Palestine in our Palestinian nation, with holy Jerusalem as its capital'.[90]

In 2012, the UN General Assembly granted Palestine the status of non-member observer State, since 132 States members of the UN accorded recognition to the State of Palestine.[91] In 2014, Sweden affirmed that Palestine had met statehood criteria.[92] This is what Nicholson has called 'state-in-context', where an entity is recognised as a State by some States but not by others.[93] The issue with this approach is that it gives recognition theory a quantitative value – that is, statehood recognition depends on the number of States recognising the entity.

In 'How to Recognise a State (and Not): Some Practical Considerations', Tom Grant has raised another interesting issue regarding recognition. Recognition may be clearly expressed in a statement (as shown in South Sudan's example) or in a treaty. However, the situation becomes complicated when a State does not formally recognise an entity as a State, but its practices suggest otherwise. How do we know whether the act is intended as an act of statehood recognition, especially when international law does not require a specific form for recognition? In other words, how can the international community interpret a State's intention in a tacit act? To illustrate this issue, Grant has provided the example of Singapore and its relations with Taiwan. The Singapore Court of Appeal had to decide whether their extensive relations inferred recognition. The Court of Appeal decided that they did not imply recognition: 'the acts must leave no doubt as to the intention to grant it'.[94] In *Cyprus* v. *Turkey*, the European Court of Human Rights held a similar position, stating that the acknowledgment of a court system in a territory does not imply recognition.[95]

More recently, the question of statehood recognition through a tacit act surfaced in the context of Lebanon-Israel relations. In October 2022, the two States signed the Maritime Border Agreement, which was brokered by the United States.[96] Technically, the two States are at war and have been since 1948 and the declaration of the State of Israel. Lebanon has not officially recognised the State of Israel, and many have wondered whether this agreement implied Lebanese recognition of Israel's statehood.[97]

There is no consensus on how to interpret a State's intention and tacit acts of statehood recognition. However, some acts are considered a form of recognition, while others are not. As Grant has pointed out, continuous contact between two entities does not necessarily mean statehood recognition. France did not recognise Viet Nam as a State in 1954, despite the lengthy negotiations and contact between the two entities.[98] Entering in agreement with an entity does not imply statehood recognition. As pointed out previously, Taiwan was not recognised as a State despite its numerous agreements with Singapore.

Despite this lacuna in international law (the absence of a required form for statehood recognition), some scholars have argued that recognition should always come from authorities who are able to represent the State on an international level,[99] a position reflected in Article 7, paragraph 2, of the 1969 Vienna Convention on the Law of Treaties.[100] In this case, the Israel-Lebanon Maritime Border Agreement would not qualify as tacit recognition of Israel's statehood, for the following reason: to celebrate the Maritime Border Agreement, former Israeli Prime Minister Yair Lapid announced that it was a political achievement because 'it is not every day that an enemy state recognises the State of Israel, in a written agreement, in front of the entire international community'.[101] Former Lebanese President Michel Aoun responded by denying that Lebanon recognised Israel's statehood through the Maritime Border Agreement; he announced that the '[d]emarcating the southern maritime border is technical work that has no political implications'.[102]

The evolution of positive laws, the wave of decolonisation and the emergence of new States in the twentieth century has pushed many scholars of international law to move away from exclusively espousing the recognition theory, due to its unreliability and relativism. For Nicholson, recognition theory has the potential of creating chaos within the international legal system: 'if a state recognises and is recognised by an entity that does not meet those criteria, the two entities thereby create a new parallel universe of norms and, in order to do so, must tacitly agree that the criteria do not apply for the purpose of their bilateral relations'.[103] In reaction to this criticism, some have argued that meeting the criteria of effectiveness alone is not sufficient and that States need to recognise an entity's statehood. In a way, it is important to hybridise the effectiveness and recognition theories since each cannot stand alone. Nicholson returned to the case of Somalia: if both theories were to apply independently, Somalia should no longer be recognised as a State since it does not meet the effectiveness criteria. And yet, its statehood continues to be recognised by the international community, which suggests that both theories are being applied concurrently. Despite this supportive example that favours hybridisation, Nicholson has recognised its shortcomings. If an entity can acquire statehood by either effectiveness or recognition, then statehood is almost always guaranteed despite all the gaps: 'Where an entity is universally recognised but there is ambiguity about whether the entity meets the effectiveness criteria, the effectiveness-or-recognition view makes it impossible to resolve the ambiguity: any deficiencies of effectiveness would in any event be repaired by recognition'.[104]

For Crawford in *The Creation of States in International Law* neither theory fully explains the reality on the ground:

> The declaratory theory assumes that territorial entities can readily, by virtue of their mere existence, be classified as having one particular legal status: it thus, in a way, confuses 'fact' with 'law' [. . .] the constitutive theory, although it draws attention to the need for cognition, or identification, of the subjects of international law, and leaves open the possibility of taking into account the relevant legal principles not based on 'fact', incorrectly identifies that cognition with diplomatic recognition, and fails to consider the possibility that identification of new subjects may be achieved in accordance with general rules or principles rather than on an ad hoc, discretionary basis.[105]

Simply put, for Crawford, declaratory theory confuses facts and law, and constitutive theory reduces statehood recognition to diplomacy, which should not be the case.[106]

The debate of effectiveness *versus* recognition theory is still ongoing and remains far from being resolved. It becomes complicated as most States have already been established. As last remarks on the topic, Nicholson has observed two situations that arise as exceptions to both effectiveness and recognition theories: self-determination and secession. They create situations that do not correspond with the criteria set by both theories, and they raise legal complications: is secession unlawful under international law? What domestic laws apply to the seceded entity? Would they be the domestic laws of the original State, or would the seceded entity have its own laws? Would occupation laws apply in this context? What about territorial integrity? Can we speak of statehood when the territory of the original State has been altered? Can we speak of statehood when the seceded territory is not recognised as independent by the original State and other States? While self-determination is presumed to be a clearer legal concept since it was heavily invoked during the decolonisation era, it generates, nevertheless, a fair number of legal questions. One of the most important questions relates to recognition: what if some States recognise the statehood of the new entity, but others do not?[107] While it is beyond the scope of this chapter to explain the details of these two exceptional cases, it is essential to note that the questions above show that neither effectiveness nor recognition theory are easily applied, and that there are situations that do not perfectly match the criteria that they created.

State and Non-State Actor

Although the Westphalian formula of territory-people-government remains widely used, it has not escaped the criticism of many scholars who have considered it out-dated and unable to reflect the realities of the twenty-first century.[108] For Nicholson, the concept of State is unstable, and he has preferred to employ the expression 'state-like entity' to be inclusive of entities that do not necessarily fit the traditional Westphalian formula.[109] Furthermore, as mentioned above, Nicholson has used the term 'states-in-context' for entities that lack universal recognition of statehood.[110] For Jure Vidmar in 'Unilateral Declarations of Independence in International Law', the criteria of territory-people-government and capacity to enter into relations with other States, which are enumerated in Article 1 of the Montevideo Convention on Rights and Duties of States (1933), 'are inadequate in the contemporary international law of statehood'.[111] For Karen Knop, there is no one formula to define a State under international law: 'In some cases, international law certifies no more than the state's effective control over its population. In other cases, the creation of the state through an exercise of self-determination makes the state an agent chosen freely by a people'.[112]

If the definition of a State is not set in stone in international law, the next logical question would be: how can one distinguish between State and non-State actors? For Yaël Ronen, this is indeed a tricky question since the category of non-State actor is defined in opposition to the State actor.[113] Within the non-State actor category, Ronen has focused on what she has called 'quasi-states', a concept close enough to Nicholson's 'state-like' entities. She has identified quasi-States, which include non-State actors (NSAs), 'by their similarity to states, including territorial control, and thus by the potential to exercise the full panoply of powers, rights and obligations of states. At the same time, quasi-states [. . .] are defined by their voluntary self-exclusion from the category of states'.[114] In other words, formally, quasi-States are not States. It is true that their existence may depend on the recognition of their hosting State. However, they do not have the rights, duties, or the personality of a State, which is highly problematic since these entities have great power without any State responsibility. Ronen has given the example of the Palestinian territories before 2012 and their acceptance into the UN General Assembly as a non-member observer State.

For Ronen, the Palestinian authorities have an identifiable people, territory and government. However, she has falsely noted that they never proclaimed their independence and therefore their statehood, and thus they qualify as a quasi-State. As pointed out above, the Palestinian authorities proclaimed their independence on 15 November 1988. In 'Land of the Three Faiths: The Little-Known History of the Palestinian Declaration of Independence', Jerome Segal has noted that it is 'shocking that the 1988 declaration, one of the most fundamental documents of Palestinian nationalism, is largely unknown, not just to the Israeli public, but to most Israeli leaders as well'.[115]

Ronen has presented other examples, such as Taiwan and Puerto Rico. Although Taiwan has diplomatic relations and representations in different States and has signed treaties binding it as an entity,[116] it is not recognised as a State independent from the State of China. For Crawford in *The Creation of States in International Law*, 'Taiwan is not a State because it still has not unequivocally asserted its separation from China and is not recognised as a State distinct from China'.[117] As for the Commonwealth of Puerto Rico, it is not a sovereign independent State. Instead, it is a territory that falls under the United States' sovereignty.[118]

Ronen has pointed out that there are times where quasi-States operate as if they were States. This is particularly true when they enter into binding agreements with other States. However, in many ways, these non-State entities benefit from their quasi-State status. A proclamation of statehood and independence from the Palestinian authorities (in relation to Israel) and Taiwan (in relation to China) would trigger a series of events that would most likely have violent outcomes. Furthermore, as Ronen has indicated, this proclamation would weaken the Palestinian authorities' position in their negotiations with Israel and the international community. As for Puerto Rico, despite the multiple referendums on its status, the benefits would include, but are not limited to, access to US citizenship, unrestricted travel to the United States and economic aid.[119]

For Ronen, in some cases the decision of not proclaiming statehood and independence may be a deliberate political choice.[120] Consequently, the quasi-State status generates legal challenges for international law. This is true when a quasi-State provides citizenship to its nationals, establishes borders control, violates human rights, or uses force against a State.[121] The issues of human rights violation and use of force are particularly interesting in the context of this book. If Hezbollah is not a State in the Westphalian sense, and if Hezbollah better fits the legal definition of a non-State actor, what would be the legal consequences when it uses force inside Lebanon? Would international humanitarian law apply, or would it be considered a matter of domestic law? What would be the legal repercussions of its use of force on an international level in Syria and against Israel? These questions are important and will be addressed in the next chapter on Hezbollah's statehood.

Ronen has ended her study on pessimistic note, stating that '[t]here is no one-stop solution to the challenges presented by NSAs in general and by quasi-states in particular'.[122] There are too many inconsistencies as circumstances and conditions vary, and to make the distinction between a State and non-State actor, it is important to proceed on a case-by-case basis.

To conclude, this chapter has offered a brief definition of statehood according to the Peace Treaty of Westphalia. It has examined the definition of personality; a State cannot exist as a legal entity without personality. It has also discussed the two opposing theories of effectiveness and recognition. For effectiveness theory, a State exists when it fulfils three general conditions: (1) it must exist as a fact that meets the effectiveness criteria; (2) it must have rights and duties as per customary law; and, finally, (3) it must contribute to the formation of customary law. To meet the effectiveness criteria, a State must at least have a territory, a people and a government. Scholars have added other criteria such as the capacity to enter into relations with other States and independence. For recognition theory, for a State to exist, it simply must be recognised as such by other States. Both theories have their benefits and limitations. This chapter has also analysed the distinction between State and non-State actors.

Despite the fluid definition of statehood, the criticism of the Westphalian model as out-dated and inadequate, the weak distinction between State and non-State actors and the continuous debate on the modality of statehood recognition, the entity of the 'state is inescapable'.[123] With all its benefits and flaws, it remains the foundation of international law and international relations. The next chapter will examine the definition of statehood in the context of Hezbollah and Lebanon. It will answer the following question: is Hezbollah a State, a quasi-State, or a non-State Actor?

Chapter 5

Hezbollah: A State Actor in Times of Peace and War?

Chapter 4 has covered the legal definition of statehood, two theories of statehood recognition, as well as the distinction between State and non-State actors. This chapter will focus on Hezbollah as an entity and aim to answer the following question: is Hezbollah a subject of international law with legal personality? Does Hezbollah fulfil the legal definition of State? These questions cannot be answered in the absolute and must be examined in specific contexts. For this reason, it is important to distinguish between Hezbollah's activities inside and outside Lebanon, as well as in times of peace and times of war. Furthermore, to borrow the language of Article 4 of the Articles on Responsibility of States for Internationally Wrongful Acts,[1] Hezbollah may be an organ of the State of Lebanon or its representative. This possible qualification will be examined in Chapter 8 on State responsibility.

Hezbollah and the Lebanese State after 1992

Hezbollah's relation with the Lebanese State is complicated. It is multi-faceted and varies between complicity, opposition and violent confrontation. The Lebanese State has worked closely with Hezbollah and collaborated with its members. It has offered legal cover for its military activities and allowed its members to access the parliament and the government. Furthermore, the LAF have collaborated with Hezbollah fighters in certain battles. However, there have also been times when Hezbollah acted against the State's interests and in violation of its constitution.

Hezbollah–Lebanon Relationship

Hezbollah Acts in Collaboration with the State of Lebanon

As pointed out in the Chapter 3, the Taif Agreement of 1989 put an end to the Lebanese Civil War;[2] this was followed by the General Amnesty

Law of 1991,[3] which re-affirmed the political power-sharing based on sectarian affiliations, allowed Syria to maintain its control over Lebanon and called for the dismantling of all militias. Furthermore, the General Amnesty Law of 1991 called for the strengthening of the armed forces, so that they could maintain Lebanon's safety and fight against the Israeli occupation in the south. The law itself did not explicitly refer to Hezbollah and was interpreted as non-applicable to the Shiite militant group. In fact, Hezbollah was considered a resistance movement with the legal and legitimate right to fight the Israeli occupation in Lebanon, and Lebanese lawmakers legalised Hezbollah's military activities inside and outside of Lebanon.

In a recent interview, President Michel Aoun – whose political party, the Free Patriotic Movement, had signed a memorandum of understanding and alliance with Hezbollah in 2006 – gave legal cover to Hezbollah by announcing that Hezbollah . . .

> . . . is a Lebanese organisation that was founded to liberate our territory from the Israeli occupation. It was created for that in 1985, and then later, in 2000, Israel withdrew from Lebanon, and we believed that the action of Hezbollah was finished [. . .] You cannot say to Hezbollah, 'We have to dismantle your organisation', since Israel is provoking Lebanon and is attacking.[4]

This close collaboration with the former Lebanese president and his political party, the Free Patriotic Movement, prompted the United States to impose sanctions on the president's family:

> The US Department of the Treasury's Office of Foreign Assets Control (OFAC) sanctioned Gibran Bassil (Bassil), the President of the Free Patriotic Movement (FPM) political party and Member of Parliament (MP), pursuant to Executive Order (E.O.) 13818, for his role in corruption in Lebanon. E.O 13818, which builds upon and implements the Global Magnitsky Human Rights Accountability Act, targets corruption and serious human rights abuse around the world.[5]

Hezbollah's political representation in parliament and the government allowed its members to speak as official members of the Lebanese State, thus combining Hezbollah's and the State of Lebanon's narratives as one. These official representatives acted in the name of the Lebanese people – or at least a good portion of the Lebanese people. In fact, Hezbollah's Secretary General Hassan Nasrallah has frequently referenced in his speeches what he considers to be the three pillars of Lebanon's statehood: the army, the Lebanese people and *al-Muqawamah* (Arabic for resistance, but in this case employed as a synonym for Hezbollah). In doing so, he linked Lebanon's statehood with Hezbollah's fighters.[6] Since 2008, this same formula of 'Army, Lebanese people, *al-Muqawamah*' has appeared in several ministerial statements,[7] which gave 'Hezbollah legitimacy within the state without the accountability required of a state institution'.[8] It also provided Hezbollah with the 'exceptional right to possess and use weapons in the name of national defence, without delineating Hezbollah's duties or responsibilities in return; this enable[d] it to use force at its own discretion under the pretext of national security'.[9]

At times, the LAF collaborated with Hezbollah. In 2011, the porous eastern border of Lebanon became a smuggling area for illegal goods, a crossing-path for undocumented Syrians fleeing the civil war and a hub for terrorism. In 2014, a group of al-Qaida jihadists and militia men of the Islamic State attacked the LAF and took hostages. 'In the following month, an implicit collaboration between Hizbullah (on the Syrian side) and LAF (on the Lebanese side) started to squeeze, surrounded and corner the jihadists in the mountainous area'.[10] Publicly, Hezbollah presented itself and the LAF as defenders of Lebanon's sovereignty. In 2017, Hezbollah collaborated once again with the LAF to fight the Hayat Tahrir al-Sham jihadist fighters: 'Hassan Nasrallah, head of Hezbollah, praised the LAF after the operation, describing it as a partner of Hezbollah and a pillar of Lebanese security. Nasrallah patronisingly noted that the LAF had played an essential supporting role in "scoring this victory"'.[11]

Once again, Hezbollah used this partnership to improve its national image as Lebanon's defender and to send a message to the international community that Hezbollah and the LAF were collaborating.[12] As regional analysist Lina Khatib has pointed out, this narrative allows for Hezbollah to legitimise its weapons and ties it to Lebanon's security. It also depicts ultra-conservative Sunnis as the only danger to the State and the LAF.[13]

Hezbollah Acts against the State of Lebanon

Despite the collaborative work, Hezbollah has acted numerous times against the State's interests. In 2000 and after Israel withdrew from the occupied Lebanese territories in the south, Hezbollah members went in to maintain law and order and to liberate those whom Israeli forces illegally detained in Khiam prison.[14] The State and its armed forces were visually absent; therefore, they failed in their own legal duties towards the occupied south. Hezbollah took advantage of this void and collaborated with the Syrian Armed Forces to bully the few LAF members out of the region.[15]

Hezbollah needed to redefine itself, and so it assigned itself a new agenda: to evict the State and gain control over more territory. Between

2000 and 2006, Hezbollah executed multiple attacks against Israel and negotiated prisoner exchanges.[16] These decisions were made outside the appropriate legal channels and without the State's intervention; yet, despite these flagrant violations, Emile Lahoud, the pro-Syrian President at the time of the exchange, welcomed the returning prisoners along with Hezbollah officials at the Beirut airport.

Furthermore, Hezbollah has acted independently of the State of Lebanon and without accountability. It has appropriated the exclusive right to declare peace and war (as we will see below). Article 49 of the Lebanese Constitution of 1926 stipulates:

> The President of the Republic is the head of the state and the symbol of the nation's unity. He shall safeguard the constitution and Lebanon's independence, unity, and territorial integrity. The President shall preside over the Supreme Defense Council and be the Commander-in-Chief of the Armed Forces which fall under the authority of the Council of Ministers.[17]

Much like his predecessors, former President Michel Aoun has given legal cover to Hezbollah, and his actions can be understood in two ways: either the president is willingly collaborating with Hezbollah, or he is being coerced to do so. Either way, the facts remain that Hezbollah is acting in violation of Lebanon's Constitution and that the State of Lebanon has no power to stop it.

In 2006, Hezbollah kidnapped two Israeli soldiers, which led to a full-scale war between Hezbollah and Israel. The UN Security Council responded to this violation by adopting Resolution 1701 which called 'for the full cessation of hostilities, the deployment of Lebanese forces to Southern Lebanon [. . .] and the establishment of a demilitarised zone between the Blue Line and the Litani River'.[18] At the end of the war, Hezbollah proclaimed 'Divine Victory',[19] but most Lebanese people blamed Hezbollah for the destruction of Lebanon. Tensions rose again between the anti-Syrian 14 March and pro-Syrian 8 March groups, which translated into tensions between the Lebanese State and Hezbollah.

This tension appeared during the discussion of Resolution 1701, when Prime Minister Siniora imposed mentioning the Shebaa Farms, a land disputed between Lebanon, Syria and Israel. Hezbollah has claimed and continues to do so to this day that the Shebaa Farms are Lebanese, and that it is within its right to fight the Israeli occupation. Israel has always rejected this claim. However, the Lebanese State's discussion of this matter on the international stage of the UN 'reveals the attempt to re-take the lead over any national sovereignty issue',[20] and '[i]n such circumstances, the mention of the Shebaa Farms in the UN resolution

1701 was seen as a victory for the Siniora government as he tried to challenge Hizbullah on the monopoly of the territorial sovereignty'.[21] Having appointed cartographers, the UN decided that the Shebaa Farms were Syrian territory captured by Israel in 1967.[22] It is interesting that, in 2011, the Syrian dictator Bashar al-Assad recognised that the Shebaa Farms were Syrian and not Lebanese, thereby undermining the role of Hezbollah as Lebanese resistance against the Israeli occupation of Lebanese soil.[23]

As pointed out earlier, in 2008 Hezbollah deployed its arms domestically against Lebanese civilians and armed militia members. Hezbollah's fighters marched in predominantly Sunni and Druze streets in Beirut and Mount Lebanon, killing and injuring several civilians. To silence the government, Hezbollah's fighters launched well-planned attacks on governmental properties and pro-government television stations and newspapers.[24] With the fear of a civil war between Sunnis and Shiites rising, the State retracted its decision to monitor Hezbollah's communication network, and officials met in Doha for peace negotiations. Hezbollah lost popularity in Lebanon and the Arab world, and it came to be referred to as 'a militia' and no longer as resistance.

This change in discourse reflected, in essence, 'a decline in the domestic popularity that Hezbollah had enjoyed'.[25] However, despite this loss, Hezbollah emerged victorious with the election of a pro-Syrian president; it also gained veto power within the government and control over a wider area in the suburbs of Beirut and the airport. This was the only instance where Hezbollah openly and violently challenged the State of Lebanon. Today, Hezbollah is participating in the war in Syria in support of the Syrian regime and al-Assad's dictatorship. Despite the numerous international calls for Hezbollah to leave Syria and the threat of sanctions, the Lebanese State did not act (or perhaps could not act) to censor Hezbollah's military activities.[26]

The Legal Classification of Hezbollah in Lebanon: Multiple Scenarios

By infiltrating almost all public institutions, Hezbollah has effectively paralysed or hijacked elements of the Lebanese State. It acts as its sole representative, especially in matters of security. It blocks its parliamentarian and governmental activities, unless the outcome fits its needs. As such, it is fair to question the legal status of Hezbollah in international law. Is it the State of Lebanon or a non-State actor? The answer to this question may vary, depending on the definition and theory used to define and recognise an entity as State. First, Hezbollah's classification will be examined based on the Westphalian traditional definition which overlaps – to a certain extent – with the effectiveness theory. Second, it will be assessed according to the recognition theory.

Hezbollah, the Westphalian Definition of State and the Effectiveness Theory

According to the traditional Westphalian definition of statehood, a State must have a territory on which to exercise its jurisdiction, a permanent population and a government. Scholars such as James Crawford have added other criteria, such as the capacity to enter into relations with other States and independence. Following the Westphalian model in its simple form of territory-people-government, it is possible to say that Hezbollah is a State entity as it satisfies these criteria. Its members participate in the government: 'From 2008 until 2019, the group effectively had veto power in the Lebanese cabinet, as its members and supporters held a third plus one of all ministerial posts'.[27] Past election results clearly indicate that the party has its own permanent population and supporters, which empowers Hezbollah to speak, nationally and internationally, in the name of the Lebanese people. Hezbollah operates within an identifiable territory that it continuously claims as its own. The safety of this territory is ensured by Hezbollah's armed members who patrol it and make sure that the LAF and other State agents are kept out. Additionally, Hezbollah positions itself as the protector of Lebanon's independence; its website tracks international violations against Lebanon's sovereignty and Hezbollah's response to these violations.

However, this tool used to assess Hezbollah's statehood is unreliable. As pointed out in the previous chapter, the Westphalian definition of State is far from perfect. Many have criticised it as inadequate and out-dated: 'The Westphalian state system is a product of a specific socio-historical moment; the states this system produced should be thought of as products of historically contingent empirics, and not as conceptual ontological givens'.[28] Its monochromatic explanation of statehood is unable to catch the different political realities and does not allow, for instance, an appropriate analysis of the Global South.[29] Furthermore, the unclear divide between State and non-State actors does not help, especially in situations where non-State actors are heavily involved in governance and where the government is almost non-existent.

Instead of re-imagining a State definition that would encompass the various nuances especially in the Global South, the legal community has clung to the Westphalian definition and decided that whatever does not fit within its criteria is either a failing or a weak State. This same legal community has not imagined criteria for a State to fall out of statehood. In other words, it has set criteria to define a State, ones that *ipso facto* exclude many States, and oddly enough it has continued to consider the weak and/or failing entities as States. In this idiosyncratic situation, the current definition of statehood is not helpful.

Lebanon can serve as an example of a State that does not fit the Westphalian definition of statehood: 'It does not have authority centralized in a unified administrative and legal body that governs over an organized community, and its government does not have a legitimate monopoly over instruments of force, and never really did since independence'.[30] In fact, Lebanon's governance system relies on the consensus of eighteen religious communities; it is a sectarian system that depends on the patronage of countries such as France, the United States, Iran and Syria.[31] It 'has been used by politicians and by local actors to deflect demands for political change, by external powers to gain influence and by local actors to cultivate autonomous power bases'.[32] It is not impartial and fosters 'sectarian identities, clientelism and corruption'.[33] The system also 'includes non-state mechanisms in the mediation of domestic crises and accommodates the interest of external actors'.[34]

On the surface, Lebanon may have an identifiable government, territory and people. However, the Lebanese State was 'born failed'.[35] It does not fit the legal definition of a modern State, nor does the definition explain the legal and political realities of Lebanon. And yet, despite this mismatch and the shortfalls of the Westphalian definition, Lebanon legally remains a State, one that is recognised by the UN and the international community. The Westphalian method cannot be fully trusted to define a State. As such, it cannot be considered an appropriate tool to assess Hezbollah's status. What about other theories such as effectiveness theory and recognition theory?

Effectiveness theory – as seen in the previous chapter – requires three attributes for an entity to be recognised as a State: the State must exist as a fact that meets the effectiveness criteria; the State must have rights and duties, and finally the State must contribute to the formation of customary law. There is some overlap between the Westphalian definition of statehood and effectiveness theory's first attribute, since both look for the criteria of territory-people-government. As argued above, it is possible to say that Hezbollah exists as a fact for it fulfils the criteria of territory-people-government. However, Hezbollah does not fulfil the effectiveness theory's second and third attributes, as it does not have the rights and duties of a State, nor does it participate in the formation of customary law. In other words, it remains an entity distinct from the

State of Lebanon. Only the State of Lebanon has international rights and duties and can participate in the formation of customary law.

Under the Westphalian model, we could potentially declare Hezbollah a State, but the Westphalian model is unreliable. When applying effectiveness theory, Hezbollah cannot be considered as State. What about recognition theory? Is Hezbollah a State according to the latter?

Measuring Hezbollah's Statehood Using Recognition Theory

As pointed out in the previous chapter, some scholars of international law have favoured the theory of recognition and argued that the recognition of an entity as State is enough for the entity to acquire statehood status. For instance, both Japan[36] and the United States[37] have recognised the Republic of South Sudan as a new State. However, there are multiple issues with this theory. On the one hand, as Nicholson has pointed out in *Statehood and the State-Like in International Law*, States might not agree on an entity's statehood and may interpret facts differently.[38] Today, Palestine would be the perfect example of different subjective interpretations of facts relevant to statehood. On the other hand, as Tom Grant has argued in 'How to Recognise a State (and Not): Some Practical Considerations', recognition may be explicitly or implicitly expressed. Although the international community seems to be favouring formal recognition, there is no consensus on the form that the State's recognition must take. Some acts are considered forms of recognition, while others are not. For instance, entering into an agreement with an entity does not automatically imply statehood recognition.[39] Despite the absence of a required form for statehood recognition, scholars of international law have agreed that recognition should always come from authorities who are able to represent the State on an international level.[40] This position is reflected in the 1969 Vienna Convention on the Law of Treaties.

As one might expect, there is no formal recognition of Hezbollah's statehood by the international community. In other words, no State has openly and formally declared Hezbollah as a State with a territory, people, government and independence. However, public statements made by Lebanese and international officials suggest as much. To begin with, lawmakers have legalised Hezbollah's military activities since the early 1990s with the General Amnesty Law of 1991, which was followed by Hezbollah's infiltration into the parliament and the government. Three consecutive presidents recognised Hezbollah as an integral part of Lebanon's statehood, as one of its pillars along with the army and the people. Former President Michel Aoun signed a Memorandum of Understanding with Hezbollah's Secretary General Hassan Nasrallah, took pictures with him and spoke in favour of Hezbollah on both national and international levels. More importantly, Iranian and Syrian officials address Lebanese leaders and Hezbollah's members in their official communications, as if they were all State representatives. They purposely conflate Hezbollah and the State of Lebanon, and they attribute Hezbollah's military activities to the Lebanese State.

For instance, on 26 May 2021, the Iranian President Hassan Rouhani and the Minister of Foreign Affairs Javad Zarif sent congratulatory messages to the Lebanese President Michel Aoun and other Lebanese officials on the anniversary of the liberation of the south from the Israeli occupation. Rouhani's message stated:

> I would like to offer my sincerest congratulations to Your Excellency and the noble people of Lebanon on the anniversary of the victorious and glorious festival of resistance and freedom that led to the liberation of the country's southern parts from the Zionist regime's aggressor forces with the self-sacrifice of the people of Lebanon.[41]

In a more recent example, Iranian authorities warned Israel of an 'obliterating war' if it were to attack Hezbollah and Lebanon.[42] This statement not only indicates a strong political interference in Lebanese affairs and the erosion of the Lebanese governing system, but also asserts the conflation of Hezbollah and the State of Lebanon.

Article 7, paragraph 2 of the 1969 Vienna Convention on the Law of Treaties stipulates:

> In virtue of their functions and without having to produce full powers, the following are considered as representing their State: (a) Heads of State, Heads of Government and Ministers for Foreign Affairs, for the purpose of performing all acts relating to the conclusion of a treaty; (b) heads of diplomatic missions, for the purpose of adopting the text of a treaty between the accrediting State and the State to which they are accredited; (c) representatives accredited by States to an international conference or to an international organisation or one of its organs, for the purpose of adopting the text of a treaty in that conference, organisation or organ.[43]

Iran signed this convention on 23 May 1969, but did not ratify it. Syria ratified it on 2 October 1970. In the examples provided above, it is possible to argue that Iranian officials, such as the head of state and cabinet members, considered Lebanon and Hezbollah members as one entity. Realistically, on the ground, Hezbollah fighters dominated the south of Lebanon and played a key role in its liberation from Israeli occupation;

the State of Lebanon and its armed forces were absent. Today, as once more war is raging between Hezbollah and Israel, the LAF remains absent from the conflict.

This conflation of Lebanon (as State) and resistance (which is employed as a synonym for Hezbollah) is not innocent and has legal ramifications. It implies the equation of the State of Lebanon with Hezbollah and as such the implicit recognition of Hezbollah's statehood by a foreign State.[44] Syrian officials made similar statements in which Hezbollah and the State of Lebanon were conflated. However, if we assume that Iran and Syria indirectly recognised Hezbollah as a State actor through their actions and public statements, does this imply a formal recognition for the rest of the international community? Like the Westphalian model, this method of assessment is flawed, for it does not clearly indicate the number of instances of a State's recognition required for an entity to become a State, and it does not stipulate solutions if the interpretation of facts differs. In other words, it is unclear whether a statehood recognition by two States is enough. Past examples and logic indicate the need for more than just two. This is the case with Ukraine and Russia, for example.

On 24 February 2022, Russia invaded Ukraine and attempted to seize some of its territories. The conflict is ongoing at the time of writing this chapter. On 29 June 2022, the State of Syria formally recognised 'the independence and sovereignty of the Luhansk and Donetsk People's Republics'.[45] Luhansk and Donetsk are part of the Donbas region in the Ukraine and harbour some Russian-supported separatists. From the standpoint of international law, Syria's proclamation is not enough for Luhansk and Donetsk to acquire statehood status, and the international community clearly does not recognise this status either.

Furthermore, this method of assessment does not offer a solution when different States assign an entity with different status. While Iran and Syria may see Hezbollah as the State of Lebanon, this is certainly not the United States' position on the matter. In fact, countries such as the United States and the United Kingdom have labelled Hezbollah in its military and political wings as a terrorist organisation. For Imad Mansour, the terrorist label automatically disqualifies Hezbollah from statehood status: 'Labelling an actor as terrorist also frames them as incapable of obtaining or serving an important legal Westphalian requirement and that is abiding by international norms, and especially the protection of their people, constituencies, and citizens'.[46]

A revision of the definition of a State is in order. To accommodate the realities of the Global South, scholars have suggested theories of 'limited statehood', 'state-like actor' or 'quasi-actor' as alternatives. While these theories have not been fully accepted by the legal community, they offer the benefit of a better representation and understanding of non-State actors who act like States and States that do not exactly fit in within the Westphalian statehood definition.

Imagining a Legal Solution: Hybrid Sovereignty and Quasi-Statehood

Although Hezbollah acts like a State, the Westphalian definition of statehood, effectiveness theory and recognition theory do not allow us to affirm with any certainty that Hezbollah is indeed a State in the positive legal sense. This does not necessarily mean that it is not acting as one. Unfortunately, this limitation in international law allows for ambiguous actors such as Hezbollah to thrive. Scholars of international law and political science have suggested other theories. As seen in the previous chapter, in *Statehood and the State-Like in International Law*, Nicholson has employed the expression 'state-like entity' to include entities that do not match the Westphalian criteria.[47] For entities that lack universal recognition of statehood, he has used the term 'states-in-context.[48] In 'Entities That Can Be States But Do Not Claim to Be', Ronen has applied the concept of the 'quasi-state' to non-State actors who act as States and have territorial control, the potential exercise of power and rights and obligations as States.[49] These theories allow for a better understanding of Hezbollah as a State-like entity in Lebanon, one that behaves like a State with its own military powers, its own governance, its own permanent population and, finally, its own claimed territory.

In 'Beyond the "Weak State": Hybrid Sovereignties in Beirut', Sara Fregonese has suggested changing the narrative about Lebanon from a failing weak state to 'a constellation of hybrid sovereignties'.[50] This hybridity would allow for the State to remain omnipresent and for a binary system of State and non-State alliance to emerge in different spheres:[51]

> The hybrid sovereignty perspective makes it possible to interpret the geographies of conflict (and, indeed, cooperation) in Lebanon and elsewhere, to think beyond the state as a container to be secured and filled with power, and to account for spaces where hybrid articulations of *both* state *and* nonstate are embedded in everyday practices and material networks.[52]

International law is not yet willing to recognise these overlapping categories of State-like or quasi-State or hybrid sovereignties.[53] Nevertheless, they offer a better explanation of cases such as Lebanon and Hezbollah. According to Ronen, quasi-States 'are defined by their voluntary self-exclusion from category of states',[54] which leads us to the last question: why has Hezbollah not declared its statehood?

The Quasi-Statehood of Hezbollah and the Absence of a Statehood Declaration

Hezbollah has never declared its statehood, and yet it acts as a State. To understand this contradiction, this chapter proposes two possible analyses: first, Hezbollah benefits from its quasi-State status. Hence, there is no need for it to declare its statehood. Second, Hezbollah does not recognise international law and therefore deliberately ignores its rules.

As to the first point, Hezbollah is thriving outside the traditional State structure. A 2019 report by the Issam Fares Institute for Public Policy and International Affairs expressed its concern over the wave of 'de-sovereignisation' in the Middle East area, particularly in conflict areas.[55] It reported that, while traditional States continue to exist, 'other social-security nets – ethnic groups or the family for example – [become] more important and establish [. . .] structural context for sectarianism to evolve within'.[56] Consequently, people distrust the State and search for substitutes which can be found in quasi-States such as Hezbollah.

As a quasi-State, Hezbollah has its own structure, governance and people; it has control over some areas in Lebanon and is attempting to gain more territory. Visually, it cultivates the image of a State-like entity with pictures that offer an alternative to the existing Lebanese State. In fact, Hezbollah uses media (whether it is broadcasting, publishing, or the internet) for propaganda and to legitimise its existence as a partner in Lebanon's statehood. For instance, Hezbollah often uses the images of young fighters killed in battles with Israel or in Syria to reinforce the narrative that Hezbollah is the only protector of Lebanon's borders and guarantor of its security. These images are often oversized prints displayed in public spaces; they transcend language barriers and are designed to trigger sympathy. Equally, Hezbollah emphasises its flag and makes sure that it is always on display in all its public appearances and public communications. For Aaron Anfinson, this is a tactic to visualise statehood and a method to legitimise a non-State actor.[57]

While Hezbollah blooms as a quasi-State, Lebanon functions as a State with limited statehood. The traditional theories of statehood recognition do not make room for the concept of limited statehood. Legal scholars have spoken of a 'failed State', but this is not the same as limited statehood. Limited statehood . . .

> . . . concerns those areas of a country in which central authorities (governments) lack the ability to implement and enforce rules and decisions and/or in which the legitimate monopoly over the means of violence is lacking. The ability to enforce rules or to control the means of violence can be differentiated along two dimensions: (1) territorial, that is, parts of a country's territorial space, and (2) sectoral, that is with regard to

> specific policy areas. It follows that the opposite of 'limited statehood' is not 'unlimited' but 'consolidated' statehood, that is, those areas of a country in which the state enjoys the monopoly over the means of violence and/or the ability to make and enforce central decisions. Statehood is not a dichotomous variable; there are degrees of limited statehood.[58]

Limited statehood does not necessarily imply weakness or lawlessness. It simply means that some services are provided by the State, while others are provided by non-State actors.

The category of quasi-State is not without legal challenges. It raises several legal questions: can a quasi-State sign a treaty instead of the State with limited statehood? Can it provide its people with its own citizenship? What would happen in case of use of force between State and quasi-State?[59] In theory, the quasi-State and State with limited statehood relationship may lead to State-building, especially when non-State actors operate within the realm of the law and provide services such as healthcare or education. However, this is not the case when the quasi-State and the State with limited statehood are competing for full control of the entity in question. One could argue that this is the scenario between Hezbollah and Lebanon: Hezbollah acts as a quasi-State and Lebanon acts with limited statehood on its territory.

Hezbollah benefits from the weak status of the Lebanese State. Hezbollah functions in this grey area of the State-like actor, with some overlap with Lebanese statehood and Lebanese institutions. Perhaps its long-term plan would be to entirely replace the failed Lebanese State. From a political science point of view, this would be considered a change in the regime rather than a legal shift from a State-like entity to a State entity. If such a move were to occur, it would force the international community to respect the will of the people and to welcome the new State of Hezbollah – formerly known as Lebanon – into its fold.

The situation would be more complicated if Hezbollah today were to declare its statehood in opposition to Lebanon's statehood. In this case, the territory of Lebanon would become a disputed land between the State of Hezbollah and the State of Lebanon, potentially triggering the implementation of laws of war. The international community's response to this scenario would be more serious and would vary between sanctions and no recognition of Hezbollah's statehood. Despite these challenges, there are benefits to being a quasi-State. Hezbollah has all the advantages of a State but none of its duties or responsibilities. It can also evade the application of international law since it cannot be party to any treaty.

Second, Hezbollah did not declare its statehood because it does not recognise the validity of international law, nor its definition of statehood.

Consequently, Hezbollah operates entirely outside the realm of international law. In fact, Hezbollah defines itself as a Lebanese Shiite political party and resistance group. Its ideology was established in its 1985 Manifesto which took the form of an open letter addressed 'to the oppressed in Lebanon and the world';[60] it called for the expulsion of Western powers from Lebanon and the destruction of the State of Israel. It also pledged allegiance to Ruhollah Khomeini, Iran's former supreme leader, and advocated the rise of an Islamic State called *al-Umma*.[61]

Al-Umma differs from the concepts of nation and State. A nation, as defined by Benedict Anderson in *Imagined Communities: Reflections on the Origin and Spread of Nationalism*, is 'an imagined political community – and imagined as both inherently limited and sovereign. It is *imagined* because the members of even the smallest nation will never know most of their fellow-members, meet them, or even hear of them, yet in the minds of each lives the image of their communion'.[62] There is often an overlap between nation and State where the same imagined community has agreed to live within a defined territory and government. Unlike the nation-State, the *Umma* has 'no racial or territorial connotations'.[63] The *Umma* is the grouping of the whole community of Muslims regardless of ethnicities, borders and governments.[64] The *Dawla* or the local government under which some of these Muslims may exist is 'non-sovereign, non-territorial, temporary political arrangement that is accountable to and responsible for the whole Umma, not only to that portion of the Umma under its jurisdiction'.[65]

Consequently, the *Dawla*, which is the Arabic word for State, is a temporary porous structure that obeys the *Umma*. A *Dawla* must have elements of statehood: population, territory and government. Population refers to Muslims and non-Muslims residing in any Islamic State. Muslims are equal in rights and duties irrespective of their origin, race, language and colour. If a Muslim moves from a Muslim State to another, he or she will be considered a citizen of this new State, with rights and duties similar to those of other citizens. As to non-Muslims, they have the right to live in Muslim States, and the authorities cannot compel them to convert to Islam. They have the right to practice their religion, as long as they do not threaten peace, harmony, or Islam. They have rights comparable to those of Muslim citizens, but they must pay a head tax or *jizyah*.

Islam makes a distinction between two territories: the territory of Islam (*dar al-Islam*) and the territory of war (*dar al-Harb*). The territory of Islam consists of any territory where Muslim citizens exist in peace. The territory of war is where Muslims are under attack. As for government, it is the stable authority that represents the people and indicates the existence of a State. This government has the right to declare war or *jihad* only to defend the Islamic faith.[66] The definition of statehood in international law presents some similarities with the *Dawla*'s definition in Islamic law. However, the major difference relates to the independence of the *Dawla*, which always answers to the *Umma* and its supreme leader. Therefore, 'the concept of *Ummah* and the elements of state in Islam [. . .] are fundamentally not in line with the concept and elements of a state as enumerated under the Montevideo Convention 1933'.[67]

This could explain why Hezbollah has no consideration for the State of Lebanon and why it acts in its place. According to its religious values and Islamic law, a State or a *Dawla* can be disregarded, and obedience is only due to the *Umma* and its supreme leader which, in this case, is Ali Khamenei. In fact, Hezbollah has repeatedly and openly rejected international law. Its leaders have accused the UN and the STL of favouring Israel and working against Lebanon's sovereignty and interests. To give an example, in 2012 UN Secretary General Ban Ki-Moon visited Lebanon and demanded the disarmament of Hezbollah.[68] In response, Hezbollah's Secretary General Hassan Nasrallah categorically rejected the call. In a televised appearance, he said:

> I affirm today, firmly, decisively and with the greatest conviction [. . .] the choice of armed resistance [. . .] These weapons, along with the Lebanese people and army, are the only guarantee of Lebanon's protection [. . .] Your concern, Secretary-General, reassures us and pleases us. What matters to us is that you are worried, and that America [. . .] and Israel are worried with you.[69]

The first part of this chapter has examined Hezbollah's activities since 1992 and its gradual infiltration into Lebanese institutions. At times, Hezbollah acted in collaboration with the State of Lebanon; other times, it acted against its interest and in violation of its constitution. Within Lebanon, Hezbollah is a State-like actor with an ambitious agenda. It cannot be firmly declared a State (or at least not yet), since the current assessment tools of statehood, as available within international law, are inadequate. What about Hezbollah's activities in armed conflicts?

Hezbollah in Armed Conflict

To understand Hezbollah's status as a State or non-State actor in its relations with Israel and Syria, it is important to review the definition of international and non-international armed conflicts and the laws that apply in both cases. International armed conflicts occur between States. Non-international armed conflicts occur between a State's armed forces and armed groups or between armed groups themselves on a State's territory. The qualification of the armed conflicts in Israel and in Syria varies, depending on the role played by Hezbollah. If Hezbollah acted as the State of Lebanon or as agent of the State of Lebanon, the conflict would be international. If Hezbollah acted as a non-State actor, the conflict would be non-international. As we will see below, the international community has exhibited mixed reactions about the qualification of the 2006 armed conflict between Israel and Hezbollah.

As to Hezbollah's participation in the Syrian war, the conflict's qualification varies, depending on whether Hezbollah acts as an agent of the State of Lebanon, as an agent of the State of Syria, or as an armed group on Syrian soil. In all scenarios, Hezbollah's status continues to shift, thereby making the conflict's qualification fluid and hard to assert with any certainty.

Qualification of Armed Conflict and Applicable Laws

International law has many branches, two of which consist of international human rights law and international humanitarian law. They both 'share the goal of preserving the dignity and humanity of all [. . .] Although different in scope, international human rights law and international humanitarian law offer a series of protection to persons in armed conflict, whether civilians, persons who are no longer participating directly in hostilities or active participants in the conflict'.[70] International human rights law offers international protection to all persons, regardless of their nationality, sex, gender, religion, language, ethnicity, or any other status. Often, it is considered a system of law applicable in times of peace. International humanitarian law is a set of rules that applies during armed conflicts. Known as 'laws of war', international humanitarian law seeks to 'protect persons who are not or are no longer participating in the hostilities, and restricts the means and methods of warfare'.[71] In other words, it organises when the use of force is permissible. It is important to note that international human rights law does not stop applying during times of war; it offers a layer additional to international humanitarian law, which becomes the primary legal regime in armed conflict.

International humanitarian law developed in the late 1800s, when Henri Dunant, a Swiss businessman, witnessed the aftermath of the Battle of Solferino in 1859 and the mistreatment of the wounded combatants and civilians. He advocated the creation of a relief society to help the wounded and argued that the society must be composed of volunteers recognisable by all armies on the field. Years later, the ICRC came to see the light, and the 1864 Geneva Convention for the Amelioration of the Condition of the Wounded in Armies in the Field was adopted.[72] The nineteenth century saw many wars and, consequently, the signing of more conventions in international humanitarian law, such as the 1899 Hague Conventions, followed by the 1907 second Hague conference, which revised the 1899 Hague Conventions and added more provisions.[73] The experiences of World War I and World War II led to the adoption of four Geneva Conventions. Universally accepted, these conventions set specific rules to protect military personnel and civilians. They have several articles in common, such as Article 3 which applies to 'conflicts of not international character'.[74] The fear of nuclear, chemical and biological warfare, the wave of decolonisation in the 1940s and the 1950s, and the Vietnam War all underscored gaps in the Geneva Conventions.[75] The ICRC acknowledged the need to add more provisions to fill these voids which led to the adoption of two additional protocols on 8 June 1977 (AP I, AP II).

In the 1950s, wars for independence raised the issue of the legal status of guerilla fighters and whether they could benefit from prisoner of war status if captured. AP I addressed this issue. Its Article 1(4) stipulates that the protocol applies to 'armed conflicts in which people are fighting against colonial domination and alien occupation and against racist régimes in the exercise of their right of self-determination as enshrined in the Charter of the United Nations and the Declaration on Principles of International Law . . . '[76] As for AP II, its preamble recognised the limits of common Article 3 of the Geneva Conventions, which applies to non-international armed conflicts. The preamble stipulates that common Article 3 'proved to be inadequate in view of the fact that about 80% of the victims of armed conflicts since 1945 have been victims of non-international conflicts and that non-international conflicts are often fought with more cruelty than international conflicts'.[77] Hence, AP II expanded the scope of international humanitarian law to apply to armed conflicts 'which take place in the territory of a High Contracting Party between its armed forces and dissident armed forces or other organized armed groups which, under responsible command, exercise such control over a part of its territory as to enable them to carry out sustained and concerted military operations . . .'[78] However, to ensure the respect of States' sovereignty, AP II does not apply to 'situations of internal disturbances and tensions, such as riots, isolated and sporadic acts of violence and other acts of a similar nature, as not being armed conflicts'.[79]

While the Geneva Conventions are widely accepted by its 196 State parties, the Additional Protocols are not. AP I has 174 State parties, and Additional Protocol II has 169 State parties. Lebanon signed both Additional Protocols in 1997, but Israel did not. In 1983, Syria ratified AP I but did not sign or ratify AP II.[80] Some rules of international humanitarian law are international customary law. This means that their practice is universally accepted, and they cannot be disputed. For instance, the legal requirements to distinguish between civilians and combatants and not to attack civilians are customary laws. Consequently, international customary law applies, whether a State is party to the Geneva Conventions and its Additional Protocols or not.

International armed conflicts occur when hostilities break out between two or more States. Common Article 2 of the Geneva Conventions defines international armed conflict as 'all cases of declared war or any other armed conflict which may arise between two or more of the High Contracting Parties'.[81] International armed conflicts also occur when 'people are fighting against colonial domination and alien occupation and against racist regimes in the exercise of their self-determination'.[82] International humanitarian law, which includes the Geneva Conventions and the Additional Protocols, applies to international armed conflicts and to signatory parties. States who have not signed these agreements must abide by international customary law in case of international armed conflict.

Non-international armed conflicts are covered by common Article 3 to the Geneva Conventions and Article 1(1) of AP II which stipulates that, for a conflict to be qualified as non-international, hostilities must occur between State armed forces and dissident armed forces or between armed groups themselves on the territory of a High Contracting Party.[83] Therefore, common Article 3 of all Geneva Conventions applies to all signatory parties, as well as AP II. With the increased number of non-international conflicts, many scholars have debated the application of international customary law in this context. The matter was settled in *Prosecutor* v. *Dusko Tadic* where the Appeals Chamber at the International Criminal Tribunal for Yugoslavia decided that international customary law also applies to internal armed conflicts. Before this decision, non-international armed conflicts were only governed by common Article 3 of the Geneva Conventions and by AP II.[84] The Appeals Chamber stated:

> [I]t cannot be denied that customary rules have developed to govern internal strife. These rules, as specifically identified in the preceding discussion, cover such areas as protection of civilians from hostilities, in

> particular from indiscriminate attacks, protection of civilian objects, in particular cultural property, protection of all those who do not (or no longer) take active part in hostilities, as well as prohibition of means of warfare proscribed in international armed conflicts and ban of certain methods of conducting hostilities.[85]

Therefore, international customary law applies to non-international armed conflicts.

To understand Hezbollah's role in the 2006 armed conflict with Israel and in the Syrian war, it is important to identify whether Hezbollah acted as a State or a non-State actor. This classification will subsequently determine whether these armed conflicts were international or non-international and thus allow us to determine the rules of law that apply to each conflict.

Israel

History of the 2006 Armed Conflict between Hezbollah and Israel

On 12 July 2006, hostilities erupted between Hezbollah fighters and the Israel Defence Forces (IDF). Hezbollah fired rockets at Israeli positions, crossed the Blue Line (a demarcation line recognised by both Lebanon and Israel and monitored by the UN), ambushed an Israeli patrol and kidnapped two soldiers.[86] This led to a full armed confrontation between Hezbollah and Israel. The Israeli Prime Minister, Ehud Olmert (1945–) considered this attack and the capture of the two soldiers as an 'act of war' by the State of Lebanon, since Hezbollah operates from Lebanon's territory and is represented in various Lebanese institutions. He said that '[t]he Lebanese government, of which Hizbullah is a member, is trying to undermine regional stability. Lebanon is responsible and Lebanon will bear the consequences of its actions'. He vowed a 'very painful and far-reaching response'.[87] Israeli Chief of Staff Dan Halutz threatened that, 'if the soldiers are not returned, we will turn Lebanon's clock back 20 years'.[88]

On 13 July 2006, the Lebanese Government informed the secretary-general and the president of the Security Council at the UN that '[t]he Lebanese Government was not aware of the events that occurred and are occurring on the international Lebanese border'. The letter added that '[t]he Lebanese Government is not responsible for these events and does not endorse them'. The Lebanese Government condemned the Israeli aggression against Lebanese civilians and Lebanon's infrastructure and asked the UN Security Council for an urgent meeting.[89] On 14 July, the Security Council held its first meeting but did not reach a resolution. While the United States called for restraint and supported Israel's right to self-defence, Iran supported Hezbollah and criticised Israel and its western allies. Amid the rise of criticism against Israel for its disproportionate response[90] and the frequent pleas from Lebanon for a cease-fire, the Security Council on 11 August 2006 adopted Resolution 1701; it called for a . . .

> . . . full cessation of hostilities based upon, in particular, the immediate cessation by Hezbollah of all attacks and the immediate cessation by Israel of all offensive military operations [. . . and] emphasizing the need to address urgently the causes that have given rise to the current crisis, including by the unconditional release of the abducted Israeli soldiers.[91]

The Human Rights Council adopted resolution S-2/1 to condemn the grave situation of human rights in Lebanon caused by Israeli military operations.[92]

After thirty-three days, the armed conflict ended on 14 August 2006. According to the ICRC and the Lebanese government, 1,191 were killed and 4,409 injured. More than 900,000 were displaced. Israel reported forty-three civilians killed, 997 injured and 300,000 displaced from northern Israel:[93]

> During the campaign, Israel's Air Force flew more than 12,000 combat missions. Its Navy fired 2,500 shells, and its Army fired over 100,000 shells destroying as a consequence large part of the Lebanese civilian infrastructure, including roads, bridges and other 'targets' such as Beirut International Airport, ports, water and sewage treatment plans, electrical facilities, fuel stations, commercial structures, schools and hospitals as well as private homes [. . .] Over 789 cluster-bomb sites have been identified in southern Lebanon, and over one million bomblets have littered the region.[94]

There is consensus among scholars that the 2006 war between Hezbollah and Israel was an armed conflict. However, it is unclear whether it was an international or non-international armed conflict. The qualification depends on the rules of law applied to this conflict and on the actors' status.

Hezbollah: A State or Non-State Actor in the Armed Conflict with Israel in 2006

Although the State of Lebanon denied prior knowledge of the attacks on Israeli forces and appealed for an immediate cease-fire, the question remains whether Hezbollah acted as the Lebanese State, thus entailing the State's responsibility.[95] Hezbollah members and their allies control a significant portion of the State institutions, such as the presidency, the government and the parliament. As pointed out above, Hezbollah at times acts as if it were the State of Lebanon or collaborated with State representatives and armed forces. It can be argued that there is a conflation of Lebanese State agents and Hezbollah, and that the latter is a State actor, which makes the armed conflict an international one. This was Israel's official position: Hezbollah is a State agent representative of the State of Lebanon, which is why Israel expanded its military actions to the entirety of Lebanon's territory and did not restrict them to the areas controlled by Hezbollah. Moreover, this interpretation of the facts allowed for Israel to invoke its right to self-defence as the armed conflict involved two States.

International law does not effectively regulate border incidents, and the conditions to apply Article 51 of the UN Charter on self-defence are unclear.[96] Any one party to a border conflict can claim self-defence. In the absence of explicit regulations, the question would be: can any border attack trigger the right to self-defence? In *Nicaragua* v. *United States of America*, the ICJ responded by making a clear distinction between the gravest forms of use of force (those constituting an armed attack) and other, less grave forms.[97] Only the gravest forms of use of force would justify the right to self-defence. Moreover, in *Oil Platforms* (*Islamic Republic of Iran* v. *United States of America*), the ICJ held that a series of attacks do not constitute a grave use of force triggering self-defence.[98]

Considering these criteria, it is possible to argue that Israel could not invoke self-defence as Hezbollah's border attack did not rise to the level of the gravest form of use of force. As for Hezbollah, a non-State actor cannot claim self-defence, unless it was acting as a State actor. Like the United States of America and the United Kingdom, Israel has labelled Hezbollah a terrorist organisation, which would give it the right to defend itself in the eventuality of terrorist attacks. Post-9/11, the world has seen an expansion of the definition of self-defence particularly in the context of terrorism. However, to this day, there is no consensus on when and how Article 51 of the UN Charter applies.

In the context of the 2006 armed conflict between Hezbollah and Israel, most States agreed that Israel had the right to defend itself, and that Hezbollah was a non-State actor:

> . . . a considerable number of states, especially with respect to the July 2006 war, in principle accepted Israel's right to use force against terrorist organisations such as Hamas or Hezbollah. Israel itself was at pains to attribute Hezbollah's conduct to Lebanon and Syria, but did not claim that these states had controlled and directed Hezbollah's conduct.[99]

To counter Israel's argument of self-defence, the Lebanese authorities denied knowing about the attacks and called for the international community to implement a cease-fire. Scholars such as Catherine Bloom have argued that the Lebanese State implicitly approved of Hezbollah's activities, and Hezbollah's actions could imply that its members acted as State agents:

> Lebanon did not investigate Hezbollah's activities, nor did Lebanon go after Nasrallah and try to stop his attacks on Israel. Israel was attacking Lebanon from every direction and the only party that responded was Hezbollah [. . .] Lebanon did not deploy its 'official' army. Instead, Lebanon fully supported its real army, Hezbollah, to defend the country against Israel.[100]

Deciding whether Hezbollah is a State or a non-State actor is not an easy task with the current limitations of international law. As seen above, the State definition and the distinction between State and non-State actor are inconclusive. The criteria set by jurisprudence do not cover the different relations between State and non-State actors. The immediate consequence to this dilemma emerges in the context of international humanitarian law: what instruments apply in the context of the 2006 armed conflict between Israel and Hezbollah?

If Hezbollah is considered a State-agent, the conflict would be international armed conflict, which would trigger the application of all the Geneva Conventions. AP I applies to Lebanon since it is a State party (as opposed to Israel), and international customary law also applies. If Hezbollah is considered a non-State actor, the conflict would be a non-international armed conflict, which would trigger the application of common Article 3 to the Geneva Conventions and international customary laws.[101]

It is worth mentioning that in its 2006 investigative reports on human rights violations in the 2006 armed conflict[102], the UN considered Hezbollah a non-State actor. This was also the position of most States; it was reiterated in the 2011 OHCHR report on the 'International Legal Protection of Human Rights in Armed Conflict'. In examining the application of international human rights law and international humanitarian law, the OHCHR clearly stated that both branches of international law applied to non-State actors. It referred to the Security Council's practice of calling on both States and non-State actors to abide by international human rights laws and international humanitarian law. The OHCHR specifically referenced the 2006 armed conflict between Israel and Hezbollah and considered it an armed conflict between a State and a non-State actor.[103]

Syria

A History of the Syrian Conflict

In February 2011, protests erupted in Syria against the repressive regime of Bashar Al-Assad (1965–). Inspired by the Arab Spring[104] and the experiences of Tunisia, Egypt and Libya, Syrians marched to demand reforms. They asked for basic human rights, such as freedom of expression, the release of political prisoners and anti-poverty measures. Mid-March, news of the detention and torture of a group of children in Dar'a over anti-government graffiti on public buildings spread in the country, and peaceful protests erupted in major cities such as Damascus, Dayr Az Zawr, Homs, Hama and others.[105] The government met the protesters with fierce violence. The Syrian Armed Forces used live ammunition, opened fire and killed several protesters.[106] The government claimed that the protesters were terrorists who planned to destabilise Syria and that it 'will not relent in pursuing the terrorist groups in order to protect the stability of the country and the security of its citizens'.[107] In response to the government's oppression of its own people, many defected from the military and security forces. Along with civilians, they created the 'Free Syrian Army'.[108]

The deteriorating situation in Syria and mounting international pressure pushed the Human Rights Council to investigate the alleged serious human rights violations in Syria. An independent international commission of inquiry was dispatched, and it gathered a 'substantial body of evidence [. . .] that these gross violations of human rights have been committed by Syrian military and security forces since the beginning of the protests in March 2011'.[109] In August 2011, the Security Council in a public statement condemned the Syrian authorities for their 'widespread violations of human rights and the use of force against civilians'. It re-affirmed its commitment to Syria's sovereignty and territorial integrity, but it called on the authorities to respect human rights, to investigate their serious violations and to prosecute those responsible. It also asked the authorities to implement the reforms they promised the Syrian people.[110] Interestingly, Lebanon dissociated itself from the Security Council's statement, stating that 'the text did not help to address the current situation in Syria [. . .] that the Lebanese people stood in support of the sovereignty and territorial integrity of Syria and the unity and safety of its people'.[111]

The European Union and the United States imposed sanctions on the Syrian regime.[112] The Arab League boycotted Syrian goods and suspended Syria's membership.[113] In contrast, Lebanon expressed concerns over the Arab League's sanctions and openly claimed that it would not participate in enforcing them.[114] The conflict became more complicated with the participation of different entities. In his essay 'The Legal Status of Hezbollah in the Syrian Conflict: An International Humanitarian Law Perspective', Mohamad Ghazi Janaby has tracked at least ten armed groups that are not representative of the Syrian State: (1) the Free Syrian Army, (2) the Supreme Military Council of the Free Syrian Army, (3) the Martyrs of Syria Brigade, (4) the Northern Storm Brigade, (5) the Islamic Front, (6) Harakat Ahrar al-Sham al-Islamiyya, (7) the Syrian Islamic Liberation Front, (8) the Ahfad al-Rasoul Brigade, (9) The al-Nusra Front, or Jabhat al-Nusra and (10) the Islamic State of Iraq and Syria (ISIS) or Islamic State of Iraq and Levant (ISIL).[115] While some groups may be labelled as rebels fighting the Syrian oppressive regime, others were known terrorist groups, such as ISIS or ISIL. Moreover, some members of these armed groups were not Syrians. This was the case with ISIS or ISIL and Hezbollah.

According to a recent report published by the Office of the High Commissioner for Human Rights, nearly 306,887 civilians were killed between 1 March 2011 and 31 March 2011 in Syria. Of these, 27,126 were children.[116] Today, with the support of Iran and Russia, the Syrian regime has taken back control of most regions in Syria. Hezbollah has been present in Syria from the beginning of the conflict, which leads to the following questions: what is Hezbollah's status in the Syrian armed conflict? Is Hezbollah acting as a State or non-State actor? If acting as a State actor, is it acting on Lebanon's or Syria's behalf? Is the conflict international and non-international?

Hezbollah: A State or Non-State Actor in the Syrian Armed Conflict

As stated above, international armed conflicts occur when hostilities break out between two or more States. International armed conflicts also occur when 'people are fighting against colonial domination and alien occupation and against racist regimes in the exercise of their self-determination'.[117] International humanitarian law, which includes the Geneva Conventions and the Additional Protocols, applies to international armed conflicts and to signatory parties. States who have not signed these agreements must abide by international customary law in case of international armed conflict.

Non-international armed conflicts are covered by common Article 3 to the Geneva Conventions and Article 1(1) of AP II, which stipulates that, for a conflict to be qualified as non-international, hostilities must occur between State armed forces and dissident armed forces or between armed groups themselves on the territory of a High Contracting Party.[118] Therefore, common Article 3 of all Geneva Conventions applies to all signatory parties, as does AP II. International customary law applies to non-signatory parties.

Does the Syrian crisis amount to an armed conflict? If so, it is an international or non-international armed conflict? What about the participation of Hezbollah fighters? Does it automatically turn the conflict into an international armed conflict? The qualification of the Syrian conflict as international or non-international armed conflict depends on the level of violence, the geographical location of the conflict and the armed groups involved.

In terms of violence, it must exceed situations 'of internal disturbances and tensions, such as riots, isolated and sporadic acts of violence and other acts of a similar nature'.[119] As many human rights organisations reported, the violence was severe and consistent. It was not sporadic nor the equivalent of rioting. As such, the conflict was without doubt an armed conflict. In terms of geographical location, initially the conflict was strictly on Syrian soil. In recent years, it spilled over the Syrian-Turkish borders, with the displacement of many Syrians to the northern border of Syria and the settlement of many in refugee camps on the Turkish border. Türkiye has openly called for the removal of the Syrian president Bashar al-Assad. Additionally, Türkiye has supported the Muslim brotherhood in Syria, an entity fiercely opposed to the Syrian regime, and has engaged in military actions at the Syrian border and against Syrian and Kurdish fighters.[120] It can be argued that the armed conflict between Syria and Türkiye amounts to international border incidents with occasional hostilities. The large portion of the conflict occurred on Syrian territory with the involvement of Syrian and non-Syrian armed groups such as Hezbollah fighters. Some scholars have argued that it can be an internationalised armed conflict or mixed armed conflict with the combination of a civil war and the intervention of foreign armed forces. In this case, the armed conflict would be both international and non-international.[121]

In July 2012, the ICRC qualified the situation in Syria as non-international armed conflict . . .

> . . . opposing Government Forces and a number of organised armed opposition groups operating in several parts of the country (including, but not limited to, Homs, Idlib and Hama). Thus, hostilities between these parties wherever they occur in Syria are subject to the rules of

> international humanitarian law. These rules impose limits on how the fighting can be conducted, with the aim of protecting the civilian population and persons, not or no longer, directly participating in the hostilities.[122]

The qualification of the Syrian armed conflict is certainly not stagnant; it evolved with the conflict and changed with the increased intensity of violence intensity and the participation of non-Syrian armed groups. Does the participation of Hezbollah render the conflict an international armed conflict? The answer depends on the qualification of Hezbollah fighters, and whether they are State or non-State actors.

In April 2013, Secretary General Hassan Nasrallah confirmed Hezbollah's role in Syria and its support for the Syrian regime: 'Syria has real friends in the region and the world that will not let Syria fall in the hands of America, Israel or Takfiri (extreme jihadi) groups'.[123] Nasrallah explained that, if Syria fell, Lebanon would fall too, and the Palestinian cause would be lost. He vowed that '[Hezbollah] will continue along the road, bear the responsibilities and the sacrifices. This battle is ours, and I promise you victory'. He recognised the legitimacy of some opposition armed groups in Syria and revealed that they rejected his call for dialogue: 'I have contacted Assad and members of the opposition to reach a settlement. Assad accepted the suggestion whereas the opposition rejected it'.[124] The rationale, however, continued to shift. At some point, Nasrallah argued that Hezbollah was defending Lebanese citizens living in Syrian villages on the Lebanese-Syrian border. In another televised appearance, Nasrallah explained that it was time to organise on the Golan Heights a resistance movement against the Israeli occupation.[125]

Hezbollah's participation in the Syrian war raises the following questions: is Hezbollah a State agent acting on Syria's behalf? Is it acting on behalf of or as the Lebanese State or as a non-State actor? According to Mohamad Ghazi Janaby, there are three possibilities: (a) Hezbollah could be considered an armed group forming part of the armed forces; (b) it could be considered an armed group belonging to a party of the armed conflict; and finally (c) it could be considered an armed group in the context of internal armed conflicts.[126]

In Article 4(1), GC III identifies an armed group of a Party to the conflict as 'members of militias or volunteer corps forming part of such armed forces'.[127] However, as Janaby has argued, for Hezbollah to be recognised as an official armed group of the Syrian armed forces, the Syrian authorities must officially recognise it first. To our knowledge, there is no such official recognition. Consequently, the first possibility does not apply. The second possibility is stated in Article 4(2) of GC III, according to which an armed group can belong to a party to the armed conflict if it operates outside or inside its territory and meets the following criteria: '(1) it is commanded by a person responsible for his subordinates; (2) it has a fixed distinctive sign; (3) it carries arms openly; (4) it respects the laws and customs of war'.[128]

Hezbollah fighters are an armed group belonging to a party in the armed conflict (in this case the State of Syria). There is a clear relationship between the Syrian authorities and Hezbollah, as recognised by its Secretary General Hassan Nasrallah. For instance, Hezbollah's fighters fought alongside Syrian officers in the infamous battle of al-Qusayr where Hezbollah and the Syrian Armed Forces attacked the Syrian opposition for seventeen days, took control of the town of al-Qusayr and returned it to the Syrian regime. 'The battle also marked the first time that Hizb Allah played a significant lead combat role in the Syria war, even though its fighters operated in Syria for at least a year prior to the Qusayr offensive'.[129]

The group has commanders and subordinates; it has distinctive signs, and it is openly armed:

> Hezbollah forces in Syria have improved their operational and tactical combat skills, trained and equipped thousands of militants as part of its growing network of Shi'a militias, and stockpiled an impressive arsenal of standoff weapons like Fateh-110/M-600 guided missiles, Karrar unmanned armed drones, Shahab-1 and Shahab-2 short-range ballistic missiles, Toophan anti-tank missiles, and possibly chemical weapons. In addition, much of Hezbollah's arms are shipped through, or potentially manufactured in, Syria – making the country a critical transit hub. Hezbollah is perhaps the best-trained, best-equipped, and most capable terrorist organisation in the world, and these developments have raised the prospects of a wider conflict in the Middle East.[130]

However, as Janaby has noted, it is not possible to affirm with any certainty whether Hezbollah fighters respect laws and customs of war. As pointed out earlier, there is serious doubt that Hezbollah recognises the legitimacy of international law. However, there were instances where Hezbollah members relied on the help of the ICRC to exchange prisoners and consequently obeyed the rules of international law.[131] Hezbollah's respect for laws and customs of war should not be the exclusive criteria to include or exclude the qualification of an armed group belonging to a party in the armed conflict since, in some cases, States party to the Geneva Conventions and their Additional Protocols have violated these same obligations. The criteria may apply to Hezbollah only loosely. Therefore, even though Hezbollah fighters may not respect laws and customs of war, they have acted in collaboration with and at times under the command of Syrian authorities. Hence, it is possible to argue that Hezbollah fighters are an armed group belonging to a party to the armed conflict.

Janaby's last scenario considers whether Hezbollah fighters are an armed group in the context of an internal armed conflict. In this case, Hezbollah would be acting independently from the States of Syria and Lebanon. Janaby has concluded that, '[d]ue to Hezbollah's heavy attacks in areas controlled by the rebels, especially near the Lebanese border, the Syrian opposition had to surrender its control to Hezbollah, which secured these areas and then handed them over to the Syrian army'.[132] In this case, Hezbollah operated independently from the Syrian and Lebanese authorities. Therefore, Hezbollah fighters are an armed group in the context of an internal armed conflict.

Clearly, Hezbollah's role in the Syrian conflict is fluid. It changes depending on the battles' needs and players. It is possible to advance the theory that Hezbollah acted in both capacities as an armed group belonging to the State of Syria, which is party to the armed conflict, and as an armed group acting independently from the States of Syria and Lebanon and in the context of internal armed conflict. Therefore, the conflict is an internationalised armed conflict with both international and non-international armed conflicts. It is certainly a non-international armed conflict due to the hostilities between Syrian armed groups and non-Syrian armed groups such as Hezbollah acting either in collaboration with or independently from the State of Syria. The conflict may shift to become international due to the rising hostilities with Türkiye, Israel and Iraq at the times of writing this chapter. So far, in all scenarios, Hezbollah is a non-State actor.

This chapter has considered Hezbollah's classification in relation to the Westphalian definition of statehood, the effectiveness theory and the recognition theory. It has argued that the current status of international law does not allow us to affirm with any certainty whether Hezbollah is a State actor. Furthermore, this chapter has examined situations where Hezbollah was engaged in armed conflict, in order to decide whether it did so in its capacity as State or non-State actor. It has concluded that Hezbollah was a non-State actor in the 2006 armed conflict with Israel and in the Syrian Civil War.

However, in my opinion, cases such as Hezbollah in Lebanon remain in the 'shadowland' and outside the reach of positive law.[133] Rigid interpretations of rules as well as a lack of interdisciplinarity and inclusivity of other factors (such as politics) weaken the definition of statehood and render it, at times, ineffective. On the ground, Hezbollah is a quasi-State on the rise to possibly become the State of Lebanon. It has its own structure, government and people. It co-exists with the failed State of Lebanon. It employs the State of Lebanon as a façade to sign treaties and enter international agreements, and it benefits from its weaknesses and dysfunction.

Conclusion to Part II

Part II has examined the question of Hezbollah's statehood; it has begun with the legal definition of statehood. Chapter 4 has focused on the origin of statehood according to the Peace Treaty of Westphalia and the two theories of statehood recognition. Furthermore, Chapter 4 has made a distinction between State and non-State actors and argued that there is no perfect definition of statehood. Despite its shortfalls, the Westphalian definition remains the one model universally employed to identify a State. However, it does not allow to capture the category of a quasi-State. Chapter 5 has employed the statehood theories outlined in Chapter 4 and discussed Hezbollah's status as a State or a non-State actor within the context of Lebanon, the 2006 armed conflict with Israel and the Syrian Civil War. Chapter 5 has concluded that, in these various scenarios, Hezbollah is not a State with legal personality, nor a subject of international law. Based on the current interpretations of international law, it remains a non-State actor.

I am of the opinion that Hezbollah is a quasi-State co-existing with the failed State of Lebanon. However, in the absence of a legal recognition of this category and for the sake of this discussion, we may agree that Hezbollah is a non-State actor. The questions that follow are: what kind of non-State actor is it? Is it an armed national liberation movement? Is it an insurgency or a terrorist organisation? More importantly, are these groups subjects of international law? What about Lebanon's legal responsibility? Can Hezbollah's actions be attributed to the State of Lebanon? Is Lebanon an accomplice in Hezbollah's unlawful activities? What about the State of Iran?

Part III
Hezbollah: A Non-State Actor

Introduction to Part III

According to the rules of international law and the Westphalian definition of statehood, Hezbollah is a non-State actor. However, there are numerous forms of non-State actors, some of which are subjects of international law. What kind of non-State actor is Hezbollah? Furthermore, what is Lebanon's responsibility regarding Hezbollah's unlawful acts?

To answer these questions, this part offers three chapters: Chapter 6 will examine the growing role of non-State actors and their different forms in the public and private sectors. It will study the relationship between non-State actors, use of force and hosting States. Chapter 7 will investigate the different legal classifications of Hezbollah as armed non-State actor and distinguish between national liberation movement, insurgency and terrorism. Moreover, this chapter will explore the position of the Special Tribunal for Lebanon (STL) on Hezbollah. Chapter 8 on State and non-State actors' responsibility will address the question of Lebanon's legal responsibility for Hezbollah's unlawful activities; it will consider Lebanon's responsibility by attribution or for complicity and differentiate between State responsibility for the wrong-doing of a non-State actor (Hezbollah) and State responsibility for the wrong-doing of another State (Iran).

Chapter 6

General Comments on Non-State Actors

Hezbollah does not fit the Westphalian definition of State and is therefore a non-State actor. However, the category of a non-State actor is broad and refers to different entities. Non-governmental organisations that advocate for human rights or defend humanitarian laws are non-State actors. Terrorist organisations and international organisations such as the World Bank or the International Monetary Fund also constitute non-State actors. The International Law Association defines a non-State actor as 'legally recognised and organised entities that are not comprised of nor governed or controlled by States nor groups of States and that actually perform functions in the international arena that have real or potential effects on international law'.[1] These non-State actors could consist of non-governmental organisations, multi-national enterprises, organised armed opposition groups, *sui generis* entities and organised indigenous peoples' groups.[2] The membership to the group of non-State actors 'is difficult to define and virtually open-ended [. . . a] grab-bag of miscellaneous players'.[3] Alston has humorously called this fact 'the "not-a-cat" syndrome' for all we know is that a non-State actor is not a State (and certainly not a cat).

What kind of non-State actor is Hezbollah? According to Lebanese law, it is a legally recognised political party, non-profit organisation and armed non-State actor. Most States would disagree with this label and consider Hezbollah a terrorist non-State actor. Understanding Hezbollah's legal status requires a general examination of the growing role of non-State actors on the national and international levels and the issue of use of force by non-State actors.

The Growing Role of Non-State Actors

For several reasons, the role of non-State actors is growing both domestically and internationally. Privatisation has moved certain responsibilities from the public to the private sector. Social welfare, healthcare, utilities, schools and even security have become the responsibility of non-State actors. Globalisation has moved some corporations to become transnational super-powers, which cannot be ignored by State actors. Finally, human rights advocacy work has stretched the role of civil society and non-profit organisations and altered their relations with States and international institutions.[4]

The rise of non-State actors can potentially be problematic, especially when non-State actors threaten or replace traditional State functions. In this case, not only do they challenge the coherence of international law, but they can also create a constitutional crisis, since it is unclear whether they are bound by international laws concerning governance, State responsibilities and human rights.[5] There are times when this expansion is welcomed. This is the case with the ICRC which dramatically contributed to the evolution of international customary law and international humanitarian law. Its work has been an undeniable positive influence on both.[6] This growth of non-State actors has been met with some regulations from international law. The UN Charter considers the possibility of sanctions, asset freezes, bans and embargos on State and non-State actors.[7] AP II mentions 'armed forces and dissident armed forces or other organized armed groups'.[8]

In 2004, the Security Council adopted Resolution 1540 in which it expressed its concerns over 'the threat of terrorism and the risk that non-State actors [. . .] may acquire, develop, traffic in or use nuclear, chemical and biological weapons and their means of delivery'. In a footnote, the Resolution defined a non-State actor as an 'individual or entity, not acting under the lawful authority of any State in conducting activities which come within the scope of this resolution'.[9] In 2016, the Security Council adopted Resolution 2325 in which it re-affirmed Resolution 1540 and expressed once again its grave concerns over the threat of terrorism and the risk of non-State actors acquiring, developing, trafficking in or using nuclear, chemical and biological weapons. The Security Council asked the 1540 Committee, which oversees the execution of Resolution 1540, to pay close attention to the work of non-State actors and their use of evolving science, technology and international commerce.[10] In 2019, the Security Council adopted Resolution 2459 in which it affirmed its commitment to the sovereignty and independence of the Republic of South Sudan, and its strong condemnation of all human rights violations by 'armed groups and national security forces' – in other words, by State and non-State actors.[11]

These legal references to non-State actors are significant. They seem to suggest that non-State actors are subjects of international law.[12] In fact, the ICJ had confirmed this position back in 1949 in *Reparations for Injuries*.[13] In 2010, in the Kosovo Advisory Opinion the ICJ stated that 'it has not been uncommon for the Security Council to make demands on actors other than UN Member States and inter-governmental organisations'.[14] Even with these random provisions, there still exist several gaps in the regulation of non-State actors. Despite their numerous legal contributions, non-State actors are not lawmakers. This formal position remains a State's exclusive right.[15] The absence of a solid definition of a non-State actor in international law (one that goes beyond the simple opposition to a State actor), the non-existence of comprehensive regulations on non-State actors' activities and the fluid distinction between the different forms of non-State actors constitute a serious obstacle in international law. These deficiencies are problematic, and they stem from international law's attachment to an outdated definition of statehood.

Non-State Actors and the Use of Force

The prohibition of use of force is the foundation of international law.[16] The UN Charter recognises two exceptions: taking measures to forcibly apply the Security Council's decisions and the right to self-defence against armed attacks.[17] On an internal level, the use of force is regulated by domestic laws. The issue of use of force becomes complicated when it emanates from a non-State actor against the hosting State or against a third State. In 'Entities That Can Be States But Do Not Claim to Be', Ronen has pointed out that, although we have laws that apply during armed conflicts and that distinguish between inter-state and intra-state conflicts, it is difficult to determine which laws apply in the case of use of force by non-State actors. This becomes more complicated when the non-State actor in question does not belong to any State or targets a third territory (a foreign State).[18] Ronen has provided a theoretical answer to this issue and argued that 'quasi-states, particularly those not within sovereign territory, *ought* to be bound by the prohibition on the use of force. If peace and security are core values that underpin the international order, it is only reasonable to expect that the use of force by NSAs[19] should be prohibited'.[20]

However, international law does not expand to apply to entities other than State actors, and non-State actors benefit tremendously from this limitation. International human rights laws apply to State actors and generate rights and obligations to these entities. This is not true for non-State actors, which might weaken a State's position and commitment to human rights. The strong presence of a non-State actor on a State's territory might act as a deterrent and discourage a State from entering a binding treaty on human rights.

International law struggles with its limitations in matters of armed conflicts and human rights, which is why international criminal law was developed to respond to these limitations. Unlike public international law, international criminal law depends on individual responsibility regardless of a State's affiliation.[21] Nevertheless, international criminal law remains limited in certain scenarios. For instance, a State has the obligation to investigate serious crimes such as genocide or war crimes, as dictated by the Geneva Conventions. However, this obligation does not extend to non-State actors. This exclusion is troubling, especially if a non-State actor is involved in the crimes. It also undermines international criminal law's efforts to ensure peace and security. Furthermore, the application of international criminal law depends on domestic laws and domestic courts, which creates a heavy burden on States, a burden about which non-State actors do not have to worry.

To remedy these serious issues, Ronen has offered four recommendations. The first solution suggests creating legal obligations to non-State actors under international human rights laws.[22] Although this proposition puts legal boundaries on non-State actors, it might legitimise the existence of a non-State actor within the hosting State; it might create a domestic conflict, especially if the non-State actor in question is a guerilla. Furthermore, this expansion might open the door for non-State actors to claim self-defence against the hosting State or a third-party State. Finally, the expansion of obligations to non-State actors may result in more legitimacy for the non-State actor but not accountability. In other words, a non-State actor might have more rights but not necessarily responsibility towards other entities.[23]

As a second proposition, Ronen has suggested imposing statehood on non-State actors. 'If it walks like a duck and quacks like a duck', then it should be considered a duck (or in this case a State). This proposal sounds interesting. However, much like her first suggestion, it generates several legal complications. For one, non-State actors will have access to statehood rights, including immunity and the capacity to enter into relations with other States and international organisations. Furthermore, imposing statehood status on a non-State actor undermines the two theories of effectiveness and recognition, dismisses objective criteria on which statehood is founded and ignores the will of the people. To elaborate further, imposing statehood on a non-State actor acting like a State violates the three basic criteria of territory-people-government, not to mention the criteria of capacity to enter binding international agreements and independence. Also, this solution violates the right to self-determination and may constitute an illegal intervention in domestic affairs. Finally, there is no guarantee that other States will agree to this change in the non-State actor's status, nor that the non-State actor in question will agree to it.[24]

As a third solution, Ronen has wondered whether it is possible to interpret some legal acts as an implicit recognition of statehood. Implicit recognition does not require a statement of recognition and occurs when a State accepts certain performed acts from non-State actors. However, as seen in the previous chapter, implicit recognition is problematic and does not mean full recognition by the international community. In other words, while some States might consider various acts such as the delimitation of maritime borders as an implicit recognition of a non-State actor's statehood, others may not. This would create what Nicholson has referred to in *Statehood and the State-Like in International Law* as a parallel universe where criteria for States' recognition are inconsistent.[25] Furthermore, an implicit recognition of statehood might be rejected by the non-State actor itself.

Finally, as a fourth solution, Ronen has suggested the recognition of statehood-for-a-limited purpose: a non-State actor may be regarded as a State in a specific context. For instance, the Palestinian authorities, Taiwan and Puerto Rico have, in some cases, acted as States and were able to enter internationally binding agreements. This is akin to Nicholson's state-in-context theory. Ronen has expressed some reservations in relation to this last suggestion. Some non-State actors have been attributed legal personalities, but this does not automatically imply statehood. As discussed above, personality signifies that an entity exists as a fact according to the norms of international law and has rights and duties.[26] However, personality alone does not meet the traditional Westphalian criteria of statehood, and therefore statehood and personality cannot be used interchangeably. Another complication emerges when we try to determine when a non-State actor is acting as a State and when it is acting as a non-State actor.

While this approach of statehood-for-a-limited-purpose may be functional, it creates inconsistencies within the non-State actor category where some are recognised as States for political reasons and others are not. This inconsistent expansion of the definition of statehood is not supported by international law, and it would be difficult to identify, for a limited purpose, the State's obligations and responsibilities regarding other States. Contractual reciprocity would be unclear and near impossible to define.[27]

The question of an armed non-State actor and the use of force is particularly interesting in relation to Hezbollah. Ronen's four recommendations would legalise Hezbollah in one way or another, especially if we interpret Hezbollah's use of force – which is by definition a State trait – as either explicit or implicit recognition of statehood or recognition of statehood for a limited purpose. If this classification is impossible, what then is Hezbollah's legal status?

Chapter 7

What Kind of Non-State Actor is Hezbollah?

Is Hezbollah a national liberation movement? Are its members insurgents? The answer depends on several factors: the definitions of national liberation movement and insurgency, the context in which the act of violence occurred and the States' position on the matter.

Hezbollah: A National Liberation Movement or Insurgents?

Armed Non-State Actor and National Liberation Movement

There is no one definition of armed non-State actor. Mahmoud Cherif Bassiouni defines it as follows:

> . . . non-governmental groups who directly or indirectly engage in support of non-governmental combatants in non-international and purely internal conflicts. These groups take a variety of forms, including: 1) Regularly constituted groups of combatants with a military command structure and a political structure; 2) Non-regularly constituted groups of combatants with or without a command structure and with or without a political hierarchical structure; 3) Spontaneously gathered groups who engage in combat or who engage in sporadic acts of collective violence with or without a command structure and with or without political leadership; 4) Mercenaries acting as an autonomous group or as part of other groups of combatants; and 5) Expatriate volunteers who engage for a period of time in combat or in support of combat operations, either as separate units or as part of duly constituted or ad hoc units.[1]

For Agata Kleczkowska, armed non-State actors are members organised to be party to an armed conflict. They have an obvious leader or multiple leaders who manage and control the group, issue orders and make members comply with their commands. It is not important whether the group has a political goal, nor whether it consists of mercenaries and volunteers. The hierarchal structure is what matters. The armed attacks of this group cannot be limited to one single attack. The attacks should be continuous, repeated and intense.[2]

International law and international humanitarian law have recognised the role of armed non-State actors in the context of decolonisation and national liberation movements.[3] The UN Charter,[4] the Universal Declaration of Human Rights,[5] common Article 1 to the ICCPR and the ICESCR,[6] as well as the Geneva Conventions and their Additional Protocols[7] have all explicitly recognised the right to resist occupation and the right to self-determination, rights that result immediately from the principle of State sovereignty and territorial integrity. [8] However, there was an assumption that these non-State actors would eventually join the governments of the newly formed States, and that they would be formally integrated. As such, not much attention was given to them.[9] Legal issues arose when some non-State actors were not formally integrated in the State structure and continued to exist in this in-between of State/non-State actors. Without clear definitions of armed non-State actor, resistance/national liberation movements, it became hard to distinguish between an act of resistance and an act of terrorism.[10]

In recent years, the ICRC has expanded the definition of armed non-State actors to apply beyond national liberation movements. It defined an armed non-State actor as 'a group that is not recognised as a State but has the capacity to cause violence that is of humanitarian concern. It includes a wide range of groups with varying goals, structures, doctrines, funding sources, military capacity, and degree of territorial control'.[11] Today, armed non-State actors are often involved in non-international armed conflicts (such as civil wars). They might oppose the hosting State and a supporting State, but the conflict in which they are engaged remains a non-international armed conflict.

Two conditions are required for a non-international armed conflict to exist: first, the clashes cannot amount to internal disturbances and tensions such as riots and isolated and sporadic acts of violence.[12] The clashes must become hostilities.[13] Second, the armed non-State actor must be organised to be a party to the armed conflict.[14] The ICRC recognises that the size, structure, capabilities and motivations of armed non-State actors continue to evolve and, '[w]hile large groups with centralised and well-defined command and control structures continue to arise and exist, other groups are decentralised in structure and operate in fluid alliances'.[15] The challenge of the armed non-State actor is that there is no international body mandated to label the existence/or absence of an armed non-State actor. States and international actors such as the ICRC engage in their own analysis, which may be problematic (not to mention political, too). The increase in the number of armed non-State actors and non-international armed conflicts makes it hard to accurately identify and label their nature.[16] In jurisprudence, the legitimacy of the conflict matters, along with other criteria such as the intensity of the group's activities, its level of organisation and the duration of its armed activities. With the increase of the intensity, duration and organisation, the armed acts of non-State actors move from acts of resistance to illegal political acts, rebellion, insurgency and, finally, belligerency.[17]

Prosecutor v. *Dusko Tadic* made the distinction between belligerency and insurgency: 'The former category applied to armed conflicts between sovereign States (unless there was recognition of belligerency in a civil war), and while the latter applied to armed violence breaking out in the territory of a sovereign State'.[18] The ICTY also noted that an armed conflict may have the characteristics of both international and non-international armed conflicts.[19] Therefore, resistance or national liberation movements cannot amount to an armed conflict. If it reaches this level, it becomes insurgency and a non-international armed conflict. If it moves any further, it becomes belligerency and an international armed conflict.[20]

Of interest here is the evolution in the UN's position on the right to self-determination and the conduct of national liberation movements. Prior to 1980, UN resolutions tended to condemn violence, while making exceptions in the context of national liberation. After the 1980s, the UN continued to recognise the right to self-determination but no longer excused the terrorist conduct of national liberation movements. In fact, it strongly condemned terrorism and rejected it under all circumstances.[21] For instance, Resolution 44/29 re-affirmed . . .

> . . . the inalienable right to self-determination and independence of all peoples under colonial and racist regimes and other forms of alien domination and foreign occupation, and the legitimacy of their struggle, in particular the struggle of national liberation movements, in accordance with the purposes and principles of the Charter and the Declaration on Principles of International Law concerning Friendly Relations and Co-operation among States in according with the Charter of the United Nations.[22]

However, it did not recognise the violent conduct of national liberation movements as an exception to the prohibition of terrorism; it even called on States to take all necessary steps to combat terrorism. Resolution 46/51 on measures to eliminate international terrorism adopted a position similar to Resolution 44/29.[23] Resolution 60/288 went even further. It referred to the right to self-determination of peoples under colonial domination or foreign occupation. However, it also added that disputes must be resolved by 'peaceful means and in conformity with the principles of justice and international law'.[24] In other words, the right to self-determination must not be interpreted as an invitation to violence and certainly not terrorism. In Resolution 1377, the Security Council re-affirmed its 'unequivocal condemnation of all acts, methods and practices of terrorism as criminal and unjustifiable regardless of their motivation, in all their forms and manifestations, wherever and by whomever committed'.[25]

Based on the analysis above, one can conclude that Hezbollah is an organised group formed of combatants with a visible structure, hierarchy and leaders. Its political and military goals are clear, and it frequently engages in intensive armed attacks in Israel and Syria. For the Lebanese State, Hezbollah is an armed non-State actor engaged in a national liberation movement against the Israeli occupation of Lebanese territory. However, with the withdrawal of Israel from the occupied south in 2000, Hezbollah's qualification has changed. As seen above, the Shebaa Farms are not Lebanese territory. After having appointed cartographers, the UN decided that they are Syrian territory, captured by Israel in 1967.[26] In 2011, the Syrian dictator Bashar al-Assad announced the Shebaa Farms as Syrian soil.[27] Furthermore, Hezbollah is fully funded by Iran. In 2008, it used its weapons internally against the Lebanese people. Hence, the label of national liberation movement does not apply to Hezbollah, at least no longer after 2000.

What other labels do apply? Are Hezbollah fighters insurgents? Are they members of a terrorist organisation?

Insurgency

Over the past decade, the study of insurgency has flourished with the rise of armed non-State actors and the various legal issues that they generate.[28] For Schindler, for insurgency to exist, 'the hostilities are meant to be of a collective character, that is, they have to be carried out not only by single groups. In addition, the insurgents have to exhibit a minimum amount of organisation. Their armed forces should be under a responsible command and be capable of meeting minimal humanitarian requirements'.[29] Insurgents are armed non-State actors that challenge their host State through armed struggle. They are not terrorists, although their violence can escalate to become terrorism. Their goal is to transform the system of governance and to dismantle the established authority. Insurgents, who are sometimes referred to as rebels or guerilla fighters, are organised with a visible structure and great military capacity. They hold control over specific territory within the State. They have their own governance and hierarchal authorities. They can compete against the State and provide public goods such as security, healthcare, education, environmental protection and trade regulation to their own groups.[30]

Insurgents also have advanced recruitment methods and access to weapons. They can operate in urban settings and become involved in organised crime. Insurgents may be State-supported. Yet, with the decline of State sponsorship, insurgents rely more often on organised to crime to fund their activities.[31] Their visibility distinguishes them from terrorist units.[32] In comparison to terrorism, insurgency operates within certain limits. Some targets are unacceptable. Although civilians may be hurt, they are not insurgents' primary target. Terrorism, however, does not have moral limits and does not distinguish between State forces and civilians.[33]

Most States threatened by insurgency are weak or failing States (such as Afghanistan). Some have argued that the goal is not always to transform or defeat the State.[34] When insurgents are unsuccessful in overthrowing the government in place, they end up co-existing with it. In Sri Lanka, the Liberation Tigers of Tamil Eelam existed unchallenged in the country's north and east and had their own governance and military. In 2006, after years of toleration, the Sri Lankan State defeated them. In 2014, the Islamic State proclaimed its statehood and sovereignty over Iraq and Syria. It launched military attacks against both States and engaged in violent acts. In the end, they were defeated. 'When insurgency reaches a certain level – where it claims territory, usurps governmental prerogatives, and actually threatens the state – it opens itself to a military backlash too powerful for most embryonic pro-states'.[35] In theory, the government should step in and address the issues that have led to insurgency in the first place. However, often States step in to squash these movements without resolving any matter.[36]

For Grasser, insurgents are involved in non-international armed conflicts that take place on a State's territory and oppose the insurgents to the government. The causes of these conflicts and the goals vary, but in all cases insurgents are opposed to their hosting State. The insurgents may also be described as 'rebels, revolutionaries, secessionists, freedom fighters, terrorists, or by similar names – [they] are fighting to take over the reins of power, or to obtain greater autonomy within the State, or in order to secede and create their own State'.[37] Some might take issue with this lack of distinction between these different forms of armed non-State actors, especially the conflation of freedom fighters (and by extension resistance and national liberation movements) and insurgents. Freedom fighters might have a legitimate cause to fight, while insurgents might simply be a violent group attempting to destabilise the State. Furthermore, for Andrew Clapham, 'it is clumsy to list N[ational] L[iberation] M[ovements] as non-state actors. Their representatives may reject the label of non-state actor, as not only may they wish to stress their putative state-like aspirations and status, but they may sometimes already be recognised as a state member in certain regional inter-governmental organisations'.[38]

Moreover, the distinction between these categories is important as it determines the laws that apply. For instance, national liberation movements are protected under international humanitarian law: they benefit from the protection of international humanitarian law if the struggle is against colonial domination, occupation, and against racist regimes (Article 1(4) of AP I). Members of national liberation movements may also benefit from the prisoner of war status, as stipulated in Article 44(3) of AP I.[39]

Considering the doctrinal definition of insurgency and the inapplicability of the label of national liberation movement to Hezbollah, it is possible to argue that Hezbollah fighters are insurgents inside Lebanon. This was particularly true in the armed struggle of May 2008. As pointed out in Chapter 2, the government ordered to monitor Hezbollah's communication network. Hezbollah violently retaliated against this State operation, deployed its weapons internally and launched attacks against the LAF. The Secretary General to Hezbollah, Hassan Nasrallah, announced the State's move 'a declaration of war'.[40] As insurgents, Hezbollah fighters aimed to control the State/its government and to gain control over its territory. Civilians were not necessarily the immediate target of their attacks. The fighters were organised, structured, well-trained and well-equipped. They were visible to anyone in Lebanon. In 2008, one could easily identify them in the streets of Beirut. They had distinctive uniforms with a patch of Hezbollah's yellow flag on their arms. Today, the State of Lebanon and Hezbollah insurgents co-exist. The State of Lebanon – or at least some public officials – tolerate them as they continue to challenge the State's legitimacy and decisions.

Hezbollah: A Terrorist Non-State Actor

Understanding Hezbollah's legal classification as a terrorist non-State actor requires an examination of the definition of terrorism according to international and regional legal instruments, domestic law and the STL.

Terrorism in International and Regional Instruments and Domestic Law

Terrorism in United Nations Instruments

It is a fallacy to believe that terrorism is a new issue in the world, as terrorist activities have existed 'since the beginning of humanity'.[41] The English word 'terrorism' comes to us from the French and originally referred to State-sponsored terrorism; it emerged in the eighteenth century when Robespierre installed *La Terreur* or the Reign of Terror and ordered the execution of thousands of people for their opposition or potential threat to the French Revolution.[42] In the nineteenth century, the term was expanded to include the terrorism of non-State actors.

The twentieth century witnessed several serious debates on international law and terrorism. In 1927, the first International Conference for the Unification of Criminal Law took place in Poland and discussed international law and the prohibition of slavery and piracy.[43] In 1937, the Convention for the Prevention and Punishment of the Crime of Terrorism attempted to define terrorism and regulate its prohibition. The Convention did not enter into force for lack of ratifications. In 1949, the Geneva Conventions and their Additional Protocols specifically sanctioned terrorism and acts of terrorism against civilians. However, they did not offer a definition of terrorism.[44]

Since 1963, the UN has adopted nineteen international legal instruments to prevent or combat terrorism. The Office of Counter-Terrorism at the UN divides these instruments into nine themes: instruments regarding civil aviation; the protection of international staff; the taking of hostages; nuclear material; maritime navigation; explosive materials; terrorist bombings; financing of terrorism; and nuclear terrorism.[45] In terms of civil aviation, in 1963 the Convention on Offences and Certain Other Acts Committed on Board Aircraft was adopted to ensure in-flight safety;[46] it authorises the aircraft commander to protect the aircraft by imposing reasonable measures such as restraining a person committing or attempting to commit a violent act on board. In 1968, members of the Popular Front for the Liberation of Palestine hijacked El Al flight 425 from Rome to Tel-Aviv and diverted it to Algeria. The hijackers demanded the release of Palestinians imprisoned in Israel.[47] To respond to this mounting threat to aircrafts, the Convention for the Suppression of Unlawful Seizure of Aircraft was adopted in 1970;[48] it makes it illegal for any passenger to seize control or attempt to seize control of the aircraft by force or any other form of intimidation. States parties to this Convention were asked to punish hijacking in their domestic laws. In 1971, the Convention for the Suppression of Unlawful Acts against the Safety of Civil Aviation was adopted.[49] Commonly known as the Montreal Convention, this instrument makes unlawful acts of violence that would endanger the safety of the aircraft, such as placing explosives. Attempts to endanger the aircraft and complicity are also punishable acts.

In the 1970s, there was a legitimate concern over kidnapping and hostage-taking. As such, the Convention on the Prevention and Punishment of Crimes against Protected Persons was adopted in 1973; it considers the head of state, minister of foreign affairs and any representative or official or a State or international organisation as an 'internationally protected person'.[50] In 1979, the International Convention against Taking of Hostages was adopted;[51] it defines the crime of taking a hostage as the unlawful seizure or detention and threats to kill, to injure, or to continue to detain another person to force a third party – whether a State, an international or governmental organisation, a natural or juridical person, or a group of persons – to perform or to abstain from performing an act in exchange for the release of the hostage.

In 1988, a Supplementary Protocol for the Suppression of Unlawful Acts against the Safety of Fixed Platforms Located on the Continental Shelf (supplementing the Convention for the Suppression of Unlawful Acts against the Safety of Civil Aviation) was adopted, extending the prohibition to terrorist acts at airports serving international civil aviation.[52] This prompted the adoption of the 2010 Convention on the Suppression of Unlawful Acts Relating to International Civil Aviation, which punishes the use of weapons, the use and transport of biological, chemical and nuclear discharge, or any other substance that could cause death, injury, or damage on the aircraft.[53] With the evolution of technology and the real threat of its use by terrorists, the convention criminalised cyber-attacks on air navigation. The convention was followed by a Protocol Supplementary to the Convention for the Suppression of Unlawful Seizure of Aircraft Protocol, which expanded its scope and included different forms of hijacking as punishable acts.[54]

The pressing need to protect civil and international aviation prompted the international community to turn its attention to maritime navigation. In 1988, the Convention for the Suppression of Unlawful Acts against the Safety of Maritime Navigation was adopted.[55] Much like the 1971 Convention for the Suppression of Unlawful Acts against the Safety of Civil Aviation, the 1988 Convention prohibits certain acts that could endanger the safety of the ship. These include, but are not limited to, the unlawful seizure or exercise of control over a ship by force, threat, or intimidation, acts of violence against a person on board of a ship and the placement of destructive substances or devices on the ship. In 2005, a protocol was added to the convention to criminalise certain unlawful acts.[56] These acts include the transport of banned materials that would cause injury, death or damage to the passengers and the ship, as well as the transport of persons who have committed acts of terrorism.

The fear of the misuse of nuclear material and explosive materials in unlawful acts such as terrorism prompted the international community to adopt the 1980 Convention on the Physical Protection of Nuclear Material,[57] which prohibits the unlawful possession, use, transfer, or theft of nuclear material, or the threat to use nuclear material. In 2005, the convention was amended, and the protection of nuclear facilities was added as a requirement binding for all States Parties.[58]

As for terrorist acts, the 1977 International Convention for the Suppression of Terrorist Bombings was adopted to prohibit the use of explosives and other lethal devices in public spaces, with the intent to kill or cause serious injury or extensive destruction of the public space.[59] Financing of terrorism was also banned in the 1999 International Convention for the Suppression of the Financing of Terrorism, which requires States Parties to combat unlawful financial acts such as money-laundering.[60] It also specifically stipulates that States Parties must identify, freeze and seize funds allocated for terrorist activities. In 2005, the International Convention for the Suppression of Acts of Nuclear Terrorism was adopted, covering multiple forms of unlawful acts or attempts to commit such crimes or to participate in them.[61]

In addition to these international treaties, the UN General Assembly adopted numerous resolutions to condemn terrorism. In 1994, the General Assembly adopted the Declaration on Measures to Eliminate International Terrorism (included in the annex to Resolution 49/60)[62] and the Declaration to Supplement the 1994 Declaration on Measures to Eliminate International Terrorism (included in the annex to Resolution 51/210).[63] In September 2006, the General Assembly adopted Resolution 60/288 in which it reiterated its strong condemnation of terrorism and detailed its strategy regarding counter-terrorism. In its latest Resolution about counter-terrorism, the General Assembly re-affirmed its commitment to Resolution 60/288 and reviewed its counter-terrorism strategy.[64] Similarly, the Security Council adopted multiple resolutions on the prohibition of terrorism. Over the past decade, some of the resolutions adopted have focused on the following topics: the prevention of kidnapping and hostage-taking committed by terrorist groups,[65] the condemnation of the Islamic State, the al-Nusrah Front (ANF) and all other individuals or groups associated with al-Qaida,[66] women and peace and security,[67] threats to international peace and security caused by terrorist acts,[68] and children and armed conflicts.[69]

In response to the terrorist attacks on the United States on 11 September 2001, the Security Council adopted Resolution 1373, one of the most interesting resolutions: it created the Counter-Terrorism Committee (CTC) and imposed various binding and non-binding obligations on all States. In fact, the resolution contains twelve binding obligations in which it dictates that all States shall prevent and suppress the financing of terrorist acts; all States shall refrain from offering safe haven to terrorists, or any type of direct or indirect support, and they shall penalise complicity in committing these unlawful acts; all States must effectively control their borders and territories to prevent unlawful acts that contribute to terrorism such as counterfeiting, forgery, or fraudulent use of identity papers and travel documents. Finally, all States are required to report to the CTC. The resolution also contains nine non-binding provisions according to which the Security Council encourages all States to collaborate with each other and to increase communication, improve their domestic laws and implement preventive counter-terrorist acts.[70]

This resolution was followed by Resolution 1377 in which the Security Council declared international terrorism as the 'most serious threats to international peace and security in the twenty-first century' and 'a challenge to all States and to all of humanity'.[71] The Security Council re-affirmed its 'unequivocal condemnation of all acts, methods and practices of terrorism as criminal and unjustifiable regardless of their motivation, in all their forms and manifestations, wherever and by whomever committed'.[72] The Security Council's role in counter-terrorism effectively commenced with Resolution 1373. Today, it has four main tasks: condemning acts of terrorism, imposing sanctions, creating universally binding counter-terrorist measures and strengthening the skills, abilities and resources in counter-terrorism at national levels.[73]

Terrorism in Regional Instruments

The Arab Convention for the Suppression of Terrorism of 1998 provides a definition of terrorism as follows:

> . . . any act or threat of violence, whatever its motives or purposes, that occurs in the advancement of an individual or collective criminal agenda and seeking to sow panic among people, causing fear by harming them, or placing their lives, liberty or security in danger, or seeking to cause damage to the environment or to public or private installations or property or to occupying or seizing them, or seeking to jeopardize a national resources.[74]

The Arab Convention then lists what constitutes acts of terrorism (unlawful acts in aircrafts and ships, crimes against international protected persons, including diplomats and taking hostages). Similarly, the Convention of the Organisation of the Islamic Conference on Combating International Terrorism of 1999 offers a general definition of terrorism and lists terrorist acts.[75] The Organisation of African Unity Convention on the Prevention and Combating of Terrorism of 1999[76] and the Inter-American Convention against Terrorism reference several international treaties on terrorism and enumerate acts of terrorism, but without providing a definition.[77]

In 1977, the Council of Europe adopted the European Convention on the Suppression of Terrorism. The goal of the convention was to facilitate the extradition of those who had committed acts of terrorism. Some of the acts listed are attacks against internationally protected persons, the hijacking of aircraft, kidnapping and taking hostages, as well as the use of explosives such as bombs, grenades, or rockets to endanger persons.[78] Beforehand, in 1957, the council had also adopted the European Convention on Extradition where its State Parties committed to extradite persons sought for criminal proceedings or for the carrying-out of a sentence. The State Parties have the right to refuse extradition in case of political offence or the risk of death penalty.[79] Related to this, in 1975, the council adopted an Additional Protocol to this convention, in which it specifically prohibited extradition in case of political offence.[80] However, in the 1977 Convention on the Suppression of Terrorism, the State Parties were encouraged not to consider as political offence any act of violence against the life, physical integrity or liberty of a person. In 2003, the Council of Europe adopted a Protocol to amend the European Convention on the Suppression of Terrorism. This protocol expanded the scope of the convention and, therefore, covers all unlawful acts contained in the UN anti-terrorist Conventions and its Protocols.[81]

In 2005, the Council of Europe adopted two important texts: (1) the Convention on the Prevention of Terrorism and (2) the Convention on Laundering, Search, Seizure and Confiscation of the Proceeds from Crime and on the Financing of Terrorism. The Convention on the Prevention of Terrorism criminalises certain acts that may lead to terrorism; it increases the effectiveness of already existing international texts and enhances national and international collaboration for the prevention of terrorism with better communication, preventive policies, mutual exchange programmes and extradition policies.[82] In 2015, this was followed by an Additional Protocol which added a number of unlawful acts, such as the participation in a terrorist group, receiving terrorist training, traveling abroad for the purposes of terrorism and financing or organising travel for this purpose. The protocol created a network of around-the-clock nation contact points to enhance communication.[83] The Council of Europe's Convention on Laundering, Search, Seizure and Confiscation of the Proceeds from Crime and on the Financing of Terrorism stipulates measures to prevent acts of terrorism through money-laundering and other unlawful financial activities. It recognises the importance of fast communication and quick access to financial information of criminal organisations and terrorist groups so as to prevent and combat terrorism.[84]

No International Agreement on How to Define Terrorism

Despite the diversity of their topics and the wide scope of application, the legal instruments listed above share some commonalities. In general, they all prohibit intentional acts of violence on international and national levels and require States to criminalise these acts in their domestic laws. Most stipulate universal jurisdiction and require States to either extradite or prosecute the offender. They also reject terrorism under all circumstances.[85] Post-9/11, treaties and State practice have shifted to focus on the perpetrators' intent to cause death, serious bodily harm, or substantial damage to property and environment; they have also required a high level of violence for the crime of terrorism to hold.[86]

Furthermore, it has been argued that the prohibition of terrorism (just like the prohibition of genocide) is a *jus cogens* norm. This means that there is no possible derogation.[87] Although there is no official statement from a higher authority proclaiming the prohibition of terrorism as a *jus cogens* norm, it has been suggested as much by the widely ratified international and regional treaties listed above and State practice.[88] The prohibition of terrorism has a certain universality to it – or as Kofi Annan, the former Secretary General to the UN, would say, 'a terrorist attack on one country is an attack on humanity as a whole'.[89]

Apart from the Arab Convention for the Suppression of Terrorism of 1998, all the instruments listed above, both international and regional, follow what is called a sectoral approach; it means that 'they do not define international terrorism in general, but rather address particular acts of terrorism, such as acts of violence on board an aircraft and its unlawful seizure . . .'[90] Even Resolution 1373 with its important legislative nature and role in counter-terrorism has failed to provide a definition of terrorism. Today, despite numerous attempts,[91] there exists no one single international definition of terrorism, and many have lamented the fragmented international legal response to terrorism.[92]

Domestic Laws on Terrorism

Many States have adopted their own definitions of terrorism. It is impossible to survey all of these laws. Consequently, this chapter will focus on States that have been seriously engaging in counter-terrorism or that have expressed their positions on Hezbollah's legal classification.

In the **United States of America**, the United States Code on Crimes and Criminal Procedure distinguishes between international and domestic terrorism. International terrorism includes violent, criminal acts committed by individuals and/or groups who are inspired by or associated with a foreign organisation or nation. The acts must be dangerous to human life or must aim to intimidate or coerce civilians or influence, intimidate, or coerce a government or affect its conduct by mass destruction, assassination, or kidnapping. They can occur either within the jurisdiction of the United States or outside, if the violence transcends the national boundaries within which the act was intended or the persons targeted.

The United States recognises armed non-State actors' terrorism and State-sponsored terrorism. Unlike international terrorism, domestic terrorism aims to further ideological goals which originate from domestic, political, religious, social, racial, or environmental influences. Domestic terrorism includes acts within the territorial jurisdiction of the United States, acts that endanger human life, as prescribed in the United States criminal laws, or acts that appear to intimidate or coerce civilians and to influence, intimidate or coerce government or to affect its conduct by mass destruction, assassination, or kidnapping.[93] The US Patriot Act of 2001 defines terrorist offences as the threat, conspiracy or attempt to hijack airplanes, boats and other vehicles; to commit violent acts against protected persons such as public officials; and to commit crimes with dangerous devices that would endanger public safety or cause substantial damage to property.[94]

In **Canada**, the Criminal Code of 1985 relies on the international instruments listed above to define terrorism in the context of civil aviation, maritime navigation, nuclear materials, protected persons, kidnapping and hostage-taking, as well as the suppression and financing of terrorism. Furthermore, under Offences against Public Order, the Criminal Code stipulates that terrorism may be an act or omission committed inside or outside of Canada, for a political, religious, or ideological purpose, through the intimidation of civilians or the public, threats to economic security against a person, a government, or an international organisation to pressure them to refrain from performing any act. The act must be intentional and aimed to cause death or serious bodily harm, or endanger the life of a person through violence, cause serious risk to public health and safety, or substantial damage to public or private property, or disruption to essential public or private services.[95]

In **Australia**, the Criminal Code Act of 1995 defines terrorism as acts intended to force, intimidate, influence, or coerce the public or any government to advance a political, religious, or ideological cause. These goals may be achieved when individuals or groups endanger the life of a person or the health of safety of the public, cause death or harm to a person, or cause serious damage to property, including serious interference, disruption, or destruction of infrastructure such as telecommunications or electricity networks.[96] The offence of terrorism includes the execution of the terrorist act, the intent to execute a terrorist act, to plan, prepare, finance, provide or receive training for a terrorist act, possess things related to terrorist acts and collect documents to facilitate terrorist acts.

In the **United Kingdom**, the Terrorism Act 2000 defines terrorism as the use of threat to influence the government or an international organisation, or to intimidate the public in order to advance a political, religious, racial, or ideological cause. This prohibited conduct includes serious violence against a person, or a threat of violence, serious damage to property, serious risk to public health and safety, as well as actions designed to disrupt public services. These actions can be within the United Kingdom's jurisdiction or outside of it. Moreover, the text enumerates the various offences that fall under terrorism, such as communicating, training and financing terrorism.[97]

In **France**, Le Code Pénal (penal code) covers the prohibition of terrorism in Title II, Articles 421-1 to 422-7. In general, the Code Pénal defines terrorism as intentional acts of violence against a person's life and integrity; kidnapping; hijacking; violence on board of an aircraft or ship; illegal transport of arms, explosives and nuclear materials; property destruction; membership in terrorist organisations; and training with and providing information and materials to a terrorist organisation.[98]

In **Lebanon**, Article 314 of the Lebanese Criminal Code defines terrorism as acts intended to create public danger and to cause a state of terror by using 'explosive devices, inflammable materials, toxic or corrosive products and infectious or microbial agents'.[99]

Finally, in **Israel**, the 1948 Prevention of Terrorism Order, the Declaration on Unauthorised Associations and Terrorist Organisations in accordance with the Defence Regulations (Emergency) 1945 and the Prohibition on Terrorist Financing Law 5765-2004, as well as the Declaration on Terrorist Organisations in accordance with the Prevention of Terrorism Ordinance No. 33 5708-1948 define terrorism as an individual or as a group of individuals who execute or threaten to execute violent and intentional acts to cause death or injury to a person so as to achieve their goals.

Terrorism also includes the promotion of hatred or contempt, or the incitement to hatred and contempt against the Israeli government or its public officials and the destruction or damage to public property. A member of a terrorist organisation is an individual who belongs to an organisation considered terrorist by the Israeli Defence Ministry, who participates in its activities, trains with its members and recruits for it, publishes its materials, participates in its propaganda, organises its activities, or collects funds or goods for its benefit.[100] The Counter-Terrorism Law of 2016 extends this definition of terrorism and terrorist acts to the cyber-space; it considers terrorism public acts demonstrating solidarity with a terrorist organisation, publications that call for the commission of terrorist acts or that praise or support a terrorist act.[101]

This is only a brief, general examination of domestic laws, as it is beyond the scope of this chapter to discuss the details of each domestic law. Despite their differences, these legislations have three key elements in common. For terrorism to exist, they all require (1) the commission of a criminal act or the threat of a criminal act (as defined either in domestic law or in the international and regional instruments listed above); (2) the intent to spread fear among civilians, public and private institutions; and (3) the goal to further or impose their own ideology or cause. In other words, they all define terrorism or terrorist offences as intentional violence or the threat of violence committed against civilians or public or private institutions so as to further a cause or goal.

In the absence of a universally agreed-upon definition, this chapter adopts Blacksley's definition, according to which terrorism is . . .

> . . . use of violence by some specific group, or government, or leadership, in order to obtain thereby some military, political, religious, or philosophical end, committed by any means against innocent individuals or their property, and for the purpose of placing them in fear, by intimidation, or coercion [. . .] violence must be aimed at or must wantonly impact on innocents. It may include the use of weapons of mass destruction.[102]

The Classification of Hezbollah as Terrorist Non-State Actor

Except for Lebanon, all the States listed above consider Hezbollah a terrorist non-State actor and organisation. Israel was among the first States to do so and has made its position clear since the 1980s. Considered the first international terrorist tribunal, the STL prosecuted some of Hezbollah's members and classified their unlawful acts as terrorism. It is worth mentioning that, as a court of law, the STL was tasked to examine Hezbollah fighters' individual criminal responsibility and not to attempt the classification of the organisation. Nevertheless, it played a role in linking Hezbollah to terrorism.

The Classification of Hezbollah in International, Regional and National Instruments

In the **United States**, the US Department of State in October 1997 listed Hezbollah as a foreign terrorist organisation,[103] and there are legal ramifications to this classification. For instance, it is unlawful for a person in the United States to provide support or resources to Hezbollah, and the

United States has the right to impose sanctions on individuals affiliated with Hezbollah.

In a recent example, the OFAC, a financial intelligence and enforcement agency of the US Treasury Department, accused nine individuals of multiple cases of money-laundering and securing goods and services to finance and support Hezbollah. Nazem Ahmad, a diamond smuggler and art collector, was identified as the main person of interest. He is facing multiple charges related to terrorism.[104] Following the US's decision, the UK's Treasury announced sanctions against Ahmad for affiliation and financing a terrorist organisation.[105] In 2022, the OFAC designated four members of an international oil-smuggling network for facilitating oil trade and financing Hezbollah and the Iranian Islamic Revolutionary Guard Corps-Qods Force. These individuals (Viktor Artemov, Edman Nafrieh, Rouzbeh Zahedi and Mohamed al-Zein) had developed an illicit network to smuggle Iranian oil in violation of international regulations, to falsify documents and to generate revenue to support the activities of two terrorist organisations.[106] In 2015, the Congress adopted the Hezbollah International Financing Prevention Act, which is specifically designed to sanction foreign financial institutions from working with or facilitating transactions or money-laundering on Hezbollah's behalf.[107] This act forced Lebanon's Central Bank to close several accounts related to Hezbollah.[108] In 2018, the Hizballah International Financing Prevention Amendments Act followed, expanding financial sanctions against Hezbollah and imposing measures on financial institutions to refrain from supporting the group.[109]

These are only some examples among many. Furthermore, since the US Department of State has labelled Hezbollah a foreign terrorist organisation, courts have convicted several individuals for their affiliations with Hezbollah. In May 2022, a New Jersey man was convicted for training with Hezbollah, as well as for marriage fraud and falsifying documents.[110] In September 2022, the United States District Court for the Eastern District of New York ordered Hezbollah to pay millions of dollars in damages to a group of Americans who had been in Israel in 2006 and had been wounded by Hezbollah's rockets. The court stated that Hezbollah is 'an FTO (Foreign Terrorist Organisation) widely known for causing the deaths of innocents, listed as such by the United States since 1997'. The court awarded the plaintiffs $111,485,900.01 in total damages, which include $37,161,966.67 in compensatory damages. [111]

Canada listed Hezbollah as a terrorist organisation in 2002.[112] It described Hezbollah as a radical Shiite group that aims to spread the Iranian Revolution in Lebanon, to liberate Jerusalem, destroy Israel and ultimately establish a revolutionary Shiite Islamic State in Lebanon.

Thus, Hezbollah is responsible for several serious terrorist attacks, such as the Beirut Barracks Bombing of 1983, the hijacking of TWA Flight 847 and continuous attacks on the Israeli forces.[113]

Based on the Criminal Code Act 1995, Division 102, **Australia** proclaimed Hezbollah a terrorist organisation for its direct or indirect involvement in the planning, preparing, assisting and fostering of terrorist acts and for advocating for terrorism. Australian National Security provided a long list of Hezbollah's involvements in terrorism, such as the continuous attacks on Israel, the public threat to US military interests, especially after the assassination of Major General Qassem Soleimani on 3 January 2020, the use of Iranian missiles and other weapons, the procurement of explosives for terrorist activities outside of Lebanon, as well as training of and assistance to other terrorist organisations in the region.[114]

The **United Kingdom**'s government labelled Hezbollah's External Security Organisation as a terrorist group in 2001. In 2008, this classification was extended to include both the military and political wings of the group. For the UK government, Hezbollah seeks to destroy Israel and to seize the entire Palestinian territories; it supports terrorism in Iraq, amasses weapons in Lebanon in direct violation of UN Security Council Resolutions 1701 and 1559, supports the Syrian regime in the Syrian conflict and violates the Lebanese Government's decision of neutrality. [115]

In 2000, **France**'s Prime Minister Lionel Jospin called Hezbollah a terrorist organisation during his visit to the West Bank. His proclamation was not well received.[116] In 2013, the French Minister of Foreign Affairs Laurent Fabius followed the United Kingdom's recommendations and asked the European Union to add Hezbollah to its list of terrorist organisations.[117] France changed its mind on Hezbollah's classification for two main reasons: (1) it disapproved of Hezbollah's support to the Syrian regime and participation in the Syrian Civil War;[118] and (2) investigations revealed that Hezbollah had been behind the July 2012 bus attack in Burgas (Bulgaria), which had killed five Israeli tourists and the Bulgarian driver and wounded more than thirty other Israelis.[119]

Hence, in the Council Implementing Regulation (EU) 2022/147 of 3 February 2022, implementing Article 2(3) of Regulation (EC) No. 2580/2001 on specific restrictive measures directed against certain persons and entities with a view to combating terrorism, and repealing Implementing Regulation (EU) 2021/1188, the Council of the **European Union** specifically listed the 'Hizballah Military Wing' as terrorist group.[120] Unlike Israel, the United States, Canada, Australia and the United Kingdom, France and the European Union have distinguished between Hezbollah's military wing and political wing and only listed the military wing on their list of terrorist organisations. By doing so, France and the European Union have reserved the right to negotiate with Hezbollah's public officials and representatives in the State of Lebanon. In other words, this distinction guarantees that the door to diplomacy remains open.[121] The United States criticised this distinction and called on the European Union to abandon it.[122]

In March 2016, the **Arab League** took the bold decision of declaring Hezbollah a terrorist organisation. The rise of sectarian violence between Sunnis and Shiites in Iraq, Syria and Yemen prompted this decision. The Arab League was also opposed to Hezbollah's support to the Syrian regime; it argued that Hezbollah was a terrorist Iranian anti-Arab organisation whose unlawful activities were aggravating the Palestinian–Israeli conflict and not solving it. In response to this classification, the Lebanese Minister of Interior, Nuhad al-Mashnouq, proclaimed that, while Lebanon agreed that Iran was destabilising the region, it rejected the label 'terrorist organisation' for Hezbollah.[123]

In this move, the Arab League followed the Gulf Cooperation Council (GCC) in its decision to label Hezbollah a terrorist organisation. Composed of six States (Bahrain, Kuwait, Oman, Qatar, Saudi Arabia and the United Arab Emirates), the GCC accused Hezbollah of recruiting young people to execute terrorist acts and of destabilising the region with its hostile unlawful activities.[124] Considering recent events, the 7 October attack on Israeli civilians and the ongoing war in Gaza, the Arab League dropped Hezbollah's terrorist label. This decision generated much discussion in the Middle East. Some have argued that it was a necessary move to negotiate a cease-fire in Gaza, the return of Israeli hostages and the cessation of Hezbollah's attacks into northern Israel.[125]

Unlike the European Union and the Arab League, the **United Nations** do not have a list of terrorist organisations. Although they have adopted resolutions strongly condemning ISIS in Iraq and Syria as well as the Taliban in Afghanistan, the UN have not clearly expressed their position on Hezbollah. This is certainly a dilemma: Lebanon has signed and ratified several of the international instruments listed above and, therefore, technically would be in violation of international law for not domestically prosecuting Hezbollah fighters.

In fact, Lebanon signed the 1963 Convention on Offences and Certain Other Acts Committed on Board Aircraft, the 1970 Convention for the Suppression of Unlawful Seizure of Aircraft, the 1971 Convention for the Suppression of Unlawful Acts against the Safety of Civil Aviation, the 1988 Protocol for the Suppression of Unlawful Acts of Violence at Airports Serving International Civil Aviation, supplementary to the Convention for the Suppression of Unlawful Acts against the Safety of Civil

Aviation, the 1973 Convention on the Prevention and Punishment of Crimes against Internationally Protected Persons, the 1979 International Convention against the Taking of Hostages, the 1980 Convention on the Physical Protection of Nuclear Material, the 1988 Convention for the Suppression of Unlawful Acts against the Safety of Maritime Navigation, the 1988 Protocol for the Suppression of Unlawful Acts against the Safety of Fixed Platforms Located on the Continental Shelf and the 1991 Convention on the Marking of Plastic Explosives for the Purpose of Detection. It is safe to say that Hezbollah fighters committed several crimes that violated these international legal instruments, particularly the hijacking of aircraft, kidnapping and taking hostages. However, there were no domestic legal consequences to their actions. This absence of accountability can be immediately tied to Lebanon's General Amnesty Law, which forgave all crimes committed prior to 1991.[126] This would explain the UN's silence on Hezbollah's crimes prior to 1991 and Lebanon's responsibility.

However, Lebanon signed and/or ratified several other legal instruments *after* the General Amnesty Law of 1991, including the 1999 International Convention for the Suppression of the Financing of Terrorism, the 2000 Convention against Transnational Organised Crime, the 2003 Convention against Corruption and the 2005 International Convention for the Suppression of Acts of Nuclear Terrorism. Although Lebanon has signed these treaties, it has not domestically prosecuted Hezbollah members for organised crimes, corruption, or financing terrorism – this despite the irrefutable national and international proof of their involvements.

Despite these flagrant violations of international law, the UN still has not voiced an opinion on Hezbollah. In Resolution 1559, the Security Council referred to Hezbollah as an armed militia.[127] In Resolution 1701, the Security Council adopted a different approach and opted not to directly classify Hezbollah. It referred to its armed attacks against Israel and asked the State of Lebanon to monopolise the use of force.[128] To some extent, one can understand the UN's position – or lack thereof – on Hezbollah. It is not within the practice of the UN to keep a list of international terrorist organisations. Furthermore, there would be serious legal consequences to and possibly complications with this classification. For instance, with the conflation of the State of Lebanon and Hezbollah, the international community would hesitate to communicate or deal with the State of Lebanon – a State with members labelled as terrorists. Finally, there would arise the issue of the applicability of international humanitarian law in the context of terrorism.

While the UN's decision is understandable, this does not mean that it is practical or effective. In fact, the lack of classification by the UN allows for Hezbollah to continue with its unlawful activities and for its members to continue to infiltrate the State of Lebanon. Moreover, it creates confusion and opens the door to contradictory practices. To give a recent example, in January 2023 Joanna Wronecka, the UN's Special Coordinator for Lebanon, tweeted to thank Ammar Moussawi, Hezbollah's head of international relations, for a fruitful discussion on Lebanon's affairs. In this example, a UN official publicly thanked a Hezbollah member, one that is considered a terrorist by many States. This tweet was severely criticised by many Lebanese and by several States, including the United States and Israel.[129]

The Special Tribunal for Lebanon

General Overview of the Special Tribunal for Lebanon

The STL was established after Lebanon had solicited the UN's help. Although Lebanon did not ratify the final agreement, the UN moved ahead with it.[130] Acting under Chapter VII of the Charter, the UN implemented the provisions of the agreement through Security Council Resolution 1757.[131] Hence, the STL was created to prosecute those responsible for the attack of 14 February 2005, which killed former Lebanese Prime Minister Rafic Hariri and twenty-one others and injured at least 226 people. It also has jurisdiction for the attacks that occurred in Lebanon between 1 October 2004 and 12 December 2005, if they are connected to the attack of 14 February 2005 and are similar in nature and gravity.[132]

Composed of Lebanese and international judges, the STL is a mixed court based in The Hague and applies Lebanese Criminal Law. The STL is unique in its kind as it prosecutes terrorism as a stand-alone crime, defining terrorism as international crime.[133] Daniel Bellemare, the former Chief Prosecutor at the STL from 2009 to 2012, has stated that . . .

> . . . [a]s the first international terrorist tribunal, the STL has no prototype. Everything is new. The investigative challenges are those of a complex terrorist investigation, compounded by several factors: the evolving political landscape of Lebanon and the region; security issues affecting potential witnesses and investigators alike; a headquarters outside the country; and a lack of domestic law enforcement tools.[134]

Initially, the STL accused five Hezbollah members of the terrorist attack on 14 February 2005. The Trial Chamber rendered its sentencing judgment on 11 December 2020 and convicted *in absentia*[135] Salim Jamil Ayyash, of conspiracy to commit terrorist acts, committing a terrorist act by means of an explosive device, the intentional homicide of Rafic

Hariri with premeditation by using explosive materials, the intentional homicide of twenty-one persons in addition to Rafic Hariri with premeditation by using explosive materials and the attempted homicide with premeditation by using explosive materials of the 226 who were intentionally injured in the 14 February attack.

The Trial Chamber decided on life imprisonment and recommended that Lebanon should establish an independent statutory compensation scheme for the victims of the 14 February 2005 attack, in compliance with Article 8 of the 1985 United Nations Declaration of Basic Principles of Justice for Victims of Crime and Abuse of Power. It also recommended the creation of a trust fund for the victims. Hassan Habib Merhi, Hussein Hasan Oneissi and Assad Hassan Sabra were acquitted of all accounts.[136] The proceedings against Mustafa Amine Badreddine were dropped following reports of his death.

On 12 January 2021, the prosecution, Ayyash's defence and the Legal Representatives for the Victims filed an appeal. On 10 March 2022, the Appeals Chamber unanimously reversed the Trial Chamber's sentencing judgment of Merhi's and Oneissi's acquittal. The Appeals Chamber stated errors of law and facts and found Merhi and Oneissi guilty beyond reasonable doubt of conspiracy aimed at committing a terrorist act, being an accomplice to the felony of committing a terrorist act, being an accomplice to the felony of intentional homicide and being an accomplice to the felony of attempted intentional homicide.[137]

The Appeals Chamber delivered its judgment *in absentia* and issued arrest warrants for Merhi and Oneissi. On 16 June 2022, both Merhi and Oneissi were sentenced to life in prison. The Appeals Chamber considered the gravity of their offences and stated that the attack involving 'the use of a large amount of military-grade explosives, which were detonated in a busy public place, in broad daylight' amounted to a terrorist act; thus, the 'death of individuals, the destruction of buildings, and the use of an explosive device were pleaded as aggravating circumstances'.[138]

It is important to note that, in 2011 and before the confirmation of the first indictment, the Pre-Trial Judge had submitted fifteen questions of law to the Appeals Chamber. The goal of these questions was to determine whether to confirm the indictment.[139] The Appeals Chamber decision came less than ten days later, in which it stated that there existed an international customary definition of terrorism, one that should be applied by STL. The Appeals Chamber's decision was criticised for being procedurally flawed. Some scholars have argued that the STL expanded its own procedural rules, which jeopardised the integrity of its decisions. It also defined terrorism beyond the provisions of the Lebanese Criminal Code.

Contrary to traditional international justice, the Appeals Chamber's decision came with no adversarial proceedings. The accused party was procedurally missing at that point, and the decision was rendered to respond to pre-trial questions, which eventually led to an indictment. Furthermore, the Appeals Chamber's decision should have been an advisory opinion, for how can it be a decision when there is no specific case?[140] Hence, the Appeals Chamber expanded its own role and power of interpretation. There are dangerous consequences to this misstep: it opens the door for judges to amend procedural rules, which are set in place to protect all those involved in the administration of justice. It also opens the door to accusations of bias and unprofessionalism.[141] The Appeals Chamber's position argued that it was its role to interpret the laws and procedures for the Pre-Trial Judge to follow.

Furthermore, Article 2 of the STL Statute[142] requires the application of Lebanese law. Article 314 of the Lebanese Criminal Code offers a narrow definition of terrorism.[143] The Appeals Chamber provided a broad definition of terrorism, one that went beyond the limits of the Lebanese Criminal Code. The Appeals Chamber justified its move by stating that these were grave times that required a broad interpretation of terrorism. Although there was no one universally agreed-upon definition of terrorism, the Appeals Chamber argued that the number of new treaties and UN resolutions and State practice allowed for a customary rule of international law to emerge and define terrorism in times of peace. Therefore, the international customary law defining terrorism includes the following:

> (i) the perpetration of a criminal act (such as murder, kidnapping, hostage-taking, arson, and so on), or threatening such an act; (ii) the intent to spread fear among the population (which would generally entail the creation of public danger) or directly or indirectly coerce a national or international authority to take some action, or to refrain from taking it; (iii) when the act involves a transnational element.[144]

Clearly, the Appeals Chamber expanded Lebanon's definition of terrorism. For Ben Saul, the STL 'invent[ed] an international crime of transnational terrorism', which constituted a dangerous precedent, as it allowed itself to create a rule of law.[145]

Finally, it is worth mentioning that the Appeals Chamber defined terrorism in times of peace, thus leaving the door open to the interpretation of crimes committed during an armed conflict. This interpretation goes against the overwhelming opinion and UN resolutions according to which terrorist crimes exist in times of both peace and armed conflict.[146]

Hezbollah and the STL

Putting aside the valid criticism of STL's procedural flaws, there is no doubt that the STL played a major role in classifying Hezbollah fighters as terrorists in the context of the 14 February 2005 attack and the three attacks that followed. It was the first court to hold an armed non-State actor and its members accountable for crimes committed on Lebanese soil and against the Lebanese people. It is noteworthy that the STL was not created to prosecute Hezbollah *per se*, nor to classify the organisation. The word Hezbollah does not appear in the UN Security Council Resolution establishing its mandate. It was asked to examine individual criminal responsibility in the context of terrorism.

Unsurprisingly, as stated in Chapter 5, Hezbollah's Secretary General Hassan Nasrallah rejected the STL's jurisdiction. He called it an 'Israeli project', doubted the integrity of the investigators and attacked STL's president, Judge Antonio Cassese, for his expression of sympathy for the State of Israel. He considered the tribunal a political tool meant to implement Resolution 1559 of 2004, which called for the disarmament of all militias.[147] He was also concerned that the STL's jurisdiction would be extended to examine crimes committed in the 1980s (prior to the General Amnesty Law of 1991). When Resolution 1757 passed in 2007, thereby establishing the STL, Shiite ministers blocked the Lebanese Government by refusing to attend meetings, and House Speaker Nabih Berri blocked the parliamentarian process by refusing to convene the Assembly, which hindered the presidential elections.[148] The situation escalated quickly in May 2008, when the Lebanese government clashed with Hezbollah fighters. The Lebanese government wanted to monitor Hezbollah's communication network, but Hezbollah violently retaliated and used force against the LAF and civilians.[149]

Furthermore, Secretary General Hassan Nasrallah threatened to 'cut off the hands' of those targeting the suspects named above. His response came when the STL handed Lebanon's Prosecutor General arrest warrants for four Hezbollah members, for their connection to the 14 February 2005 attack. Nasrallah went even further and defied the Lebanese State, stating that '[n]o Lebanese government will be able to carry out any arrests whether in 30 days, 30 years or even 300 years'.[150] In a separate and concurring opinion to *The Prosecutor vs. Salim Jamil Ayyash*, Judge David Re referenced Secretary General Hassan Nasrallah's threat to the STL and deplored Hezbollah's interference in the administration of justice.[151]

Unfortunately, the STL faced several serious issues that impacted its effectiveness. In general, the Lebanese people have little faith in international justice, especially when many international decisions and UN resolutions are either ineffective or not enforced. Lebanon is not party to the International Criminal Court and therefore lacks the tradition of international law. The long list of unsolved crimes has made the Lebanese distrust the judicial system. Furthermore, the STL's opponents were powerful and managed to spread misinformation about the STL, thus discrediting its credibility. Despite its expansive outreach programme, the STL was misunderstood locally, and its mission remained subject to debate.[152] The STL also confronted severe budgetary constraints: 51 per cent of the tribunal expenses were covered by voluntary contributions from States, while the rest was covered by Lebanon's government. In spite of aggressive fundraising, the STL remained in deficit;[153] it ceased to exist on 31 December 2023.

This chapter has offered general comments on the growing role of non-State actors and the issue of the use of force. Although prohibited, the use of force is the exclusive domain of the State and applicable under specific conditions. However, the use of force becomes problematic when exercised by a non-State actor. Since an armed non-State actor cannot explicitly or implicitly be recognised as a State (as suggested by Ronen), the question of its classification for the use of force remains: is Hezbollah a national liberation movement? Is it an insurgency group? Is it a terrorist organisation?

This chapter has argued that Hezbollah cannot claim to be a national liberation organisation, especially after the withdrawal of Israel from the south of Lebanon. Considering the amount of violence that it has generated internally and the legal challenges that it has created for the State of Lebanon, it is possible to recognise Hezbollah members as an insurgency group. Considering Blacksley's definition of terrorism as 'use of violence by some specific group, or government, or leadership, in order to obtain thereby some military, political, religious, or philosophical end, committed by any means against innocent individuals or their property, and for the purpose of placing them in fear, by intimidation, or coercion',[154] this chapter agrees with general State practice and considers Hezbollah a terrorist organisation. In other words, Hezbollah's use of force amounts to insurgency and terrorism.

Often, acts of violence cannot be reduced to one label, as it all depends on the parties involved, their legal standing, the territory on which the acts of violence are taking place, the level of cooperation and the level of hostility, among other criteria such as political gains and bargains.[155] Thus, it is important to acknowledge that 'patterns of violence and abuse vary in important and measurable ways across conflicts, over time and across space within conflicts, and across belligerent groups'.[156] This is to say, one group cannot be locked in under one label, as it may vary with time. Therefore, Hezbollah can be classified as insurgency and terrorist organisation. In both cases, it cannot be a subject of international law and lacks legal personality. At no point, it acts as a higher authority, one that is completely independent from the State of Iran. However, Hezbollah members continue to have rights and duties in international law. In fact, '[i]ndividuals became subjects of [international law] after World War II by virtue of the establishment of their criminal responsibility under international law'.[157]

Lebanon's relationship with Hezbollah is complex. As seen above, it shifts between tolerance, opposition and complete endorsement. This raises the question of Lebanon's responsibility. Is Lebanon an accomplice in Hezbollah's unlawful acts? Can Hezbollah's acts be attributed to the State of Lebanon? Can the responsibility of the State of Iran be engaged?

Chapter 8

State and Non-State Actors' Responsibility

In April 2021, the American law firm Levy Firestone Muse issued a damning report claiming that France had supported the Rwandan allies in the commission of genocide, even when their intentions to exterminate the Tutsi minority were clear. The report added that the 'French government bears significant responsibility for enabling a foreseeable genocide', as France had failed to act to prevent the genocide from happening and was therefore responsible for the crimes committed in Rwanda.[1] The United States' responsibility has been invoked, too, for its support to the Saudi-led coalition in Yemen.[2]

The question of State responsibility is not new, as there have been attempts to regulate it since 1920.[3] State responsibility may take different forms, depending on the source of the wrong-doing, its content and its place of execution – among other criteria. The complex relationship between Lebanon and Hezbollah also raises this question of State responsibility. On the international scene, is Lebanon responsible for Hezbollah's wrongful acts? If so, to what extent is Lebanon responsible? Is Lebanon responsible by attribution, which means that Hezbollah's wrongful acts can be fully attributed to Lebanon? Or is Lebanon an accomplice in Hezbollah's wrongful acts? To understand Lebanon's responsibility in Hezbollah's wrong-doings on an international level, this chapter will offer a general definition of complicity and an examination of its different forms. The chapter will then proceed to distinguish between State complicity in the wrongful acts of a non-State actor, as well as State complicity in the wrongful acts of another State, with a focus on the 2006 armed conflict between Hezbollah and Israel.

A General Definition of Complicity

The legal definition of complicity varies, depending on the legal system examined. In its simple form, complicity is the participation in the wrong-doing of another actor.[4] Complicity is therefore a form of contribution that requires two conditions: (1) the intention to help the principal actor execute the wrong-doing, and (2) the exercise of influence on the principal actor in making their decision. This means that complicity cannot occur after the fact. Chronologically, it must take place before the execution of the wrongful act. In international law, complicity is 'a derivative form of responsibility of participation in wrong-doing committed by another actor. Wrong-doing, in this sense, may refer to the commission of any legal wrong, whether equitable, criminal, civil, or international'.[5] However, much like a contract between two parties cannot impose obligations on a third party, the same concept applies to States through the *pacta tertiis* rule, which is clearly stipulated in Articles 34 and 35 of the Vienna Convention on the Law of Treaties:[6] a treaty cannot create obligations to a third State without its consent.[7]

Complicity in the wrong-doing raises several questions: who is responsible for the wrong-doing? Are all participants responsible? If so, are they all equally responsible? Criminal law advances two theories, of unitary and differentiated participation.[8] In the unitary model, responsibility lies with . . .

> . . . every person who contributes to the carrying out of a crime in whatever way and degree as 'perpetrator', without distinguishing in any way between different types of true 'actors' or mere 'accomplices'. This 'expansive' notion of perpetratorship[,] based on the assumption that whoever contributes any cause to the commission of a crime, regardless of how close to or distant the cause is from the final result, must be considered as (co-)author of the crime.[9]

The differentiated model distinguishes between perpetratorship and mere participation, while recognising that the borderline that separates both varies according to domestic law and circumstances. In any case, the differentiated model remains a . . .

> . . . 'restrictive' theory of perpetratorship [. . .] based on the observation that, except for the case of truly equal cooperation of various persons in the commission of the crime, the causal contributions can be so different in weight and closeness to the accomplishment of a crime that it would be unjust to treat all persons involved in the same way.[10]

For Jackson, the unitary model of responsibility, which holds both author and accomplice equally responsible for the wrong-doing, may be easier from a forensic standpoint. Incriminating evidence can apply to all parties. However, while the unitary model may be easier to apply, it is important to distinguish between the principal actor of wrong-doing and the accomplice, which is why some domestic criminal laws differentiate between the attribution of responsibility and punishment among participants. In fact, it is considered unfair to hold both principal actor and accomplice equally responsible. Furthermore, it is legally and morally wrong to hold one responsible for acts that they did not commit. In other words, one can only be responsible for their own actions.[11]

This rule can be and has been expanded to States. In fact, Article 2 of the Articles on Responsibility of States for Internationally Wrongful Acts (ARSIWA) stipulates: 'There is an internationally wrongful act of a State when conduct consisting of an action or omission: (a) is attributable to the State under international law; and (b) constitutes a breach of an international obligation of the State'.[12] If Article 1 of ARSIWA states the basic principle of State responsibility for a wrongful act, then Article 2 specifies the conditions needed to establish State responsibility: (a) the State conduct in question and (b) the conduct's qualification as a breach of an international legal obligation.[13] These elements are an immediate result of State sovereignty, which implies that . . .

> . . . a state is not responsible for acts of another state (or more generally another legal person). Just as international criminal law rejects the concepts of collective responsibility or guilt by association, instead relying on the principle of individual autonomy to limit responsibility to individuals only for their actual conduct, states resist principles of responsibility that require them to be responsible for conduct other than their own.[14]

Although the differentiated model of responsibility seems to prevail, it is possible to consider a third option where complicity is penalised on its own, independently from the principal's wrong-doing. In both the unitary and differentiated models, complicity is punished when the principal act has been executed. In this third theory, the execution of the wrong-doing becomes irrelevant. This would be the case of criminal facilitation where a person aids a prisoner held on a felony charge or conviction to escape prison. Whether the operation is successful is irrelevant, for the aiding on its own is a punishable offence. The advantage of this approach is that it makes complicity a crime on its own, with no need to distinguish the different levels of participation in the wrong-doing.

However, as Jackson has pointed out, the challenge with this third theory is that it shifts from complicity to fall into the question of liability. When complicity is dependent on a wrong-doing for responsibility to be established, liability is not, and therefore it exists on its own and generates responsibility independently from the principal act.[15] There is no doubt that complicity in wrong-doing must be punished. However, how can one recognise complicity especially in the context of international law? What are the punishable forms of complicity? Is assistance required? What about influence? How can States' relations be assessed?

Forms of Complicity

There are different forms of complicity, and it is vital to distinguish between them as they generate different legal consequences. Unlike domestic law, international law does not detail different forms of complicity. Nevertheless, there are some important provisions relevant to State complicity and responsibility. For instance, Article 2(5) of the UN Charter stipulates: 'All Members shall give the United Nations every assistance in any action it takes in accordance with the present Charter, and shall refrain from giving assistance to any state against which the United Nations is taking preventive of enforcement action'.[16] The General Assembly's Declaration on Friendly Relations of 1970 adds:

> States have a duty to refrain from acts of reprisal involving the use of force.
>
> Every State has the duty to refrain from organising or encouraging the organisation of irregular forces or armed bans, including mercenaries, for incursion into the territory of another State.
>
> Every State has the duty to refrain from organising, instigating, assisting or participating in acts of civil strife of terrorist acts in another State or acquiescing in organized activities within its territory directed towards the commission of such acts, when the acts referred to in the present paragraph involve a threat or use of force.[17]

In *Democratic Republic of the Congo* v. *Uganda*, the Court considered this rule as customary international law.[18]

Article 25(3) of the Rome Statute on individual criminal responsibility enumerates the different forms of participation in wrong-doing. It stipulates:

> In accordance with this Statute, a person shall be criminally responsible and liable for punishment for a crime within the jurisdiction of the Court if that person:
>
> (a) Commits such a crime, whether as an individual, jointly with another or through another person, regardless of whether that other person is criminally responsible;
>
> (b) Orders, solicits or induces the commission of such a crime which in fact occurs or is attempted;

(c) For the purpose of facilitating the commission of such a crime, aids, abets or otherwise assists in its commission or its attempted commission, including providing the means for its commission;
(d) In any other way contributes to the commission or attempted commission of such a crime by a group of persons acting with a common purpose. Such contribution shall be intentional and shall either:
  (i) Be made with the aim of furthering the criminal activity or criminal purpose of the group, where such activity or purpose involves the commission of a crime within the jurisdiction of the Court; or
  (ii) Be made in the knowledge of the intention of the group to commit the crime;
(e) In respect of the crime of genocide, directly and publicly incites others to commit genocide;
(f) Attempts to commit such a crime by taking action that commences its execution by means of a substantial step, but the crime does not occur because of circumstances independent of the person's intentions. However, a person who abandons the effort to commit the crime or otherwise prevents the completion of the crime shall not be liable for punishment under this Statute for the attempt to commit that crime if that person completely and voluntarily gave up the criminal purpose.

3 bis. In respect of the crime of aggression, the provisions of this article shall apply only to persons in a position effectively to exercise control over or to direct the political or military action of a State.[19]

For Kai Ambos, Article 25(3) of the Rome Statute makes the immediate distinction between three forms of participation: direct or immediate perpetration 'as an individual', co-perpetration 'jointly with another' and perpetration 'through another person'. The reference to direct perpetration is somewhat confusing, as it simply means individual responsibility.[20] Co-perpetration, or co-authorship of the wrong-doing, is not a form of complicity since it is 'recognised as an autonomous form of perpetration'.[21] The perpetration by means implies that the person who commits the crime is used as a tool or instrument by the indirect perpetrator or the mastermind of the crime. This person may be innocent and unaware of the criminal act and therefore irresponsible. However, the perpetrator by means may also be responsible for a criminal act, especially in organised crimes where the perpetrator performs an act that is necessary for the wrong-doing to be fully executed. This type of responsibility raises the question of the relationship between the indirect perpetrator and the direct perpetrator and requires an examination of the hierarchy between them and the organisational structure.[22]

Moreover, Article 25(3) enumerates different forms of participation. In subparagraph (b), criminal responsibility and liability exist when a person 'orders' or 'solicits' or 'induces' the commission of a crime. This implies a relationship of subordination between a direct and an indirect perpetrator.[23] Subparagraph (c) criminalises aiding, abetting and other forms of assistance in a wrong-doing. While these forms of complicity are common, they are hard to apply, as it is difficult to determine the minimum required for a participation to become a criminal act.[24] For Ambos, 'aiding and abetting encompasses any assistance, physical or psychological, that has a substantial effect on the commission of the crime. Thus, the only limiting element is the 'substantial effect' requirement'.[25]

Subparagraph (d) is 'an almost literal copy' of the 1998 International Convention for the Suppression of Terrorist Bombing.[26] One might assume that this subparagraph is broad and applies to all forms of participation. However, this is not the case since it applies only to crimes committed by groups or persons, which automatically excludes the simplest forms of participation, such as providing knowledge that aids in the commission of a wrong-doing. This subparagraph requires a group with a common purpose and intentions.[27] Subparagraph (e) criminalises direct and indirect participation in genocide, which brings to mind Article 3(c) of the 1948 Genocide Convention.[28] Subparagraph (f) criminalises attempts to commit all crimes that fall under the jurisdiction of the International Criminal Court. By attempt, legislators implied 'the commencement of execution [. . .] by means of a substantial step'.[29] It is important to note that the Rome Statute exclusively focuses on acts of complicity before the commission of the crime. There are no stipulations on acts that occur after the wrong-doing.[30]

When regulating complicity, there are two main approaches to the question of forms. Some have opted for a legal enumeration of all possible forms (as seen in the Rome Statute), but there are risks attached to this method, mainly the difficulty of imagining all scenarios and the possibility of creating rigid laws. The second method is to limit the enumeration to easily recognisable forms of complicity, such as financing terrorism or participating in acts of aggression.[31]

Of all the possible forms of complicity, omission remains the most complex. Can the failure to act be considered a form of complicity triggering legal responsibility? International humanitarian law sanctions the failure to act in specific circumstances, such as the repatriation of prisoners of war,[32] or the repression of grave breaches to the Geneva Conventions and their protocols.[33] In criminal law, negligence could be a form of criminal omission. For Jackson, '[i]f we are willing to accept that certain omissions are the legal cause of a resulting harm, there is no reason that certain omissions should not be seen to constitute complicity in the bringing about of the harm by another actor. In some cases, distinguishing the two might be difficult'.[34] This may be true for domestic criminal law and individual criminal responsibility. However, complicity among States remains hard to determine, especially given that Article 16 of ARSIWA requires a positive act for a State to be held responsible.

State Complicity in the Wrong-Doing of a Non-State Actor

This relationship is complex as a State can participate in the wrong-doing of a non-State Actor, a non-State actor can participate in the wrong-doing of a State and, finally, the wrong-doing of a non-State actor can be attributed to a State. Despite the seriousness of these scenarios, international law does not offer a good answer to the question of complicity between a State and a non-State actor and has often considered a State's participation in a non-State actor's wrong-doing as a violation of a State's obligation to protect and not do harm. In other words, a State's participation is often examined under the lens of the obligation of due diligence rather than complicity.

For instance, in *Bosnia and Herzegovina* v. *Serbia and Montenegro*, the Court was called upon to examine Serbia's role in the genocide at Srebrenica; it concluded that the respondent . . .

> . . . did nothing to prevent the Srebrenica massacres, claiming that they were powerless to do so, which hardly tallies with their known influence over the VRS. As indicated above, for a State to be held responsible for breaching its obligation of prevention, it does not need to be proven that the State concerned definitely had the power to prevent the genocide; it is sufficient that it had the means to do so and that it manifestly refrained from using them. Such is the case here. In view of the foregoing, the Court concludes that the Respondent violated its obligation to prevent the Srebrenica genocide in such a manner as to engage its international responsibility.[35]

The question of State responsibility in the wrong-doing of a non-State actor becomes complicated as international law does not offer a clear definition of a non-State actor, and there are instances where the lines between State and non-State actor are rather blurred.[36]

In the context of Lebanon and Hezbollah, the question worth examining relates to Lebanon's responsibility for Hezbollah's wrong-doings: does Hezbollah's wrong-doing engage the responsibility of the State of Lebanon? If so, is it engaged for complicity, or can the non-State actor's wrong-doing be attributed entirely to the hosting State? This is particularly interesting in the context of the 2006 armed conflict between Hezbollah and Israel. To answer these questions, it is important to make a distinction between attribution and complicity.

Attribution

Article 4 of ARSIWA stipulates:

1. The conduct of any State organ shall be considered an act of that State under international law, whether the organ exercises legislative, executive, judicial or any other functions, whatever position it holds in the organisation of the State, and whatever its character as an organ of the central Government or of a territorial unit of the State.
2. An organ includes any person or entity which has that status in accordance with the internal law of the State.[37]

According to the commentary on Article 4 of ARSIWA, the conduct of an organ of the State is attributed to that State. A 'State organ' consists of any individual or collective entity which makes up the organisation or acts on its behalf.[38] Therefore, a State cannot be responsible (or at least not fully) for the wrongful act of a non-State actor since a non-State actor is not a State representative.

For Jackson, this non-attribution implies limited State responsibility. To determine its extent, jurisprudence has often looked at the level of agency and dependence between the two to decide on their responsibilities. In *Nicaragua* v. *United States*, the Ambassador of the Republic of Nicaragua to the Netherlands filed a complaint against the United States of America, arguing for its responsibility for military and paramilitary activities in and against Nicaragua. In 1986, the ICJ decided that a State may be held responsible for the actions of its State agents, if they were acting in their official capacity. However, some standards need to be met before holding a State responsible for the actions of its non-State actors: the State in question must have 'effective control'[39] over the non-State group. The State must also be 'recruiting, training, arming, equipping, financing, supplying and otherwise encouraging, supporting, aiding, and directing military and paramilitary actions'.[40]

In 1994, the case *Prosecutor* v. *Dusko Tadic* loosened the standards based on *Nicaragua* v. *United States of America*. The Appeals Chamber held that . . .

> . . . [b]y contrast, control by a State over subordinate armed forces or militias or paramilitary units may be of an overall character (and must comprise more than the mere provision of financial assistance or military equipment or training). This requirement, however, does not go so far as to include the issuing of specific orders by the State, or its direction of each individual operation. Under international law it is by no means necessary that the controlling authorities should plan all the operations of the units dependent on them, choose their targets, or give specific instructions concerning the conduct of military operations and

> any alleged violations of international humanitarian law. The control required by international law may be deemed to exist when a State (or, in the context of an armed conflict, the Party to the conflict) has a role in organising, coordinating or planning the military actions of the military group, in addition to financing, training and equipping or providing operational support to that group. Acts performed by the group or members thereof may be regarded as acts of *de facto* State organs regardless of any specific instruction by the controlling State concerning the commission of each of those acts.[41]

If we apply the strict *Nicaragua* v. *United States of America* standards to Lebanon-Hezbollah relations in the context of the 2006 armed conflict with Israel, it is possible to say that Lebanon is not responsible for Hezbollah's actions: although Hezbollah exists as both political party and armed group inside Lebanon, and although the Lebanese State has legalised its existence as non-militia as per the Taif Agreement of 1989 and the General Amnesty Law of 1991, Hezbollah is not an agent representative of the Lebanese State, nor a 'State organ' as required in Article 4 of ARSIWA. Furthermore, the Lebanese State does not have much control over Hezbollah, and the Lebanese State does not recruit, train, arm, equip, or supply Hezbollah members. There is no doubt that the Lebanese State encourages, supports and aids Hezbollah members. However, this is not enough to satisfy the other criteria dictated in *Nicaragua* v. *United States of America*.

Under both *Nicaragua* v. *United States of America* and *Prosecutor* v. *Dusko Tadic*, for a State to be responsible for a non-State actor, it must have a role in financing, training and equipping the group.[42] It is common knowledge that the Iranian State finances most of Hezbollah's activities. In 2016, Hezbollah's Secretary General Hassan Nasrallah in a televised speech openly recognised that 'Hezbollah's budget, its income, its expenses, everything it eats and drinks, its weapons and rockets, come from the Islamic Republic of Iran'.[43] Such a statement opened the door for questioning the responsibility of the Iranian State for wrongful acts in Lebanon and the neighbouring States. The two Court decisions above and Article 2 of ARSIWA allow us to conclude that Hezbollah's wrongful acts cannot be attributed to the State of Lebanon and therefore cannot engage its responsibility. However, at a minimum, the State of Lebanon is in violation of international customary law and the Declaration on Friendly Relations of 1970, since it did not refrain from encouraging the organisation of irregular forces and their attacks on the territory of another State.[44]

Attribution, Self-Defence and Terrorism

The general rule of attribution varies in the case of armed attacks. For the ICJ, the right of self-defence is exclusive to States and cannot be claimed by non-State actors. However, in *Nicaragua* v. *United States of America*, the ICJ referenced Article 3, paragraph (g), of the Definition of Aggression annexed to General Assembly Resolution 3314 and decided that the interpretation of armed attacks can be extended to include 'the sending by or on behalf of a State of armed bands, groups, irregulars or mercenaries, which carry out acts of armed force against another State of such gravity as to amount to an actual armed attack conducted by regular forces or its substantial involvement.[45] Therefore, the Court opened the door for a State victim of aggression to invoke self-defence in case of a non-State actor's armed attacks, ones that can be attributed to the hosting State.[46]

In 2005, the Court offered an unclear response on a similar matter. In *Democratic Republic of the Congo* v. *Uganda*, the ICJ noted that it 'has no need to respond to the contentions of the Parties as to whether and under what conditions contemporary international law provides for a right of self-defense against large-scale attacks by irregular forces',[47] especially given that the ICJ found that the preconditions for self-defence did not exist in this case, and that Uganda could not claim self-defence since the armed attacks could not be attributed to the Democratic Republic of the Congo. If they had been, then Uganda would have had the right to self-defence.

As Jackson has noted, since the 1980s and 1990s, State practice has dramatically departed from this narrow legal interpretation of the right to self-defence as dictated in Article 51 of the UN Charter.[48] Armed attacks by non-State actors are more quickly attributed to the hosting State, thus triggering an immediate response and self-defence by the State victim of the aggression. This was the United States' position following the terrorist attacks on Rome's and Vienna's airports in 1985. The United States held Libya responsible for these attacks, claiming that it provided the terrorists with the materials used in the aggression against the United States.[49] Some States opposed this expansive practice of self-defence and wanted to limit it exclusively to inter-State relations. However, the terrorist attacks of 9/11 re-opened the door to a broad interpretation. On 12 September 2001, the Security Council adopted Resolution 1368 in which it condemned the terrorist attacks of 9/11 and proclaimed the inherent right of individual or collective self-defence.[50] As the attacks were planned by al-Qaida, the United States announced its right to self-defence and started its military action against the Taliban in Afghanistan in October 2001. Their military actions were internationally supported.

State practice has shifted in the way in which scholars have interpreted the use of force when emanating from non-State actors. In some instances, these attacks have been attributed to the hosting State, thus triggering its responsibility and potentially the right to self-defence from the State victim of aggression. In other cases, these attacks are not attributed to the hosting State, but they nevertheless trigger the right to self-defence from the State victim of aggression. On these grounds, the question of attribution became irrelevant. This was the case with the United States' response to 9/11. In 2006, Israel adopted a position similar to that of the United States regarding the kidnapping of two Israeli soldiers by Hezbollah members. Israel attributed this armed attack to the State of Lebanon and claimed its right to self-defence against the entirety of the Lebanese territory. Lebanon denied knowledge of the attacks and requested an immediate cease-fire.

As pointed out in Chapter 5, international law is lacking in its regulation of border incidents and self-defence. In *Nicaragua* v. *United States of America*, the ICJ distinguished between the gravest forms of use of force (those constituting an armed attack) and other, less grave forms.[51] It held that only the gravest forms of use of force would justify the right to self-defence. In *Oil Platform*, the ICJ held that a series of attacks did not necessarily constitute a grave use of force triggering self-defence.[52] Legally, and based on these two court decisions, Israel could not invoke the right to self-defence since Hezbollah's acts could not be attributed to the State of Lebanon, and since they did not rise to the level of the gravest form of use of force. However, the international community responded differently and supported Israel in its right to self-defence, thereby holding Lebanon indirectly responsible for Hezbollah's acts. For Jackson, this State practice is problematic. Without the distinction between attribution and complicity, armed attacks between a State and non-State actor might escalate quickly to become an international armed conflict between two States almost immediately.[53]

Complicity

While attribution implies that the entirety of the wrongful act is assigned to the State, complicity does not take away the non-State actor's responsibility. In fact, it requires a relationship between the State and non-State actor, where the non-State actor has committed the wrongful act, and the State actor has participated in it. The legal question to ask is whether a State can be an accomplice and therefore responsible for the wrong-doing of a non-State actor. This question is particularly hard to answer, as international law regulates States' relations and has not offered a unifying definition of a non-State actor.

The question of complicity has been examined in the context of genocide. In the *Bosnia and Herzegovina* v. *Serbia and Montenegro*, the Federal Republic of Yugoslavia provided political, financial and military aid to the

Republika Srpska, a non-State entity in Bosnia and Herzegovina, which committed genocide against the Muslim population of Srebrenica. The ICJ was tasked to address the question of State complicity in the genocide: was the Federal Republic of Yugoslavia complicit in the genocide committed by Republika Srpska? In other words, can a State be an accomplice and therefore responsible for a genocide committed by a non-State actor? ICJ answered this question in the affirmative. To begin with, States must not commit genocide in peace or war, as stipulated in the Convention on the Prevention and Punishment of the Crime of Genocide.

As for complicity, the ICJ referenced Article III(e) of the Genocide Convention and international customary law, as codified in Article 16 of ARSIWA on Aid or Assistance in the Commission of an Internationally Wrongful Act. Article 16 stipulates:

> A State which aids or assists another State in the commission of an internationally wrongful act by the latter is internationally responsible for doing so if:
> (a) that State does so with knowledge of the circumstances of the internationally wrongful act; and
> (b) the act would be internationally wrongful if committed by that State.[54]

The ICJ argued that there should not be a distinction between complicity to commit genocide and State responsibility for 'aid and assistance' in a wrongful act.[55] In other words, 'complicity in genocide' is equivalent to complicity in 'aid or assistance', which therefore engages State responsibility. The ICJ thus criminalises State complicity in committing genocide, even if the genocide is committed by a non-State actor.

Therefore, a State is responsible when it facilitates the commission of a crime, as stated in Article 16 of ARSIWA. The crime can be genocide or any other crime. For the ICJ, there is no reason to make the distinction, as long as a State has offered aid and assistance in the commission of a wrongful act. It is worth mentioning that this aligns with the commentary on Article 16 of ARSIWA, according to which State responsibility may incur if a State provides material aid to a State which will use it to commit human rights violations. This would be the case of military assistance to countries that seriously violate human rights.[56]

Some have criticised the ICJ's broad interpretation of complicity. For Cassese, the Court . . .

> . . . has instead adopted an expansive interpretation on the Convention. It has preferred to look upon the Convention as a treaty that also imposes on contracting states themselves – as international subjects – specific obligations relating to their own behaviour towards groups protected under

> Article 11(1) (national, ethnical, racial or religious groups). This leads the Court to advance the notion that the Convention upholds 'a duality of responsibility' for genocide: according to the Court the same acts may give rise both to individual criminal liability and state responsibility.[57]

For Jackson, Cassese's second argument reads more like a defence of the ICJ's expansive definition 'rather than a plea for restrained interpretation of the obligations imposed by the Genocide Convention'.[58]

Other criticism included the ICJ's choice not to address the level of knowledge required to engage a State's responsibility in the commission of a genocide. 'It remains unclear whether knowledge of the perpetrator's specific intent or a shared specific intent is required'.[59] Furthermore, the ICJ relied on Article 16 of ARSIWA to define complicity and did not refer to international criminal law, which defines complicity more broadly. For Jackson, there is a historical reason for this omission. International criminal law regards complicity as both assistance and influence. However, State responsibility cannot be engaged on the simple basis of influence, as that would be a violation of the State's sovereignty.[60]

This may be true in case of States' relations and responsibility. What about State and non-State actors? Is influence excluded as a form of State complicity? Several UN documents refer to a State's duty not to incite or encourage non-State actors to commit wrongful acts. For instance, the Declaration on Principles of International Law Concerning Friendly Relations and Co-Operation among States in accordance with the Charter of the United Nations stipulates: 'Every State has the duty to refrain from organizing or encouraging the organisation of irregular forces or armed bands, including mercenaries, for incursion into the territory of another State'.[61] The General Assembly Resolution 40/61 of 1985 '[c]alls upon all States to fulfil their obligations under international law to refrain from organizing, instigating, assisting or participating in terrorist acts in other States, or acquiescing in activities with their territory directed towards the commission of such acts'.[62]

If complicity by influence is prohibited, what about omission? Can a State be held responsible for omitting actions to prevent the commission of a wrongful act by a non-State actor? The ICJ does not seem to condemn complicity by omission,[63] especially in that it relies on Article 16 of ARSIWA to define complicity. As stated above, Article 16 requires specific actions and does not mention omission. For Jackson, this is problematic as international criminal law punishes complicity by omission.[64]

Based on the broad interpretation above of Article 16 of ARSIWA, it is possible to argue for Lebanon's responsibility as accomplice in

Hezbollah's wrongful acts. There is no doubt that Lebanon is aiding, assisting and encouraging Hezbollah's activities: Hezbollah members in the parliament and the government as well as their allies openly speak in support of Hezbollah's activities. Lebanese officials – or at least some of them – are aware of the wrongful activities occurring on Lebanon's and neighbouring territories (Syria, Israel and beyond). However, as stated above, the level of knowledge required to retain a State's responsibility is unclear. Furthermore, from a forensic point of view, it would be hard to prove the extent of Lebanese officials' knowledge. Therefore, in theory, Lebanon's responsibility can be retained for its positive actions taken in support of a non-State actor's wrongful acts. However, in practice, it is nearly impossible to prove what information was shared and approved by State officials.

If Lebanon's responsibility cannot be engaged for positive participatory acts, can it be retained for its omission to act and control or censure Hezbollah's wrongful acts? It is true that Lebanon is not taking any measures to limit or control Hezbollah's activities in Lebanon and beyond. However, the answer to the question of responsibility by omission remains negative. As stated earlier, Article 16 requires positive actions to engage the responsibility of an accomplice. It is interesting to note that Article 2 of ARSIWA considers a State's responsible for both actions and omissions – which is not the case of complicity as dictated in Article 16.

State Complicity in the Wrong-Doing of Another State Actor

Lebanon's responsibility for Hezbollah's wrongful acts, whether by attribution, complicity, or omission seems elusive. It is a known fact that the State of Iran recruits, trains, arms, equips, finances, supplies, encourages, supports, aids and directs Hezbollah's paramilitary actions. In other words, the State of Iran has effective control over Hezbollah fighters; thus, it is logical to wonder whether the State of Iran is responsible by either attribution or complicity for Hezbollah's wrongful acts in Lebanon and in other States.

Iran's Responsibility by Attribution or Complicity

Considering the more conservative criteria of *Nicaragua* v. *United States of America*, it is possible to attribute Hezbollah's wrongful acts to Iran and therefore hold the State responsible. However, Hezbollah maintains a level of autonomy in several sectors: 'domestic politics within Lebanon, upgrading Hezbollah's military capabilities, conducting of military operations and formulation of military strategies, policies relating to organisational hierarchy, institution building and provision of services, etc'.[65] This autonomy is not absolute, for Iran remains the provider of all sources. This nuance is important as it alters the level of Iran's responsibility in Hezbollah's wrongful acts: while the State of Iran in certain cases is responsible by attribution, in other cases it may be responsible by complicity. This occurs when Hezbollah independently executes a wrongful act, but with Iran's participation and support.

What about the State of Lebanon? Is it an accomplice in Iran's wrongful acts through Hezbollah? These questions are particularly relevant in the context of armed attacks between Hezbollah and Israel as they involve three States and one non-State actor: Hezbollah, a non-State actor fully funded and supported by the State of Iran, operating from Lebanon's territory and launching armed attacks against Israel.

Lebanon's Responsibility for Iran/Hezbollah's Wrongful Acts

Article 2 of the UN Charter requires all States to respect their respective sovereignty and to resolve disputes by peaceful means. It prohibits the use of force against the territorial integrity or political independence of any State or giving assistance against a State subject of preventive or enforcement actions by the UN.[66] Annexed Article I of the General Assembly Resolution 3314, adopted by consensus on 14 December 1974, echoes Article 2(4) of the Charter and defines aggression as 'the use of armed force by a State against the sovereignty, territorial integrity or political independence of another State, or in any other manner inconsistent with the Charter of the United Nations, as set out in this Definition'.[67]

Article 3 offers a non-exhaustive list of acts of aggression, which include the following: invasion attacks by a State on the territory of another State or any military occupation; bombardment or the use of any weapons by a State against the territory of another State; blockade of ports or coasts; attack on land, sea, or air; and the use of armed forces of one State on the territory of another State and contrary to agreement between the two States.[68] Paragraphs (f) and (g) of Article 3 are the most relevant to this study. Paragraph (f) adds '[t]he action of a State in allowing its territory which it has placed at the disposal of another State, to be used by that other State for perpetrating an act of aggression against a third State'. Paragraph (g) adds '[t]he sending by or on behalf of a State of armed bands, groups, irregulars or mercenaries, which carry out acts of armed force against another State of such gravity as to amount to the acts listed above, or its substantial involvement therein'.[69] Article 3(f) is confirmed by general State practice. For instance, Switzerland rejected the United States' request to use its airspace to launch attacks against Iraq in 2003.[70] In more recent examples, Lebanon filed multiple complaints with the UN for the violation of its airspace by Israeli warplanes in their aggression against Syria.[71] The European Union accused Belarus of acts of aggression and complicity in war crimes for allowing Russia to use its territory to launch attacks against Ukraine.[72]

The question to ask here is whether Lebanon is responsible for placing its territory at the disposal of Iran and Hezbollah. There are multiple answers to this question, depending on Hezbollah's legal definition and affiliation: (1) Hezbollah is a representative of the State of Lebanon, and its wrongful acts are fully attributed to Lebanon. In this case, Hezbollah/Lebanon are fully responsible for the armed attacks against the State of Israel. (2) Hezbollah is a non-State actor with wrongful acts supported by the States of Iran and Lebanon. In this case, the States of Iran and Lebanon are responsible as accomplices. (3) Hezbollah is a representative of the State of Iran operating on Lebanese soil with the approval of the Lebanese State. In this case, Lebanon is an accomplice to Hezbollah/Iran's wrongful acts and aggression against the State of Israel. (4) Hezbollah is a representative of the State of Iran operating on Lebanese soil against the will of the Lebanese State. In this case, both the States of Lebanon and Israel are victims of aggression by the State of Iran.

State practice seems to favour the third scenario. Iran is often accused of funding terrorism in the region of the Middle East, while Lebanon is often criticised for its porous borders and lack of control over Hezbollah's wrongful acts, as well as for allowing its territory to be used for terrorist purposes. There are other considerations that come into play and that may complicate these scenarios. First, there is the question of self-defence. Before 2000, the south of Lebanon was still under Israeli occupation, which allowed for Lebanon to claim self-defence. As seen above, Israel has also claimed self-defence to justify its use of force. Claiming self-defence renders the question of responsibility by attribution or complicity void.

Second, there is the procedural question of the approval to use a State's territory for aggression against another State. How does a State express its approval for its territory to be used by a State for the aggression against a third State? Is formal permission required? General practice indicates that knowledge is required for a State to be considered an accomplice in acts of aggression. A State cannot be held responsible if not previously informed or made aware of the use of its territory to attack a third State. However, what if a State does not explicitly express its approval for the use of its territory in acts of aggression? Would it qualify as implicit authorisation?[73] An examination of Lebanon-Hezbollah relations seems to suggest as much: Lebanon recognises the legality of Hezbollah on its soil as a political party and armed group, and some Lebanese officials approve of Hezbollah's acts and are fully aware that Hezbollah members are funded, aided, recruited and trained by Iran.

In this case, it is possible to conclude that Lebanon's silence signifies implicit authorisation for Hezbollah fighters – and by extension the State of Iran – to use its territory for attacks against Israel. Furthermore, and to our knowledge, Lebanon never filed any official complaint against the State of Iran for funding and arming Hezbollah, nor for using its territory. However, this conclusion may contradict the rules on State responsibility, which require positive actions. Therefore, Lebanon's responsibility may not be engaged for silence or omission as it would be a violation of its sovereignty. Yet, it is possible to claim that Lebanon violated its obligation of due diligence and do no harm by not verbalising its disapproval of the use of its territory for acts of aggression.

Finally, as a third consideration, there is the question of military aid and how to interpret it in the context of aggression. Is military aid a simple transaction between States, one that must be respected as the result of sovereignty, or does it engage the responsibility of the recipient State for complicity?

In the case of Iran, the question is almost moot, as there are multiple national and international restrictions that limit Iran's ability to import and export weapons and nuclear materials. In 2010, the Security Council adopted Resolution 1929 which prohibited Iran from engaging in activities involving uranium mining, the production or use of nuclear materials and technology listed by the UN, as well as activities related to ballistic missiles capable of delivering nuclear weapons, along with other activities and materials.[74] This resolution was expanded and renewed multiple times until 2015, when the Security Council adopted Resolution 2231, which lifted all previous sanctions, provided that Iran remains in compliance with its responsibilities in the nuclear deal.[75] Despite this lift, several States maintained their sanctions on Iran. For instance, the United States has restrictions on activities with Iran since 1979 and the seizure of the US embassy in Tehran.[76]

It is hard to provide one solid answer when it comes to Lebanon's responsibility for Hezbollah's wrongful acts. For the question of responsibility by attribution in the context of the 2006 armed conflict between Hezbollah and Israel, it is possible to argue that Lebanon was not responsible for Hezbollah's armed attacks. Based on *Nicaragua* v. *United States of America* and *Prosecutor* v. *Dusko Tadic*, the armed attacks could not be attributed to the State of Lebanon. Yet, this was not Israel's position: it considered Hezbollah a representative of the State of Lebanon and therefore claimed its right to self-defence against a State's aggression. The international community supported Israel in its right to defend its territory. However, it did not attribute Hezbollah's wrongful acts to the State of Lebanon, and it did not label the conflict as an international armed conflict between two States.

As for the question of complicity, there is a difference between Lebanon's complicity in Hezbollah's wrongful acts and Lebanon's complicity in Iran's wrongful acts. In theory, one can argue in favour of Lebanon's responsibility as accomplice in Hezbollah's wrongful acts. However, in practice, this complicity is hard to prove, as the extent of the knowledge that the State has of Hezbollah's activities remains unclear. As to Lebanon's complicity in Iran's wrongful acts, it is a well-known fact that Hezbollah is under Iran's effective control. As such, it is possible to argue that Lebanon is an accomplice in Iran/Hezbollah's wrongful acts against Israel for allowing the use of its territory in acts of aggression. René Värk has claimed that, '[i]f a state tolerates the presence of a private armed group and takes advantage of its activities abroad – i. e., the terrorist group is "doing the job" instead of the state – that state should bear some responsibility for such activities'.[77] State practice along with Israel's narrative seems to suggest as much.

The main issue remains Lebanon's responsibility by omission: Lebanon has not formally complained against Hezbollah activities on its soil or beyond; Lebanon has neither approved nor disapproved the use of its territory by Iran/Hezbollah against Israel; Lebanon has taken no action to restrict or control Hezbollah's activities. International law, the ICJ and State practice require positive actions to engage a State's responsibility. Retaining responsibility by omission may violate State sovereignty. In all these possibilities, there is no doubt that Lebanon has violated and continues to violate its obligation of due diligence as dictated by customary international law and the Declaration of Friendly Relations.

This conclusion seems uncertain. However, its fluidity stems from the gaps in international law, which remains the law that regulates State relations. Non-State actors may be acting as if they were States, thus blurring the lines between the two entities. However, this does not imply that international law can apply to all their situations. In fact, its transposition onto State/non-State actors' relations, especially when it comes to the question of responsibility, can be 'artificial and inadequate'.[78]

Conclusion to Part III

Chapter 6 has offered general comments on the growing role of non-State actors, their different forms and the issue of their use of force. Chapter 7 and 8 have focused on Hezbollah's legal classification and Lebanon's responsibilities in Hezbollah's wrong-doings. Chapter 7 has affirmed that Hezbollah is an armed non-State actor that acts as insurgent and/or terrorist organisation, depending on the context in which it is operating. Chapter 8 has examined multiple scenarios distinguishing between Lebanon's responsibility for the wrong-doing of a non-State actor and Lebanon's responsibility for the wrong-doing of another State.

Chapter 8 has also asserted that Hezbollah's unlawful acts cannot be attributed to the State of Lebanon. However, Lebanon's responsibility can be engaged for complicity in the wrong-doing of a non-State actor, for Lebanon is aiding, assisting and encouraging Hezbollah's activities. Lebanon's responsibility can be engaged for allowing Iran/Hezbollah to use its soil for unlawful acts (especially the use of force). Realistically, these theories on Lebanon's responsibilities are hard to prove. Regarding Lebanon's responsibility for the wrong-doing of a non-State actor, the law is unclear on the level of knowledge required to retain a State's responsibility. Furthermore, it is hard to prove what Lebanese officials know about Hezbollah's activities and what they are covering without an investigation that has the potential of violating Lebanon's sovereignty. Regarding Lebanon's responsibility for the wrong-doing of another State (Iran, of which Hezbollah is an extension), this remains hard to prove. Some Lebanese officials have repeatedly deplored Iran's plans in Lebanon and its abuse of Lebanon's sovereignty. However, there has never been a formal complaint from Lebanon to the UN. The law is unclear on how to interpret Lebanon's silence.

If Lebanon's responsibility cannot be engaged for the wrong-doing of a non-State actor or the wrong-doing of another State, it can be engaged for violations of the obligation of due diligence, as dictated in customary international law and the Declaration of Friendly Relations.

Chapter 9

General Conclusion

This book has offered a comprehensive analysis of Hezbollah's legal status and its relationship with Lebanon. Part I has studied the history of Lebanon's Civil War and the rise of Hezbollah. According to Lebanese laws, Hezbollah is a legal entity: it is a political party and an armed group operating in the State of Lebanon.

The General Amnesty Law of 1991 called for the dismantling of all militias. However, this was not applied to Hezbollah, for it was not considered a militia but a legal resistance against the Israeli occupation of southern Lebanon. In 2000, Israel withdrew from the occupied south, but this withdrawal did not lead to a revision of Hezbollah's legal status in Lebanon. Hezbollah continued to exist as an armed group and political party with official representatives in parliament and in the government.

Part II has examined the definition of statehood and the two theories of effectiveness and recognition, which have set criteria according to which an entity can be identified as a State. Part II has noted that there is no perfect definition of statehood. The Westphalian model, which remains in effect today, is out-dated and does not cover cases of hybrid sovereignties where a State and a non-State actor share powers. The ambiguity of this situation complicates Hezbollah's classification in the context of armed conflict. In both the 2006 armed conflict with Israel and the Syrian conflict, the international community seemed to classify Hezbollah as a non-State actor. However, this position was not unanimous. Israel and the United States considered Hezbollah as a State actor in the 2006 armed conflict; they held Lebanon responsible for Hezbollah's attacks on Israeli soldiers and asserted Israel's right to self-defence and right to target all of the Lebanese territories and infrastructure. With the new wave of violence in the region after the 7 October attack on Israeli civilians, the same question arises once more: is Hezbollah the State of Lebanon in this new armed conflict?

Part III has examined the different forms of non-State actors and made a distinction between national liberation movements, insurgency and terrorism. It has argued that, after 2000, Hezbollah could no longer be considered a national liberation movement, especially when its fighters acted as insurgents in the 2008 conflict in Lebanon; they are also terrorists in violation of numerous international and regional instruments as well as national legislations. Although the STL did not qualify Hezbollah, it did however prosecute some of its fighters for terrorism.

Part III has also focused on State responsibility for the wrong-doing of a non-State actor and State responsibility for the wrong-doing of another State. It has distinguished between attribution and complicity, arguing that Lebanese officials may be prosecuted for assisting Hezbollah in its unlawful activities. However, this is nearly impossible to implement, for it requires either the collaboration of the Lebanese State in gathering evidence or the violation of its sovereignty. Furthermore, Part III has examined Lebanon's responsibility for the wrong-doing of the State of Iran for funding Hezbollah and promoting its terrorism. It has argued that Iran/Hezbollah may be using Lebanese soil for their unlawful activities. Yet, Lebanon never officially expressed its opposition, and the law is unclear on how to interpret a State's silence. Despite the ambiguity of international law on complicity by omission or silence, Lebanon's responsibility can be retained for violations of the obligation of due diligence, as dictated in customary international law and the Declaration of Friendly Relations.

The gradual hybridisation of Hezbollah from a paramilitary group to a political party with elected public officials, its complex relationship with the State of Lebanon, the inadequacy of the Westphalian definition, the inapplicability of the two theories on statehood recognition and the limitations of international law all benefit Hezbollah and its fighters and allow them to evade responsibility. Today, Hezbollah is a non-State actor and terrorist organisation. Despite its international presence, as well as its members' rights and duties, Hezbollah is not a subject of international law and lacks legal personality. It does not act as a high authority and continues to answer to the State of Iran. More importantly, it cannot be a source of international law, nor participate in its making.

In *State Responsibility for Non-State Actors: Past, Present and Prospects for the Future,* Richard MacKenzie-Gray Scott has deplored what he has called 'responsibility gaps [which] come into existence as a matter of international law when establishing non-state actor responsibility is not possible, and establishing state responsibility does not happen (despite it being possible), for conduct that is contrary to an international rule'.[1] The international community is afraid of accidently legalising armed non-State actors. Thus, it responds to the conundrum that they create by avoiding legislating altogether. Since armed non-State actors are not subjects of international law and do not have legal personality, they cannot be held responsible for their wrong-doings on an international platform. Furthermore, it is hard to prove State responsibility for the wrong-doings of armed non-State actors. Consequently, armed non-State actors benefit from the responsibility gaps created by none other than international law, and therefore they continue to flourish.

Should international law decide to address these responsibility gaps and update the traditional definition of statehood, then the legal scene would be quite different. In that case, Hezbollah would count as a quasi-State, one that co-exists with the failed State of Lebanon, shares its sovereignty and may potentially be held responsible for its wrongful acts.

Notes

Chapter 1

1. Yola Verbruggen, 'The Israel-Hamas Conflict', *International Bar Association*, 30 November 2023.
2. John Hudson, Yasmeen Abutaleb and Shane Harris, 'Israel's Talk on Expanding War to Lebanon Alarms US', *The Washington Post,* 7 January 2024; Ronen Bergman, Aaron Boxerman, Adam Rasgon and Thomas Fuller, 'Israel Prepares for Expected Attacks by Iran and Hezbollah', *The New York Times*, 8 August 2024.
3. Barak Ravid, 'Israel Told US Hezbollah Will Pay "Disproportionate Price" if Attack Hits Civilians', *Axios,* 7 August 2024.
4. David Bederman and Chimene Keitner, *International Law Frameworks (Concepts and Insights)*, 4th edition (St Paul, MN: Foundation Press, 2016), 83.
5. Ibid.
6. Guido Acquaviva, 'Subjects of International Law: A Power-Based Analysis', *Vanderbilt Journal of Transnational Law*, vol. 38, no. 2 (2005), 347.
7. Bederman and Keitner, *International Law Frameworks*, 83.
8. Peter Malanczuk, 'Multinational Enterprises and Treaty Making', in *Multilateral Treaty-Making: The Current Status of Challenges to and Reforms Needed in the International Legislative Process*, edited by Vera Gowlland-Debbas, Hassiba Hadj-Sahraoui and Nobuo Hayashi (Leiden: Brill, 2000), 19.
9. Jean d'Aspremont, 'Non-State Actors from the Perspective of Legal Positivism', in *Participants in the International Legal System: Multiple Perspectives on Non-State Actors in International Law*, edited by Jean d'Aspremont (Abingdon: Taylor & Francis, 2011), 25–27.
10. Melissa Loja, *International Agreements between Non-State Actors as a Source of International Law* (Oxford: HART, 2022), 10.
11. Acquaviva, 'Subjects of International Law', 354–55.
12. Ibid., 362.
13. Ibid., 365–66.
14. Ibid., 380.
15. In politics, some States are more powerful than others. Therefore, they are considered superior. Despite this political reality, international law looks at all States as peers and equal.

16. Advisory Opinion, Interpretation of the Agreement of 25 March 1951 between the WHO and Egypt, Advisory Opinion, 28 May 1980, ICJ Reports 1980, 73.
17. Ibid., 37; Acquaviva, 'Subjects of International Law', 384.
18. Advisory Opinion, Reparation for Injuries Suffered in the Service of the United Nations, Advisory Opinion, 11 April 1949, ICJ Reports 1949, 174; Yuen-li Liang, 'Notes on Legal Questions Concerning the United Nations Reparation for Injuries Suffered in the Service of the United Nations', *American Journal of International Law*, vol. 43, no. 3 (1949), 460.
19. Ibid., 390.
20. Ibid., 393.
21. Montevideo Convention on the Rights and Duties of States, Montevideo, 26 December 1933.
22. James R. Crawford. *The Creation of States in International Law*, 2nd edition (Oxford: Oxford University Press, 2006).
23. Rowan Nicholson, *Statehood and the State-Like in International Law* (Oxford: Oxford University Press, 2019).
24. Yaël Ronen. 'Entities That Can Be States But Do Not Claim to Be', in *Statehood and Self-Determination: Reconciling Tradition and Modernity in International Law*, edited by Duncan French (Cambridge: Cambridge University Press, 2013), 23–59.
25. Katharine Fortin and Ezequicl Heffes, 'Introduction: An Exploration of the Shadowland of Armed Groups and International Law', in *Armed Groups and International Law: In the Shadowland of Legality and Illegality*, edited by Katharine Fortin and Ezequiel Heffes (Cheltenham: Edward Elgar, 2023), 2.
26. Ibid., 7.
27. Ibid., 8.
28. BBC, 'Israel-Hezbollah Conflict in Maps: Ceasefire in Effect in Lebanon', 27 November 2024; L'Orient Today, 'Israel to Keep Troops at Five "Strategic Points" in Lebanon beyond Tuesday', 17 February 2025.
29. Maurits Berger, 'Islamic Views on International Law', in *Culture and International Law (From Peace to Justice Series)*, edited by Paul Meerts (The Hague: Hague Academy Press, 2008), 107.
30. Ibid., 109.
31. Ibid., 110.
32. David A. Westbrook, 'Islamic International Law and Public International Law: Separate Expressions of World Order,' *Virginia Journal of International Law,* vol. 33 (1993), 833.

Chapter 2

1. Aurora Ortega, 'Hezbollah in Colombia: Past and Present Modus Operandi and the Need for Greater Scrutiny', *The Washington Institute for Near East Policy*, 28 March 2022; H. R. No. 112-35 (2011), *Hezbollah in Latin America: Implications for US Homeland Security, before the Subcommittee on Counterterrorism and Intelligence of the Committee of Homeland Security*

(statements by Patrick Meehan, a Representative in Congress from the State of Pennsylvania and Jackie Speier, a Representative in Congress from the State of California).

2. Michael Berdine, *Redrawing the Middle East: Sir Mark Sykes, Imperialism and the Sykes-Picot Agreement* (London: Bloomsbury, 2018).
3. The Lebanese Constitution, promulgated on 23 May 1926 with its Amendments 1995, art. 9.
4. Alexander D. M. Henley, 'Religious Authority and Sectarianism in Lebanon', *Carnegie Endowment for International Peace*, 16 December 2016.
5. Rania Maktabi, 'The Lebanese Census of 1932 Revisited: Who are the Lebanese?', *British Journal of Middle Eastern Studies*, vol. 26, no. 2 (1999): 219–41.
6. United States Department of State, Office of International Religious Freedom, 'International Religious Freedom Report for 2019: Lebanon', 3.
7. This is the new spelling of Turkey as adopted by Turkish official authorities. The name spelling has also changed at the United Nations. See Juliana Kim. 'The State Department Will Start Spelling Turkey as Türkiye', *NPR*, 8 January 2023.
8. Robert Fisk, *Pity the Nation: Lebanon at War* (Oxford: Oxford University Press, 2001), 14–15.
9. Balfour Declaration, 2 November 1917, *Jewish Virtual Library: A Project of AICE.*
10. In July 1956, Egyptian President Gamal Abdel Nasser nationalised the Suez Canal. In October 1956, Israel invaded the Egyptian Sinai Peninsula, joined by France and Great Britain. At the end of the conflict, Egypt won. David Tal, 'The 1956 Sinai War: A Watershed in the History of the Arab-Israeli Conflict', in *Reassessing Suez 1956: New Perspectives on the Crisis and its Aftermath*, edited by Simon C. Smith (London: Routledge 2016), 132–45.
11. In response to the rise of the State of Israel and the exodus of Palestinians, neighbouring Arab States such as Egypt, Syria and Jordan started building their arsenals. On 5 June 1967, Israel launched a pre-emptive air assault on the Egyptian and Syrian air forces. Israel came out victorious and captured the Sinai Peninsula, the Gaza Strip, the West Bank, the Old City of Jerusalem and the Golan Heights. To this date, the status of these territories remains disputed. Guy Laron, 'From the Local to the Global', in *Six Day War: The Breaking of the Middle East* (New Haven: Yale University Press, 2017), 15–21; Mireille Rebeiz, 'Deadly Strike in the Golan Heights Risks Opening New Front in Long-Disputed Territory', *The Conversation*, 30 July 2024.
12. Lamia Rustum Shehadeh, *Women and War in Lebanon* (Gainesville: University Press of Florida, 1999), 16.
13. The Cairo Agreement, 2 November 1969, *United Nations Relief and Works Agency for Palestine Refugees in the Near East.*
14. Kamal Bayramzadeh, 'Non-State Actors and the Security of Small States: The Case of Hezbollah in Lebanon', *Journal of South Asian and Middle Eastern Studies*, vol. 41, no. 1 (2017), 59.

15. Juan de Onis, '22 Palestinians Killed in Beirut', *The New York Times*, 14 April 1975.
16. The assassination of Rafic Hariri and its legal consequences will be examined in the section on the Special Tribunal for Lebanon.
17. Jeffrey Feltman, 'Hezbollah: Revolutionary Iran's Most Successful Export', in *The Ripple Effect of Iran's Revolution across the Middle East*, edited by Suzanne Maloney (Washington DC: Brookings Institution Press, 2020), 145.
18. The Taif Agreement of 1989 and the General Amnesty Law of 1991 will be examined in Chapter 3.
19. ICTJ, 'Lebanon's Legacy of Political Violence: A Mapping of Serious Violations of International Human Rights and Humanitarian Law in Lebanon, 1975–2008' (September 2013), 11; May Tamimova, 'The Black Saturday Massacre of 1975: The Discomfort of Assembling the Lebanese Civil War Narrative', *Contemporary Levant*, vol. 3, no. 2 (2018): 123–36.
20. Thomas W. Lippman, 'Palestinians Lose Another Lebanese Refuge', *The Washington Post*, 18 May 1977.
21. ICTJ, 'Lebanon's Legacy of Political Violence', 13.
22. Ibid., 22–23.
23. Ibid., 23.
24. Ibid., 25.
25. Ibid., 28–29.
26. Judith P. Harik, 'Change and Continuity among the Lebanese Druze Community: The Civil Administration of the Mountains, 1983–90', *Middle Eastern Studies*, vol. 29, no. 3 (1993): 377–98; Itamar Rabinovich, 'Postscript: The Lebanese Crisis in 1983', in *The War for Lebanon, 1970–1983* (Ithaca: Cornell University Press, 1984), 174–82.
27. ICTJ, 'Lebanon's Legacy of Political Violence', 44–45.
28. Dalia Dassa Kaye, 'The Israeli Decision to Withdraw from Southern Lebanon: Political Leadership and Security Policy', *Political Science Quarterly*, vol. 117, no. 4 (2002–3): 561–85; August Richard Norton, 'Hizballah and the Israeli Withdrawal from Southern Lebanon', *Journal of Palestine Studies*, vol. 30, no. 1 (2000): 22–35. After the 7 October attack on Israeli civilians, violence erupted between Hezbollah and Israel. Nearly a year after, Israel launched an intense air campaign and ground invasion of southern Lebanon. A cease-fire was implemented on 26 November 2024. In February 2025, Israel announced that its forces would remain in five strategic points inside Lebanon, despite the terms of the cease-fire which had set a deadline for Israel's full withdrawal. At the time of writing this book, Israel still occupies these five points. See BBC, 'Israel-Hezbollah Conflict in Maps: Ceasefire in Effect in Lebanon', 27 November 2024; L'Orient Today, 'Israel to Keep Troops at Five "Strategic Points" in Lebanon beyond Tuesday', 17 February 2025.
29. ICTJ, 'Lebanon's Legacy of Political Violence', 65.
30. Ibid., 67.
31. Nora Boustany, 'Aoun Leaves Lebanon to Live in Exile', *The Washington Post*, 30 August 1991.

32. Amnesty International, 'Extrajudicial Executions, Lebanon: Over 30 People Captured and Executed by Syrian Forces', 21 October 1990.
33. ICTJ, 'Lebanon: Failing to Deal with the Past: What Cost to Lebanon?' (January 2014), 1.
34. The Taif Agreement of 1989, Taif, October 1989.
35. Hala Jaber, *Hezbollah: Born with a Vengeance* (New York, Columbia University Press, 1997), 47.
36. Alyssa Fetini, 'A Brief History of Hizballah', *Time*, 8 June 2009.
37. Augustus R Norton, *Amal and the Shia: Struggle for the Soul of Lebanon* (Austin: University of Texas Press, 1987), 16–23.
38. Fouad Ajami, *The Vanished Imam: Musa al Sadr and the Shia of Lebanon*, 1st edition (Ithaca: Cornell University Press, 1986), 86.
39. Bruce Riedel, *Beirut 1958: How America's Wars in the Middle East Began* (Washington DC: Brookings Institution Press, 2019).
40. Augustus Richard Norton, *Hezbollah: A Short History* (Princeton: Princeton University Press, 2007), 20.
41. Ibid., 19.
42. Ibid., 21.
43. Ibid.
44. Joe Stork, 'The War of the Camps, the War of the Hostages', *Middle East Research and Information Project: Critical Coverage of the Middle East since 1971*, June 1985; ICTJ, 'Lebanon's Legacy of Political Violence', 51.
45. Marc R. DeVore and Armin B. Stähli, 'Explaining Hezbollah's Effectiveness: Internal and External Determinants of the Rise of Violent Non-State Actors', *Terrorism and Political Violence*, vol. 27, no. 2 (2015), 345.
46. Nora Boustany, 'Hezbollah, Syrian Forces Clash in Beirut Suburbs', *The Washington Post*, 14 May 1988; 'Amal Forces Push Hezbollah', *The Washington Post*, 27 November 1988.
47. DeVore and Stähli, 'Explaining Hezbollah's Effectiveness', 342.
48. Albert Hourani, *Syria and Lebanon: A Political Essay* (London: Oxford University Press, 1946), 122.
49. Kamal Bayramzadeh, 'Non-State Actors and the Security of Small States: The Case of Hezbollah in Lebanon', *Journal of South Asian and Middle Eastern Studies*, vol. 41, no.1 (2017), 62.
50. Hezbollah, 'Open Letter Addressed to the Oppressed in Lebanon and the World, 16 February 1985', in *Hezbollah's Documents: From the 1985 Open Letter to the 2009 Manifesto*, by Joseph Alagha (Amsterdam: Pallas Publication; Amsterdam University Press, 2011), 41.
51. Ibid., 55.
52. Ibid., 43.
53. Ibid., 46–47.
54. Ibid., 50–51.
55. Ibid., 122.
56. Ibid., 126–27.
57. Rafid Fadhil Ali, 'New Hezbollah Manifesto Emphasizes Political Role in a United Lebanon', *Terrorism Monitor*, vol. 7, no. 38 (2009): 3–4; Nadim

Ladki, 'Hezbollah Cuts Islamist Rhetoric in New Manifesto', *Reuters*, 30 November 2009.

58. Lara Deeb, 'Hizballah: A Primer', *Middle East Research and Information Project*, 31 July 2006.
59. Nicholas Blandford, 'Twenty-Eight Years Ago Hezbollah's Leader Was Assassinated, and Israel Paid a Price', *Atlantic Council*, 6 January 2020.
60. Sarah Dadouch and Nader Durgham, 'Hezbollah and Allies Lose Majority in Lebanon's Parliamentary Elections', *The Washington Post*, 17 May 2022.
61. Leonard Weinberg and Ami Pedahzur, 'Suicide Terrorism', *Religion Compass*, vol. 4, no. 4 (2010), 236.
62. In 'The Readiness to Kill and Die: Suicidal Terrorism in the Middle East', Ariel Merari has argued that some drivers were 'fooled couriers' tricked by Hezbollah fighters to drive trucks full of explosives without fully understanding their fate. The bombs were detonated remotely. Ariel Merari, 'The Readiness to Kill and Die: Suicidal Terrorism in the Middle East', in *Origins of Terrorism*, edited by Walter Reich (New York: Cambridge University Press, 1990), 192–207.
63. DeVore and Stähli, 'Explaining Hezbollah's Effectiveness', 347.
64. For a detailed history of the Multinational Peacekeeping Members' arrival to Lebanon, see Benis M. Frank, *US Marines in Lebanon, 1982–1984* (Washington DC: History and Museum Division Headquarters, US Marine Corps, 1987).
65. Mireille Rebeiz, 'What We Choose to Remember Depends on Who is Calling the Shots', *PennLive*, 18 October 2021; 'Veterans Like Jeff Have Stories to Tell: Americans Need to Hear Them', *PennLive*, 2 November 2022; 'Beirut Barracks Bombing of 1983: Is Justice Possible after 40 Years', *PennLive*, 14 March 2023; 'Death of Marine Commander Scarred by 1983 Beirut Bombing Serves as Reminder of Risks US Troops Stationed in the Middle East Still Face', *The Conversation*, 22 April 2024; Timothy J. Geraghty (Ret. Col. USMC), 'Suicide Bombings and Aftermath', in *Peacekeepers at War: Beirut 1983: The Marine Commander Tells His Story* (Washington DC: Potomac Books, an imprint of the University of Nebraska Press, 2009): 91–123; Patrick J. Sloyan, 'Burying the Marines', in *When Reagan Sent in the Marines: The Invasion of Lebanon* (New York: Thomas Dunne Books, 2019), 135–51.
66. DeVore and Stähli, 'Explaining Hezbollah's Effectiveness', 349.
67. James M. Markham, 'US Ambassador and Aide Kidnapped and Murdered in Beirut Combat Sector', *The New York Times*, 17 June 1976.
68. Frederic J. Frommer, 'Steve Kerr's Life was Shaken by Gun Violence When It Took His Father', *The Washington Post*, 25 May 2022.
69. Margalit Fox, 'First Lebanon Hostage, David Dodge, Dies at 86', *New York Times*, 30 January 2009.
70. Greg Botelho, 'Since His Hostage Years, Terry Anderson Relishes "Very, Very Good Life"', *CNN*, 9 February 2016.
71. Buckley's date of birth is unavailable. Some of his information remains classified. Central Intelligence Agency, 'Heroes: William Buckley'.

72. Norton, *Hezbollah: A Short History*, 42. For a chronological list of targeted attacks, car bombs, abductions, assassinations, disappearances, arbitrary detentions and torture, see ICTJ, 'Lebanon's Legacy of Political Violence', 53–63. For a detailed account of the skyjacking of TWA flight 847, see Leo C. Byron, *From Tourist to Hostage: A Traveler's Tale of Terrorism* (Hatfield: Penn Valley Printing, 1988).
73. Norton, *Hezbollah: A Short History*, 73.
74. H. R. No. 390 (1996) 104th Cong., 2d Session, *Concerning the Prohibition on the Use of United States Passports for Travel to Lebanon* (1996) (enacted).
75. The US Department of State, Bureau of Counterterrorism, 'Foreign Terrorist Organisations: Hizballah', 8 October 1997.
76. Ronen Bergman, 'Mossad Sheds New Light on Argentina Terrorist Attacks in 1990s', *The New York Times*, 22 July 2022.
77. Stoyan Nenov, 'Israel Blames Iran for Bulgaria Bus Bomb That Killed Six', *Reuters*, 18 July 2012.
78. Imad Mansour, 'The State of Hezbollah? Sovereignty as a Potentiality in Global South Contexts', *Oxford Research Encyclopaedias: Politics* (2017), 10.
79. Daniel Meier, 'Hizbullah's Shaping Lebanon Statehood', *Small Wars and Insurgencies*, vol. 29, no. 3 (2018), 519.
80. Brian Whitaker, 'By Unpopular Demand', *The Guardian*, 6 September 2004.
81. UN Security Council, S/RES/1559 (2004), 2 September 2004.
82. UN Security Council, S/RES/1583 (2005), 28 January 2005, para. 4.
83. The assassination of Prime Minister Rafic Hariri and the legal consequences that followed will be examined in Part III.
84. The New York Times, 'Lebanese Government Resigns amid Protests', 28 February 2005.
85. The New York Times, 'Pro-Syrian Protests Gather in Beirut', 8 March 2005.
86. See Ersun N. Kurtulus, '"The Cedar Revolution": Lebanese Independence and the Question of Collective Self-Determination', *Journal of Middle Eastern Studies*, vol. 36, no. 2 (August 2009): 195–214; Marius Deeb, *Syria, Iran, and Hezbollah: The Unholy Alliance and Its War on Lebanon* (Palo Alto: Hoover Institution Press, 2013).
87. Anthony Shadid and Nora Boustany, 'Blast Kills Anti-Syrian Journalist in Lebanon', *The Washington Post*, 3 June 2005.
88. Lawrence Joffe, 'George Hawi', *The Guardian*, 21 June 2005.
89. Michael Slackman, 'Car Bomb Kills Anti-Syrian Lawmaker in Beirut', *The New York Times*, 12 December 2005.
90. Rania Abouzeid and Megan K. Stack, 'Lebanese Official Hurt in Motorcade Bombing', *Los Angeles Times*, 13 July 2005.
91. Craig S. Smith, 'Critic of Syria Loses a Hand and a Foot, But Not Heart', *The New York Times*, 15 April 2006.

92. Esther Pan, 'Lebanon: Elections Results', *Council on Foreign Relations*, 21 June 2005; L'Orient-le Jour, 'Législatives au Liban: Retour sur les scrutins de 2005 et 2009', 4 Mai 2018.
93. For a detailed analysis of this war and Hezbollah's status as a State or non-State actor in international armed conflict, see Chapter 5.
94. See Hussein Dakroub, 'Three-Month Battle Ends as Army Takes over Refugee Camp', *The Guardian*, 3 September 2007; Samer Abboud, 'The Siege of Nahr Al-Bared and the Palestinian Refugees in Lebanon', *Arab Studies Quarterly*, vol. 31, no. 1/2 (2009): 31–48.
95. Mansour, 'The State of Hezbollah', 11–12.
96. France 24, 'Beirut Street Clashes Turn Deadly', 9 May 2005.
97. UN Security Council, S/2008/392 (2008), 10 June 2008. Letter dated 22 May 2008 from the Permanent Observer of the League of Arab States to the United Nations, addressed to the President of the Security Council.
98. Martin Chulov, 'Lebanon's Unity Government Collapses', *The Guardian*, 12 January 2011.
99. Justyna Pawlak and Adrian Croft, 'EU Adds Hezbollah's Military Wing to Terrorism List', *Reuters*, 22 July 2013.
100. Laila Bassam and Erika Solomon, 'Suicide Bombings Kill 23 Near Iran Embassy in Beirut', *Reuters*, 19 November 2013.
101. Tasnim News Agency, 'Iran's Velayati Hails Election of Aoun as Lebanon's President', 31 October 2016.
102. Fares Halabi, 'From "Overthrowing the Regime" to "All Means All": An Analysis of the Lebanonisation of Arab Spring Rhetoric', *Arab Reform Initiative*, 18 December 2019.
103. Amnesty International, 'Lebanon Protests Explained', 22 September 2020, https://www.amnesty.org/en/latest/news/2019/11/lebanon-protests-explained/
104. OHCHR, 'UN Experts Call for International Investigation into 2020 Beirut Explosion', August 2022.
105. Rania Abouzeid, 'How Corruption Ruined Lebanon', *The New York Times*, 28 October 2021.
106. Brady Knox, 'Lebanon's Once-Thriving Christian Population Dwindling as Country Approaches Collapse', *Washington Examiner*, 11 February 2023; Todd M. Johnson, Gina A. Zurlo, 'Ongoing Exodus: Tracking the Emigration of Christians from the Middle East', *Harvard Journal of Middle Eastern Politics and Policy*, vol. 3 (2013–14): 39–49.
107. The World Bank Data, *Lebanon: Poverty More than Triples over the Last Decade Reaching 44% under a Protracted Crisis*, 23 May 2024, https://www.worldbank.org/en/news/press-release/2024/05/23/lebanon-poverty-more-than-triples-over-the-last-decade-reaching-44-under-a-protracted-crisis
108. The UN Refugee Agency (UNHCR), *Lebanon at a Glance*, 2024, https://www.unhcr.org/lb/at-a-glance
109. Charbel Nahas, 'Study Warns of "Drastic Change in Lebanon's Demographic Fabric"', *L'Orient Le Jour*, 11 January 2024.

Chapter 3

1. Article 20, The Universal Declaration of Human Rights, https://www.un.org/en/about-us/universal-declaration-of-human-rights#:~:text=Article%20 20,to%20belong%20to%20an%20association.
2. Article 21, International Covenant on Civil and Political Rights, https://www.ohchr.org/sites/default/files/ccpr.pdf
3. Article 22, ibid.
4. *Sidiropoulos and Others* v. *Greece*, Judgment No. 57/1997/841/1047, ECtHR, 10 July 1998, para. 40.
5. Article 24, The Arab Charter of Human Rights, 2004. The original text is available in Arabic. The translation was provided by the League of Arab States to the United Nations Office of the High Commissioner of Human Rights.
6. The Lebanese Constitution was adopted in 1926 under the French Mandate and was inspired by French Constitutional Law. For more, see Antoine Hokayem, *La Genèse de la Constitution Libanaise de 1926: Le Contexte du Mandat Français, les Projets Préliminaires, les Auteurs, le Texte Final (Beyrouth: Éditions Universitaires du Liban, 1996);* Marc Makary, *The Lebanese Constitution of May 23rd, 1926 and the Constitutional Laws of the 3rd French Republic: A Comparative Approach (unpubl. Thesis,* Library of the Saint Joseph University School of Law and Political Sciences, Beirut, 2006).
7. Loi du 1er Juillet 1901 sur le Statut des Associations / Law of July 1st, 1901, on Statues of Association in France.
8. The Lebanese Constitution, promulgated on 23 May 1926 with its Amendments 1995, art. 13.
9. Art. 2, 1909 Law on Associations. The original text is in Arabic. The translation is provided by Aline Bazouni in *Internal Governance for NGOs in Lebanon* (Beirut: Ministry of Social Affairs, 2004).
10. Art. 6, 1909 Law on Associations.
11. Marc Makary, 'Notification or Registration? Guarantees of Freedom of Association in Non-Democratic Environments: Case Studies of Lebanon and Jordan', *The International Journal of Not-for-Profit Law*, vol. 10, no. 1 (December 2007), [n. p.].
12. State Council, No. 135/2003-2004, November 18, 2003, *Association for the Defense of Rights and Liberties* v. *State*, Al Adl, vol. 2 (2004), 191.
13. Art. 8, 1909 Law on Associations.
14. Author's translation from Arabic to English.
15. Mazhar El-Harak, 'The Legal Framework of Associations in Lebanon', in *International Governance for NGOs in Lebanon* (Beirut: Ministry of Social Affairs, 2004), 19.
16. Ibid., 25.
17. Art. 3, 1909 Law on Associations.
18. Art. 4, 1909 Law on Associations.
19. Art. 7, 1909 Law on Associations.
20. Art. 11, 1909 Law on Associations.

21. Art. 18, 1909 Law on Associations.
22. Shawn Teresa Flanigan and Mounah Abdel-Samad, 'Hezbollah's Social Jihad: Nonprofits as Resistance Organisations,' *Middle East Policy*, vol. 16 (2009): 122–37; Ahmad Hamzeh, *In the Path of Hizbullah* (Syracuse: Syracuse University Press, 2004); Eitan Azani, 'The Hybrid Terrorist Organisation: Hezbollah as a Case Study', *Studies in Conflict and Terrorism*, vol. 36 (2013): 899–916.
23. Flanigan and Abdel-Samad, 'Hezbollah's Social Jihad', 124.
24. Mazhar El-Harak, 'The Legal Framework', 16; Decision of French Colonial Powers No. 60, Official Gazette No. 3273, 29 April 1936, 2–6.
25. Author's translation from Arabic to English.
26. The international legal community has for a long time discussed the legal status of international organisations and whether they are subjects of international law. As mentioned in Chapter 1, it has been concluded that they are subjects of international law under certain conditions: when they operate as high authority, when they have a legal personality with rights and duties, and when they can contribute to the making of international law. This legal debate is easy in the case of universal or regional organisations with State members. There is no doubt that the United Nations and the World Health Organisation are subjects of international law. However, the issue becomes more complicated when dealing with small non-profit organisations whose members are private individuals, businesses and non-profit groups. Generally, these non-profit international organisations have no legal power. (See International Center for Not-For-Profit Law, 'Legislation for Non-Profit Organisations: Recognition and Protection of NGOs in International Law', *The International Journal of Not-For-Profit Law*, vol. 2, no. 2 (1999), https://www.icnl.org/resources/research/ijnl/international-developments). While they may have a legal personality with rights and duties, they do not operate as a high authority, and they certainly do not contribute to the making of international law. Therefore, they cannot be considered subjects of international law. This would be the case with Hezbollah's non-profit international organisations, some of which have been accused of unlawful activities on an international level. For instance, the Qard al-Hasan Association – which operates as a social cooperation fund, offers interest-free loans and transfers funds at no cost – has been accused of money-laundering. In fact, in July 2007, the US Department of Treasury imposed sanctions, noting its illegal financial activities in the banking system (see Tony Badran and Emanuelle Ottolenghi, 'Hezbollah's al-Qard al-Hasan and Lebanon's Banking Sector', *Foundation for Defense of Democracies*, 11 May 2021.) Based on these sanctions, a 2019 civil lawsuit against Lebanese banks was filed in the Eastern District of New York by families of Americans who had been killed or injured by Hezbollah operations in Iraq between 2004 and 2011. They alleged that Qard al-Hassan was engaged in unlawful transactions and used financial institutions for money-laundering and to fund terrorist activities. See *Bartlett, et al. v. Société Générale de Banque au Liban SAL, et al.*, EDNY, 13 December 2020.

27. Hezbollah. 'Open Letter Addressed to the Oppressed in Lebanon and the World, 16 February 1985', in *Hezbollah's Documents: From the 1985 Open Letter to the 2009 Manifesto*, edited by Joseph Alagha (Amsterdam: Pallas Publication; Amsterdam University Press, 2011), 41.
28. EU, 2023/2742(RSP), 12 July 2023.
29. The Taif Agreement of 1989, Taif, October 1989.
30. Law No. 84, 26/08/1991, General Amnesty Law.
31. Art. 2, para. D, The Taif Agreement of 1989, Taif, October 1989.
32. Second Section, Spreading the Sovereignty of the State of Lebanon over all Lebanese Territories, para. A, The Taif Agreement of 1989, Taif, October 1989.
33. Second Section, Spreading the Sovereignty of the State of Lebanon over all Lebanese Territories, para. C, The Taif Agreement of 1989, Taif, October 1989.
34. Third Section, Liberating Lebanon from the Israeli Occupation, The Taif Agreement of 1989, Taif, October 1989.
35. On the legal status of Hezbollah as a State or non-State actor, see the following chapters.
36. The Lebanese Constitution, promulgated on 23 May 1926 with its Amendments 1995, art. 53, cl. 9.
37. Amnesty International, 'Report on Lebanon: Human Rights Developments and Violations' (8 October 1997), 7.
38. Sandra Geahchan, 'Beyond the Failure of Justice: Lebanon's General Amnesty Law of 1991 and Access to Redress for Victims of the 1975–1990 Civil War', *SOAS Law Journal* 6, no. 1 (2019), 24.
39. Ibid., 7.
40. According to the ICTJ, the Justice Council is a legal body that 'tries criminal cases pertaining to national security threats; it only receives cases referred to it by the Cabinet of Ministers, and its decisions cannot be appealed.' ICTJ, 'Lebanon: Failing to Deal with the Past: What Cost to Lebanon?', 9.
41. The legal status of Hezbollah as a State or non-State actor will be analysed in Part II. Geahchan, 'Beyond the Failure of Justice', 26.
42. The right to a remedy (including reparation) has been recognised by the ICCPR; it was adopted on 16 December 1966 and entered into force on 23 March 1976. Lebanon ratified it on 3 November 1972.
43. Geahchan, 'Beyond the Failure of Justice', 53–54.
44. Philomene Nasr, 'Dirassat Hawla Kanun al-Afu al-Aam an al-Jaraeim al-Mortakaba kabla Tareekh 28 Azar 1991 [Study of the Amnesty Law of the Crimes Committed before 28 March 1991]', *Revue Juridique de l'USEK*, vol. 2 (1993): 63–89. Author's translation of the title and transliteration of this note.
45. Ibid., 87.
46. Geahchan, 'Beyond the Failure of Justice', 30; L'Orient-le Jour, 'Les Commissions Apportent des Amendements Mineurs au Projet d'Amnistie Générale', 23 August 1991.
47. Human Rights Watch (HRW), 'World Report: Syria and Syrian-Controlled Lebanon' (New York, 1992).

48. Geahchan, 'Beyond the Failure of Justice', 24
49. In 2002, Al-Jazeera released a thirteen-episode documentary titled *Harb Lubnan* (translated as *The War of Lebanon*) where politicians, warlords, militia members, witnesses and survivors were interviewed. The documentary, which included archival footage and political analysis, was well received in the Arab world, including in Lebanon, demonstrating the Lebanese people's need to know what happened during the years of the civil war. Many documentaries followed, such as *Lebanon Wins the World Cup* (2015) by the directors Anthony Lappé and Tony Khoury, and the documentary *About a War* (2019) by the directors Abi Weaver and Danielle Rugo.
50. See Legal Action WorldWide and UN Women, 'Gendered Crimes during the Lebanese Civil War. Apr 13, 1975–Oct 13, 1990', https://storymaps.arcgis.com/stories/70164462cc66465db317c63516e21168.
51. Kaveh Waddell, 'The Desperate Search for Lebanon's Mass Graves', *The Atlantic*, 22 April 2018.
52. The topic of the disappeared during the Lebanese Civil War is consistently revisited by local and international organisations. Most recently, the ICRC launched the platform 'The Missing Persons Lebanon Community' to ensure a proper communication between different stake-holders (such as family members, local non-governmental and governmental agencies) regarding the fate of those who disappeared during the Lebanese Civil War. The ICRC has consistently reminded the Lebanese Authorities of the families' right to know the truth about what happened to their loved ones. ICRC, 'ICRC Launches the Missing Persons Lebanon Community and Calls for the Swift Operationalization of the National Commission for the Missing and Forcibly Disappeared', last modified 30 August 2021, https://www.icrc.org/en/document/icrc-launches-missing-persons-lebanon-community-and-calls-swift-operationalization-national
53. Uti Ojah Egbai and Jonathan O Chimakonam, 'Protecting the Rights of Victims in Transitional Justice: An Interrogation of Amnesty', *African Human Rights Law Journal*, vol. 19, no. 2 (2019), 615.
54. Ibid., 615.
55. In addition to the Sabra and Shatila case brought to justice in Belgium, Geahchan has pointed out the case of Mr X vs Australia. Mr X is a Palestinian born in Lebanon. He sought asylum in Australia, claiming to have been the witness to the right-wing Christian militia's criminal activities, particularly the Sabra and Shatila massacre. He argued that his deportation to Lebanon would imply his arrest and torture; consequently, Australia would be violating his rights under Article 3 of the Torture Convention. The United Nations Committee against Torture dismissed the case, not only for lack of evidence supporting Mr X's claims, but also on the ground of the General Amnesty Law of 1991. Geahchan, 'Beyond the Failure of Justice', 40. *Mr X* v. *Australia*, The Committee against Torture, 30 April 2009, CAT/C/42/D/324/2007.
56. The New York Times, '117 Bodies Found in Lebanese Village Recaptured from Christians', 17 February 1984.
57. Geahchan, 'Beyond the Failure of Justice', 49.

Chapter 4

1. Part of this chapter has appeared as Mireille Rebeiz, 'The Israel-Lebanon Maritime Border Agreement: Does Lebanon Implicitly Recognise the State of Israel?' *Dickinson Law Review*, vol. 128 (2023): 197–231.
2. Duncan French, 'Introduction', in *Statehood and Self-Determination: Reconciling Tradition and Modernity in International Law*, edited by Duncan French (Cambridge: Cambridge University Press, 2013), 1.
3. Ibid., 3.
4. Michel Miaille, *Une introduction critique au Droit* (Paris: F. Maspero, 1976), 146.
5. Vaughan Lowe, *International Law: A Very Short Introduction* (Oxford: Oxford University Press, 2015), 3.
6. Ibid., 2.
7. For a historical account, see Joachim Whaley, *Germany and the Holy Roman Empire, Vol. 1: Maximilian I to the Peace of Westphalia, 1493–1648* (Oxford: Oxford University Press, 2011).
8. Münster, § 1: 'I: That there shall be a Christian and Universal Peace, and a perpetual, true, and sincere Amity, between his Sacred Imperial Majesty, and his most Christian Majesty; as also, between all and each of the Allies, and Adherents of his said Imperial Majesty, the House of Austria, and its Heirs, and Successors; but chiefly between the Electors, Princes, and States of the Empire on the one side; and all and each of the Allies of his said Christian Majesty, and all their Heirs and Successors, chiefly between the most Serene Queen and Kingdom of Swedeland, the Electors respectively, the Princes and States of the Empire, on the other part. That this Peace and Amity be observ'd and cultivated with such a Sincerity and Zeal, that each Party shall endeavour to procure the Benefit, Honour and Advantage of the other; that thus on all sides they may see this Peace and Friendship in the Roman Empire, and the Kingdom of France flourish, by entertaining a good and faithful Neighbourhood'. Eric David, 'Brèves Remarques sur Les Origines du Droit International', in *The Roots of International Law/ Les Fondements du Droit International*, edited by Pierre-Marie Dupuy and Vincent Chetail (Leiden: Brill, 2014), 444–46.
9. Münster, § 121: 'CXXI. That it never shall be alledg'd, allow'd, or admitted, that any Canonical or Civil Law, any general or particular Decrees of Councils, any Privileges, any Indulgences, any Edicts, any Commissions, Inhibitions, Mandates, Decrees, Rescripts, Suspensions of Law, Judgments pronounc'd at any time, Adjudications, Capitulations of the Emperor, and other Rules and Exceptions of Religious Orders, past or future Protestations, Contradictions, Appeals, Investitures, Transactions, Oaths, Renunciations, Contracts, and much less the Edict of 1629. or the Transaction of Prague, with its Appendixes, or the Concordates with the Popes, or the Interims of the Year 1548. or any other politick Statutes, or Ecclesiastical Decrees, Dispensations, Absolutions, or any other Exceptions, under what pretence or colour they can be invented; shall take place against this Convention, or any

of its Clauses and Articles neither shall any inhibitory or other Processes or Commissions be ever allow'd to the Plaintiff or Defendant'.

10. Münster, § 123: 'CXXIII: That nevertheless the concluded Peace shall remain in force, and all Partys in this Transaction shall be oblig'd to defend and protect all and every Article of this Peace against any one, without distinction of Religion; and if it happens any point shall be violated, the Offended shall before all things exhort the Offender not to come to any Hostility, submitting the Cause to a friendly Composition, or the ordinary Proceedings of Justice'.
11. Münster, § 118: 'CXVIII: Finally, that the Troops and Armys of all those who are making War in the Empire, shall be disbanded and discharg'd; only each Party shall send to and keep up as many Men in his own Dominion, as he shall judge necessary for his Security'.
12. '[L]'on s'accorde généralement à faire remonter aux traités de Westphalie de 1648, venant clore la guerre de trente ans, la naissance d'une conception moderne de l'État souverain, articulée sur les principes de territorialité, et d'égalité: chacun possède désormais l'exclusivité et la généralité des compétences à l'intérieur de son propre territoire, dans les mêmes conditions que tous les autres États, quelle que soit sa taille ou sa puissance réelle.' Dupuy, *The Roots of International Law/Les Fondements du Droit International*, 400.
13. Crawford, *The Creation of States in International Law*, 10.
14. Nicholson, *Statehood and the State-Like in International Law*, 24.
15. Ibid., 4. It is important to acknowledge that Nicholson has based his definition of personality on Wesley Newcomb Hohfeld's works from 1913 and 1917 where he makes the distinctions between legal concepts such as privilege, duty, right, liability and so on. W. N. Hohfeld, 'Some Fundamental Legal Conceptions as Applied in Judicial Reasoning [Part 1]', *The Yale Law Journal*, vol. 23, no. 1 (1913): 16–59; 'Some Fundamental Legal Conceptions as Applied in Judicial Reasoning [Part 2]', *The Yale Law Journal*, vol. 26, no. 8 (1917): 710–70.
16. Nicholson, *Statehood and the State-Like in International Law*, 11.
17. Ibid., 4.
18. W. N. Hohfeld, 'Some Fundamental Legal Conceptions as Applied in Judicial Reasoning [Part 1]', 44; quoted in Nicholson, *Statehood and the State-Like in International Law*, 18.
19. Ibid., 18.
20. Ibid.
21. Ibid., 19.
22. Crawford, *The Creation of States in International Law,* 5. According to Kelsen's Pure Theory of Law, the law is strictly composed of norms; non-legal elements do not belong to the legal realm. Therefore, the legal personality cannot be the result of rights and obligations; it is simply a bundle of norms, a legal construct and not a natural reality. Hans Kelsen, *Pure Theory of Law* (Berkley: University of California Press, 1967), 174–77. In 'Non-State Actors from the Perspective of the Pure Theory of Law', Jörg

Kammerhofer has criticised Kelsen's reductive definition of the law as it excludes questions related to legal personality and subject of international law. He has added that, according to Kelsen's Pure Theory of Law, '[s]tates are merely legal persons of international law and international law defines their existence'. Human rights are no longer natural rights but a legal construct. Jörg Kammerhofer, 'Non-State Actors from the Perspective of the Pure Theory of Law', in *Participants in the International Legal System: Multiple Perspectives on Non-State Actors in International Law*, edited by Jean d'Aspremont (Abingdon: Taylor & Francis, 2011), 57.

23. Nicholson, *Statehood and the State-Like in International Law*, 21.
24. Nicholson has given the example of the Treaty of Paris of 30 March 1856, which ended the Crimean War between the Russian Empire, the Ottoman Empire, Great Britain, the Second French Empire and the Kingdom of Sardinia. This treaty generated an important debate on the international recognition of the Ottoman Empire by the European States and the signing of an agreement between Muslim and non-Muslim entities. Nicholson, *Statehood and the State-Like in International Law*, 56. See Mustafa Serdar Palabi, 'The Emergence of the Idea of "International Law" in the Ottoman Empire before the Treaty of Paris', *Middle Eastern Studies*, vol. 50, no. 2 (2014): 233–51.
25. For Crawford, statehood recognition was not an issue before the middle of the eighteenth century: 'The reason for this was clear: sovereignty, in its origin merely the location of supreme power within a particular territorial unit *(suprema potestas)*, necessarily came from within and did not require the recognition of other States or princes'. In its early form, statehood recognition depended on domestic laws and not on the will of other States. In the era of positive laws, this form of recognition was no longer valid, especially that statehood recognition implied rights and duties on an international level: 'If a new State subject to international law came into existence, new legal obligations would be creating for existing States. The positivists' premise seemed to require consent to the creation of the State or to its being subjected to international law so far as other States were concerned'. Moving forward, statehood recognition was no longer a domestic affair, but one tied to international entities. Crawford, *The Creation of States in International Law*, 12–15.
26. United Nations Conference on International Organisation, Amendments and Observations on the Dumbarton Oaks Proposal, 4 May 1945, UNIO, Doc. 2, G/7; Tom Grant, 'How to Recognise a State (And Not): Some Practical Considerations', in *Sovereignty, Statehood and State Responsibility: Essays in Honor of James Crawford*, edited by Christine Chinkin and Freya Baetens (Cambridge: Cambridge University Press, 2015), 194.
27. UN Security Council, SC/15670 (2024), 18 April 2024.
28. UN General Assembly, A/ES-10/L.30/Rev.1 (2024), Illegal Israeli Actions in Occupied East Jerusalem and the Rest of the Occupied Palestinian Territory, 10 May 2024.
29. Jure Vidmar, *Democratic Statehood in International Law: The Emergence of New States in Post-Cold War Practice* (Portland: Bloomsbury, 2013), 10.

30. Ibid., 238.
31. Anthony Carty, *The Decay of International Law? A Reappraisal of the Limits of Legal Imagination in International Affairs* (Manchester: Manchester University Press, 1986), 43.
32. French, *Statehood and Self-Determination*, 2.
33. Gëzim Visoka, 'Statehood and Recognition in World Politics: Towards a Critical Research Agenda', *Cooperation and Conflicts*, vol. 57, no. 2 (2021), 1.
34. Ibid., 15.
35. Math Noortmann, 'Towards an Interdisciplinary Approach to Non-State Participation in the Formation of Global Law and Order', in *Participants in the International Legal System: Multiple Perspectives on Non-State Actors in International Law*, edited by Jean d'Aspremont (Abingdon: Taylor & Francis, 2011), 76–81.
36. Crawford, *The Creation of States in International Law*, 20.
37. Nicholson, *Statehood and the State-Like in International Law*, 113, 114.
38. Ibid., 92.
39. Crawford, *The Creation of States in International Law*, 22. On recognition as a legal act or political act, see Eric Wyler, *Théorie et pratique de la reconnaissance d'État: Une approche épistémologique du droit international* (Bruxelles: Éditions Bruylant, 2013), 50–62.
40. Montevideo Convention on the Rights and Duties of States, Montevideo, 26 December 1933.
41. Crawford, *The Creation of States in International Law*, 46.
42. *Deutsche Continental Gas-Gesellschaft* v. *Polish State*, Germano-Polish Mixed Arbitral Tribunal, 1 August 1929; *Annual Digest of Public International Law Cases: Being a Selection from the Decisions of International and National Courts and Tribunals Given during the Years 1929 and 1930*, edited by H. Lauterpacht (Cambridge: Grotius, 1981), 13.
43. *Deutsche Continental Gas-Gesellschaft* v. *Polish State*, 15.
44. Crawford, *The Creation of States in International Law*, 49. For Israel, there was the question of its recognition in 1948. Today, international lawyers are still debating its final borders, especially with the disputed areas of the West Bank and Gaza (considered part of the Palestinian Territories), the Golan Heights (considered part of Syria) and the Shebaa Farms (disputed between Lebanon and Syria). On the Israeli–Palestinian conflict, see John B. Quigley, *The Case for Palestine: An International Law Perspective*, 2nd edition (Durham, NC: Duke University Press 2005); Raffaela A. Del Sarto, *Fragmented Borders, Interdependence and External Relations: The Israel-Palestine-European Union Triangle* (London: Palgrave Macmillan, 2015); Yigal Kipnis, *The Golan Heights: Political History, Settlement and Geography since 1949*, 1st edition (Abingdon: Routledge, 2013); Mireille Rebeiz, 'Deadly Strike in the Golan Heights Risks Opening New Front in Long-Disputed Territory', *The Conversation*, 30 July 2024. On the Iraqi-Kuwait border conflict of 1958–61 and the Iraqi invasion of Kuwait in 1991, see Nahla Yassine-Hamdan and Frederic Pearson, *Arab Approaches to Conflict Resolution: Mediation, Negotiation and Settlement of Political*

Disputes, 1st edition (Oxfordshire: Routledge, 2017). On the Senegalese-Mauritanian border conflict of 1989, see Miguel de Larramendi, 'Mauritania's Challenges', in *Political Regimes in the Arab World: Society and the Exercise of Power*, edited by Ferran Izquierdo Brichs, 1st edition (Abingdon: Routledge, 2013), 122–25. On Belize, see Zelena Jones, 'Culture's Ties to the Land: The Belize-Guatemala Border Conflict's Implications for the Maya Communities in Light of the UN Declaration', *Wisconsin International Law Journal*, vol. 29, no. 4 (2012): 773–806.

45. The World Bank Data, *Population, Total: Small States*, https://data.worldbank.org/indicator/SP.POP.TOTL?locations=S1-NR
46. Crawford, *The Creation of States in International Law*, 52. Crawford has pointed out that the question of nationality is different from the number of persons permanently living on the State's territory.
47. Karen Knop, 'Statehood: Territory, People, Government', in *The Cambridge Companion to International Law*, edited by James Crawford and Martti Koskenniemi (Cambridge: Cambridge University Press, 2012), 101.
48. Knop, 'Statehood', 97.
49. Ibid., 100.
50. In 2003, the General Assembly asked the ICJ for an advisory opinion on this questions: 'What are the legal consequences arising from the construction of the wall being built by Israel, the occupying Power, in the Occupied Palestinian Territory, including in and around East Jerusalem, as described in the Report of the Secretary-General, considering the rules and principles of international law, including the Fourth Geneva Convention of 1949, and relevant Security Council and General Assembly resolutions?' On 9 July 2004, the ICJ rendered its Advisory Opinion stating that the construction of the wall was illegal, as it was happening within the Palestinian territories, territories that are occupied and do not belong to the State of Israel. The ICJ also held that this illegal construction violated the Palestinian people's right to self-determination. As a side note, it is interesting that the ICJ did not refer to the Palestinian people as a State entity. ICJ, Legal Consequences of the Construction of a Wall in the Occupied Palestinian Territory, Advisory Opinion 2004.
51. Article 1 of Chapter 1 on Purposes and Principles of the 1945 UN Charter stipulates: 'The Purposes of the United Nations are: (2) To develop friendly relations among nations based on respect for the principle of equal rights and self-determination of peoples, and to take other appropriate measures to strengthen universal peace'. Article 1 of Part I of the 1966 ICESCR stipulates: '1. All peoples have the right of self-determination. By virtue of that right they freely determine their political status and freely pursue their economic, social and cultural development [. . .] 3. The States Parties to the present Covenant, including those having responsibility for the administration of Non-Self-Governing and Trust Territories, shall promote the realization of the right of self-determination, and shall respect that right, in conformity with the provisions of the Charter of the United Nations'.

52. Knop, 'Statehood', 106. On the notion of earned sovereignty, see Michael P. Scharf, 'Earned Sovereignty: Juridical Underpinnings', *Denver Journal of International Law and Policy*, vol. 31, no. 3 (2003): 373–85; Paul R. Williams, Abigail Avoryie and Carlie Armstrong, 'Earned Sovereignty Revisited: Creating a Strategic Framework for Managing Self-Determination Based Conflicts', *ISLA Journal of International and Comparative Law*, vol. 21, no. 2 (2015): 1–27.
53. Knop, 'Statehood', 105.
54. Crawford, *The Creation of States in International Law*, 56.
55. Nicholson, *Statehood and the State-Like in International Law*, 115–16. This theory seems to be supported by political scientists as well. In 'Dysfunctional State Institutions, Trust, and Governance in Areas of Limited Statehood', Tanja A. Börzel and Thomas Risse have argued that there exists a conflation of governance and statehood. 'For instance, the "fragile states index" which is widely used to determine states at risk, associates governance indicators (basic infrastructure, economic development, and the like), regime type, and state capacity indicators. As a result, it becomes impossible to examine the relationship between statehood and (good) governance. Statehood is about the capacity to implement and enforce central decisions, including maintaining a monopoly over the means of violence. Governance refers to institutionalized modes of social coordination to solve collective action problems, and provide binding rules and regulations, as well as public good and services'. Tanja A. Börzel and Thomas Risse, 'Dysfunctional State Institutions, Trust, and Governance in Areas of Limited Statehood', *Regulation and Governance*, vol. 10 (2016): 149–50.
56. Crawford, *The Creation of States in International Law*, 57. On the independence of the Democratic Republic of Congo, see Alanna O'Malley, *The Diplomacy of Decolonisation: America, Britain and the United Nations during the Congo Crisis, 1960–1964*, 1st edition (Manchester: Manchester University Press, 2018); Lazlo Passemiers, *Decolonisation and Regional Geopolitics: South Africa and the 'Congo Crisis', 1960–1965*, 1st edition (Abingdon: Routledge, 2019).
57. Crawford, *The Creation of States in International Law*, 57.
58. Ibid., 59.
59. A/RES/43/160 [A] (1988), Observer Status of National Liberal Movements Recognised by the Organisation of African Unity and/or the League of Arab States, 9 December 1988.
60. Mr F. D. Berman, 'Statement of Mr. FD Berman', *British Yearbook of International Law* 55 (7 December 1984), 446; quoted in Crawford, *The Creation of States in International Law*, 61.
61. Crawford, *The Creation of States in International Law*, 62.
62. Article 3, Montevideo Convention on the Rights and Duties of States.
63. Some scholars have argued that international law prohibits secession to protect territorial integrity. See Alexander Orakhelashvili, 'Statehood, Recognition and the United Nations System: A Unilateral Declaration of Independence in Kosovo', *Max Planck Yearbook of United Nations Law*,

vol. 12 (2008): 1–44. As Orakhelashvili has pointed out, the international legal system has seen multiple successful and unsuccessful attempts of unilateral declarations of independence. For example, Bangladesh seceded from Pakistan. After serious human rights violations and crimes, multiple States recognised Bangladesh as an independent State, and it was admitted into the United Nations in 1974. Biafra attempted to secede from Nigeria. However, it was re-integrated into Nigeria in 1970 due to the civil war and the rise of violence. Orakhelashvili has concluded that 'the principle of territorial integrity has survived post-1989 parade of declarations of independence, and international law does not authorize the unilateral secession of the territory from the state' (8). Jure Vidmar in 'Unilateral Declarations of Independence in International Law' has argued that unilateral declarations of independence may be a domestic affair and that international law steps in only to accept or reject such declaration. Thus, it is important to distinguish between the unilateral declaration of independence itself and its consequences on an international level. Vidmar has argued that international law is neutral regarding the unilateral declaration of independence: 'Only the question of *acceptance* of a declaration of independence is (partly) regulated by international law. It is a matter of the law of state responsibility that under some circumstances a declaration of independence must not be accepted. At the same time, international law does not foresee any circumstances in which states would be under an obligation to accept a declaration of independence'. In *Statehood and Self-Determination: Reconciling Tradition and Modernity in International Law*, edited by Duncan French (Cambridge, Cambridge University Press, 2013), 63.

64. Crawford, *The Creation of States in International Law*, 63.
65. PCIJ ser. A/B no. 41 (1932), 57–58; quoted in Crawford, *The Creation of States in International Law*, 65–66. See Alexander P. Fachiri, 'The Austro-German Customs Union Case', *British Yearbook of International Law*, vol. 13 (1932): 68–75.
66. Crawford, *The Creation of States in International Law*, 66.
67. Ibid., 88–89; quoted in Nicholson, *Statehood and the State-Like in International Law*, 96.
68. Crawford, *The Creation of States in International Law*, 72; quoted in Nicholson, *Statehood and the State-Like in International Law*, 96.
69. Crawford, *The Creation of States in International Law*, 74.
70. Ibid., 76.
71. These questions will be re-examined in the next chapter in the context of Lebanon-Hezbollah relations; some Lebanese politicians and civilians consider Lebanon as an extension of Syria and Iran.
72. Crawford, *The Creation of States in International Law*, 76.
73. Crawford has given the example of the Malay States before 1948, when the sultan agreed that all political foreign relations and administrative issues would go through the British government. Subsequently, this raised the issue of the sultan's immunity in British courts. Crawford, *The Creation of States in International Law*, 77.

74. Ibid., 78.
75. Ibid., 81.
76. Ibid., 83.
77. Ibid., 85.
78. Nicholson, *Statehood and the State-Like in International Law*, 98.
79. In 'Sovereignty as a Legal Value', Crawford has argued that sovereignty is an important state attribute and that it must be protected. He has defined the term as 'supreme power within the state'. 'Sovereignty as a Legal Value', in *The Cambridge Companion to International Law*, edited by James Crawford and Martti Koskenniemi (Cambridge: Cambridge University Press, 2012), 118. On a domestic level, a State has powers, and these powers are separated between the legislative, the executive and the judicial branches, but altogether form a sovereign State. International law does not concern itself with this internal division of powers, but it rather regards the State as one sovereign entity. Sovereignty, thus, 'is the standard operating assumption of a decentralized international system' (132). This is certainly an interesting dichotomy since sovereignty constitutes an international law concept founded on an entity dependent of domestic law. Crawford makes the distinction between a sovereign State and non-State entities such as individuals, non-governmental agencies and international governmental organisations. They all have rights and duties under international law. International governmental organisations have legal capacity and can sign treaties. However, none of these entities have sovereignty. It is true that an international governmental organisation can speak in a State's name, but its mandate remains limited and not representative of sovereignty. As such, sovereignty is an exclusive State attribute (119). Furthermore, sovereignty is a protected right under international law. Article 2(4) of the UN Charter stipulates: 'All Members shall refrain in their international relations from the threat or use of force against the territorial integrity or political independence of any state, or in any other manner inconsistent with the Purposes of the United Nations'. Despite this protection, international law is assumed to be weak for its inability to hold some States accountable and impose sanctions in certain contexts (such as the use of force against another State or human rights violation). Some have argued that sovereignty is, in fact, a fictional trait of statehood, and if it truly exists, it is gradually eroding with all the foreign interventions, privatisations and globalisation. Some even have gone so far as to employ the term 'failed State' to refer mostly to Third-World States in crisis. To these critics, Crawford has responded that '[r]eports of the death of sovereignty are much exaggerated' (132). He has strongly rejected the expression 'failed State' for it conflates statehood and government in crisis. He has added that '[t]o talk of states as "failed" sounds like blaming the victims' (127).
80. Montevideo Convention on Rights and Duties of States; quoted in Nicholson, *Statehood and the State-Like in International Law*, 101.
81. In 'Non-State Actors from the Perspective of Legal Positivism: The Communitarian Semantics for the Secondary Rules of International Law', Jean d'Aspremont has argued that legal positivism as a legal theory restricts

the source of international law to States only. In fact, the law is identified by virtue of its source, and it is often reduced to State's practice. Greater attention must be paid to other sources, sources that apply positive laws and understand them well. This would be the case with non-State actors, especially those that have legal personality and are a subject of international law. In fact, non-State actors such as the ICRC play a vital role in law practice. Nevertheless, despite their contribution to the field, they are not considered lawmakers. Only States are. Jean d'Aspremont, 'Non-State Actors from the Perspective of Legal Positivism', in *Participants in the International Legal System: Multiple Perspectives on Non-State Actors in International Law*, edited by Jean d'Aspremont (Abingdon: Taylor & Francis, 2011), 23–40.

82. Nicholson, *Statehood and the State-Like in International Law*, 103.
83. Ibid., 105.
84. Ibid.
85. Ibid.
86. Nicholson has also given the example of Vatican City, which is treated as a State due to a very broad interpretation of the statehood criteria. Ibid., 111.
87. Statement of the Foreign Minister of Japan on the Independence on the Republic of South Sudan, 9 July 2011, para. 2.
88. Statement of the US Department of State on US Relations with South Sudan, Bilateral Relations Fact Sheet, Bureau of African Affairs, 21 January 2022.
89. Nicholson, *Statehood and the State-Like in International Law*, 115.
90. Youssef M. Ibrahim. 'PLO Proclaims Palestine to Be an Independent State; Hints at Recognising Israel', *The New York Times*, 15 November 1988; United Nations, 'The Question of Palestine', https://www.un.org/unispal/history/
91. UN News, 'General Assembly Grants Palestine Non-Member Observer State Status at the United Nations', 29 November 2012.
92. Government Offices of Sweden, 'Sweden Recognises Palestine and Increases Aid', 30 October 2014.
93. For Nicholson, 'if an entity acquires statehood solely under the recognition norm and it the entity is recognised universally, the term "state" can be used without further qualification; but is the entity is recognised by just one or several states, it is better to use the term "state-in-context". States-in-context can be thought as another category of state-like entities (in addition to states properly so called) that have personality in international law'. Nicholson, *Statehood and the State-Like in International Law*, 92.
94. *Civil Aeronautics Administration* v. *Singapore Airlines*, 14 January 2004 [2004] SGCA 3 (Singapore Court of Appeals), para. 36. Repr. 133 *International Law Reports*, 371, 383–384; quoted in Tom Grant, 'How to Recognise a State (and Not): Some Practical Considerations', in *Sovereignty, Statehood and State Responsibility: Essays in Honor of James Crawford*, edited by Christine Chinkin and Freya Baetens (Cambridge: Cambridge University Press, 2015), 199.

95. *Cyprus* v. *Turkey*, Application No. 25781/94, ECtHR, 10 May 2001, para. 238, repr. 120, *International Law Reports*, 10, 76; quoted in Grant, 'How to Recognise a State', 199.
96. Israel-Lebanon Maritime Border Agreement, *Haaretz*, 12 October 2022.
97. Mohammed Zaatari, 'Has Lebanon Recognised Israel by Striking a Maritime Border Deal?' *Al-Jazeera*, 27 October 2022.
98. Grant, 'How to Recognise a State', 202.
99. Ibid., 204.
100. Article 7, paragraph 2 of the 1969 Vienna Convention on the Law of Treaties stipulates: 'In virtue of their functions and without having to produce full powers, the following are considered as representing their State: (a) Heads of State, Heads of Government and Ministers for Foreign Affairs, for the purpose of performing all acts relating to the conclusion of a treaty; (b) heads of diplomatic missions, for the purpose of adopting the text of a treaty between the accrediting State and the State to which they are accredited; (c) representatives accredited by States to an international conference or to an international organisation or one of its organs, for the purpose of adopting the text of a treaty in that conference, organisation or organ'.
101. Mohammed Zaatari, 'Has Lebanon Recognised Israel by Striking a Maritime Border Deal?'
102. Ibid.
103. Nicholson, *Statehood and the State-Like in International Law*, 121.
104. Ibid., 129.
105. Crawford, *The Creation of States in International Law*, 5.
106. As a reminder, Nicholson has called Crawford's constitutive theory recognition theory and Crawford's declaratory theory effectiveness theory.
107. For Duncan French, statehood is both the outcome of self-determination and a potential threat or challenge to it. Duncan French, 'Introduction', in *Statehood and Self-Determination: Reconciling Tradition and Modernity in International Law*, edited by Duncan French (Cambridge: Cambridge University Press, 2013), 5.
108. A. Claire Cutler, 'Critical Reflections on the Westphalian Assumptions of International Law and Organisation: A Crisis of Legitimacy', *Review of International Studies*, vol. 27, no. 2 (April 2001): 133–50.
109. Nicholson, *Statehood and the State-Like in International Law*, 3.
110. As a reminder, Nicholson gives the example of Palestine, which claimed its independence in 1988 (Nicholson, *Statehood and the State-Like in International Law*, 115). In 2012, the United Nations General Assembly granted Palestine the status of 'non-member observer State'. In 2014, Sweden affirmed that Palestine had met statehood criteria and recognised it as a State. See Youssef M. Ibrahim. 'PLO Proclaims Palestine to be an Independent State; Hints at Recognising Israel', *The New York Times*, 15 November 1988. United Nations, 'The Question of Palestine', https://www.un.org/unispal/history/; UN News, 'General Assembly Grants Palestine Non-Member Observer State Status at the United Nations', 29

November 2012, https://news.un.org/en/story/2012/11/427052-general-assembly-grants-palestine-non-member-observer-state-status-un
111. Vidmar, 'Democratic Statehood in International Law', 62, note 6.
112. Knop, 'Statehood', 107
113. Ronen, 'Entities', 23–24.
114. Ibid., 24.
115. Jerome Segal, '"Land of Three Faiths": The Little Known History of the Palestinian Declaration of Independence', *Haaretz*, 15 November 2017.
116. For instance, Taiwan signed a Peace Treaty with Japan on 28 April 1952 and is a member of the World Trade Organisation.
117. Crawford, *The Creation of States in International Law*, 219.
118. Ronen, 'Entities', 27.
119. Ibid., 29.
120. This reminds of Nicholson's position on the Islamic State.
121. Ronen, 'Entities', 31.
122. Ibid., 59.
123. Knop, 'Statehood', 114.

Chapter 5

1. UN Gen. Ass. Res 56/83 of 12 December 2001, corrected by document A/56/49 (Vol I) Corr. 4; International Law Commission, 'Responsibility of States for Internationally Wrongful Acts', 2001, vol. II (Part Two).
2. The Taif Agreement of 1989, Taif, October 1989.
3. Law No. 84, 26/08/1991, General Amnesty Law.
4. Al-Monitor, 'Aoun Sees Role for Hezbollah until Threats to Lebanon Cease', 21 September 2017.
5. US Department of the Treasury, Press Release, 'Treasury Targets Corruption in Lebanon', 6 November 2020.
6. Armed forces are not necessarily a criterion of statehood. However, they participate in creating the image of a strong State. They can function as a reflection of a powerful executive branch, one that has control over the State's territory and borders. In referencing the armed forces, Hezbollah is equating them with a strong State and government.
7. The text of the Ministerial Statement is available in Arabic: The Lebanese Republic, Office of the Prime Minister, Ministerial Statement of 9 November 2009.
8. Lina Khatib, 'How Hezbollah Holds Sway Over the Lebanese State', Research Paper in *Middle East and North Africa Program* (June 2021), 25.
9. Khatib, 'How Hezbollah Holds Sway over the Lebanese State', 4.
10. Meier, 'Hizbullah's Shaping Lebanon Statehood', 530.
11. Carla E. Humud, 'Lebanon', *Congressional Research Service* (2017): 11–12.
12. Meier, 'Hizbullah's Shaping Lebanon Statehood', 531; Nicholas Blandford, 'The United States-Lebanese Armed Forces Partnership: Challenges, Risks, and Rewards', *Atlantic Council* (2018): 1–15; Aram Nerguizian,

'The Lebanese Armed Forces and Hezbollah: Military Dualism in Post-War Lebanon', *Malcom H. Kerr Carnegie Middle East Center*, 30 October 2018, https://carnegie-mec.org/2018/10/30/lebanese-armed-forces-and-hezbollah-military-dualism-in-post-war-lebanon-pub-77598

13. Lina Khatib, 'The Political and Security Fallout of the Battle in Arsal', *Malcom H. Kerr Carnegie Middle East Center*, 14 August 2014, https://carnegie-mec.org/2014/08/16/political-and-security-fallout-of-battle-in-arsal-pub-56408
14. Meier, 'Hizbullah's Shaping Lebanon Statehood', 521; see Lizzie Porter, 'A Legacy of Torture: Inside of Lebanon's Khiam Jail', *Al-Jazeera*, 14 August 2017.
15. 'Through its allies in Lebanon's cabinet and parliament, Syria guaranteed Hezbollah's smooth operation, helping it to maintain security zones that were inaccessible to government forces, constantly replenishing its arms caches, and circumventing state laws as the group expanded its network of social services. With the Syrians watching its back in Lebanon's domestic politics, Hezbollah transformed itself into a purely anti-Israel force'. Hussain Abdul-Hussain, 'Hezbollah: A State within a State', *Current Trends in Islamist Ideology*, vol. 8 (2009), 71.
16. CNN, 'Israel, Hezbollah Swap Prisoners', 29 January 2004.
17. The Lebanese Constitution, promulgated on 23 May 1926 with its Amendments 1995, art. 49.
18. UN Security Council, S/RES/1701 (2006), 11 August 2006.
19. William M. Arkin, 'Divine Victory to Whom? Airpower in the 2006 Israel-Hezbollah War', *Strategic Studies Quarterly*, vol. 1, no. 2 (2007): 98–141.
20. Meier, 'Hizbullah's Shaping Lebanon Statehood', 522.
21. Ibid., 524. Unfortunately, the Shebaa Farms have remained disputed territory until today. The UN and Israel claim that they fall within the Syrian borders. Therefore, Lebanon has no claim to these lands.
22. Evelyn Leopold, 'UN Cites Confusion over Maps of Shebaa Farms', *Reuters*, 19 January 2007.
23. Frederic C. Hof, 'Assad: The Shebaa Farms are Syrian, Whatever Hezbollah Claims', *Newlines Magazine*, 7 April 2021; Michael Young, 'Leaving Hezbollah Hanging', *Malcom H. Kerr Carnegie Middle East Center*, 13 April 2021, https://carnegie-mec.org/diwan/84303
24. Sara Fregonese, 'Beyond the "Weak State": Hybrid Sovereignties in Beirut', *Environment and Planning D: Society and Space*, vol. 30 (2012), 668.
25. Mansour, 'The State of Hezbollah', 12.
26. Yeganeh Torbati, 'US Imposes Sanctions on Hezbollah Officials for Syria Support', *Reuters,* 21 July 2015; Nisan Ahmado, 'US Sanctions on Syria Leave Hezbollah More Isolated in Lebanon', *Voxnews*, 19 July 2020.
27. Khatib, 'How Hezbollah Holds Sway over the Lebanese State', 8.
28. Mansour, 'The State of Hezbollah', 3.
29. Ibid., 3.
30. Ibid., 8.
31. Ibid., 8–9.

32. Daniela Huber and Eckart Woertz, 'Resilience, Conflict and Areas of Limited Statehood in Iraq, Lebanon and Syria', *Democratization*, vol. 28, no. 7 (2021), 1267.
33. Ibid., 1267.
34. Ibid., 1272.
35. Mansour, 'The State of Hezbollah', 8.
36. Statement of the Foreign Minister of Japan on the Independence of the Republic of South Sudan, 9 July 2011, para. 2.
37. Statement of the US Department of State on US Relations with South Sudan, Bilateral Relations Fact Sheet, Bureau of African Affairs, 21 January 2022.
38. Nicholson, *Statehood and the State-Like in International Law*, 115.
39. Grant, 'How to Recognise a State', 202.
40. Ibid., 204.
41. Tehran Times, 'Iran Congratulates Lebanon on Anniv. of Victory against Israel', 26 May 2021.
42. Al-Jazeera, 'Iran Warns Israel of "Obliterating War" If It Attacks Lebanon', 29 June 2024.
43. Vienna Convention on the Law of Treaties of 1968, art. 7, para. 2.
44. As mentioned in the introduction to Chapter 5 and according to Article 4 of the Articles on the Responsibility of States for Internationally Wrongful Acts, Hezbollah may be considered an organ of the State of Lebanon. See Chapter 8 on State responsibility.
45. Eyad Kourdi, 'Syria Formally Recognises Independence of 2 Pro-Russian Separatist-Held Regions in Ukraine's Donbas', *CNN*, 29 June 2022.
46. Mansour, 'The State of Hezbollah', 6.
47. Nicholson, *Statehood and the State-Like in International Law*, 3.
48. As a reminder, Nicholson has given the example of Palestine who claimed its independence in 1988 (Nicholson, *Statehood and the State-Like in International Law*, 115). In 2012, the United Nations General Assembly granted Palestine the status of 'non-member observer State'. In 2014, Sweden affirmed that Palestine had met statehood criteria and recognised it as a State.
49. Yaël Ronen, 'Entities That Can Be States But Do Not Claim to Be', in *Statehood and Self-Determination: Reconciling Tradition and Modernity in International Law*, edited by Duncan French (Cambridge: Cambridge University Press, 2013), 23–24.
50. Fregonese, 'Beyond the "Weak State"', 659.
51. Ibid., 659.
52. Ibid.
53. In this book, the author uses quasi-State, State-like entity and hybrid sovereignty interchangeably.
54. Ronen, 'Entities', 23–24.
55. Issam Fares Institute for Public Policy and International Affairs, 'Report of the Focus Group with Stakeholders in the Middle East', Menara Working Document, no. 6, May 2019, file:///C:/Users/mgreb/Downloads/menara_wd_6.pdf
56. Huber and Woertz, 'Resilience, Conflict and Areas of Limited Statehood', 1263–64.

57. Aaron Anfinson, 'The Treachery of Images: Visualizing "Statehood" as a Tactic for the Legitimization of Non-State Actors', *Terrorism and Political Violence*, vol. 23, no. 4 (2021), 720.
58. Stephen D. Krasner and Thomas Risse, 'External Actors, State-Building, and Service Provision in Areas of Limited Statehood: Introduction', *Governance: An International Journal of Policy, Administration, and Institutions*, vol. 27, no. 4 (2014), 549.
59. On the question of the use of force, see Chapter 5.
60. Joseph Alagha, *Hizbullah's Documents: From the 1985 Open Letter to the 2009 Manifesto* (Amsterdam: Pallas Publication, 2011), 39.
61. Tamim El-Barghouti has provided a definition of the term *umma*. It derives 'from the stem Amm which, as a verb, means to head for, to quest, to lead, to guide, or to mean and to intend. As a noun it means destination, purpose, pursuit, aim, goal and end. The Umma also means the way, the main road, or the law, tradition and religion'. See *The Umma and the Dawla: The Nation-State and the Arab Middle East* (London: Pluto Press, 2008), 37. It is important to note that, while Hezbollah supports the idea of *al-Umma* and obedience to *Wali-al-Fakih* or the Supreme Leader, it also gives value to the will of the people and claims that *al-Umma* is their preferred model of governance, but only if the people want it. The manifesto also invites Christians to convert to Islam. On 30 November 2009, Hezbollah issued a political document updating the 1985 Manifesto. There was much discussion on whether Hezbollah continued its allegiance to Iran and its leader. Naim Qassem (1953–), the Secretary General's Deputy, told the Lebanese newspaper *Daily Star* that they remained committed to their principles. Rafid Fadhil Ali, 'New Hezbollah Manifesto Emphasizes Political Role in a United Lebanon', *Terrorism Monitor*, vol. 7, no. 38 (2009): 3–4; Nadim Ladki, 'Hezbollah Cuts Islamist Rhetoric in New Manifesto', *Reuters*, 30 November 2009.
62. Benedict Anderson, *Imagined Communities: Reflections on the Origin and Spread of Nationalism,* Revised Edition (London: Verso, 2006), 5–6.
63. El-Barghouti, *The Umma and the Dawla*, 37.
64. Hassan, Fareed Mohd, Mohd Izzat Amysar Mohd Arif, Hisham Hanapi and Muhammad Syahlan bin Shafie, 'The Concept of State under International Law and Islamic Law Perspective', *The International Journal of Business Management and Technology*, vol. 3, no. 1 (2019), 66–67.
65. El-Barghouti, *The Umma and the Dawla*, 2.
66. Ahmad Al-Dawoody, *The Islamic Law of War: Justifications and Regulations* (New York: Palgrave Macmillan, 2011), 71; Asma Nasar Chattha, 'Perspective of the Islamic Law of War on the Armed Non-State Actor's Militancy', *Journal of Islamic Thought and Civilization*, vol. 11, no. 2 (2021): 345–60.
67. Ibid., 70. Some Muslim scholars have argued that the difference in definitions does not prevent Islam and Muslims to agree to the international law concept of statehood and respect States and their people. See Sheikh Wahbeh al-Zuhili, 'Islam and International Law', *International Review of the Red Cross*, vol. 87, no. 858 (2005), 276.

68. Alistair Lyon, 'Disarm Hezbollah, UN Chief Tells Lebanon', *Reuters*, 13 January 2012.
69. Dominic Evans, 'Hezbollah Rejects Call by UN's Ban to Disarm', *Reuters*, 14 January 2012.
70. OHCHR, 'International Legal Protection of Human Rights in Armed Conflict', New York and Geneva, 2011, 1.
71. Ibid., 3.
72. Emily Crawford and Alison Pert, *International Humanitarian Law*, 2nd edition (Cambridge: Cambridge University Press, 2020), 4–7.
73. The new treaties revised and adopted were: Hague I – Pacific Settlement of International Disputes; Hague II – Limitation of Employment of Force for Recovery of Contract Debts; Hague III – Opening of Hostilities; Hague IV – Laws and Customs of War on Land; Hague V – Rights and Duties of Neutral Powers and Persons in Case of War on Land; Hague VI – Status of Enemy Merchant Ships at the Outbreak of Hostilities; Hague VII – Conversion of Merchant Ships into War Ships; Hague VIII – Laying of Automatic Submarine Contact Mines ; Hague IX – Bombardment by Naval Forces in Time of War; Hague X – Adaptation to Maritime War of the Principles of the Geneva Convention; Hague XI – Restrictions With Regard to the Exercise of the Right of Capture in Naval War; Hague XII – Creation of an International Prize Court; Hague XIII – Rights and Duties of Neutral Powers in Naval War; Declaration (XIV) prohibiting the Discharge of Projectiles and Explosives from Balloons. Emily Crawford and Alison Pert, *International Humanitarian Law*, 2nd edition (Cambridge: Cambridge University Press, 2020), 12–13.
74. Crawford and Pert, *International Humanitarian Law*, 16.
75. Ibid., 16.
76. AP I, art. 1(4). It is interesting that Article 4(A)(2) of the GC III relative to the Treatment of Prisoners of War stipulates that prisoners of war are '[m]embers of other militias and members of other volunteer corps, including those of organized resistance movements, belonging to a Party to the conflict and operating in or outside their own territory, even if this territory is occupied, provided that such militias or volunteer corps, including such organized resistance movements, fulfil the following conditions: (a) that of being commanded by a person responsible for his subordinates; (b) that of having a fixed distinctive sign recognisable at a distance; (c) that of carrying arms openly; (d) that of conducting their operations in accordance with the laws and customs of war'. In contrast, AP I only required for a fighter to be recognised as prisoner of war if captured to openly carry their arms during combat. See Crawford and Pert, *International Humanitarian Law*, 17.
77. AP II, Preamble.
78. Protocol II, art. 1(1).
79. AP II, art. 1(2).
80. These are the numbers of State parties at the time of writing this chapter in September 2022.
81. GC I, art. 2.

82. AP I, art. 1(4).
83. Protocol II, art. 1(1).
84. Catherine Bloom, 'The Classification of Hezbollah in Both International and Non-International Armed Conflicts', *Annual Survey of International and Comparative Law*, vol. 14, no. 1 (2008), 73.
85. *Prosecutor* v. *Tadic*, Case No. IT-94-1-AR72, Decision on the Defence Motion on Jurisdiction in the Trial Chamber of the International Tribunal, 127 (2 October 1995) (Appeal on Jurisdiction).
86. Greg Myre and Steven Erlanger, 'Israeli Forces Enter Lebanon after 2 Soldiers Are Seized', *The New York Times*, 12 July 2006.
87. Chris McGreal, 'Capture of Soldiers Was "Act of War" Says Israel', *The Guardian,* 12 July 2006.
88. Human Rights Watch, 'How Does Law Protect in War? Israel/Lebanon/Hezbollah Conflict in 2006', *Casebook ICRC*, 2007, https://casebook.icrc.org/case-study/israellebanonhezbollah-conflict-2006
89. Caroline Ziade, 'Identical Letters Dated 13 July 2006 from the Chargé d'affaires a.i. of the Permanent Mission of Lebanon to the United Nations Addressed to the Secretary-General and the President of the Security Council', *United Nations Digital Library*, 13 July 2006.
90. Ewen MacAskill, Patrick Wintour, Nicholas Watt and Tania Branigan, 'West Flounders as Old Divisions Resurface', *The Guardian*, 17 July 2006.
91. UN Security Council, S/RES/1701 (2006), 11 August 2006.
92. OHCHR, A/HRC/RES/S-2/1, 11 August 2006.
93. Human Rights Watch, 'How Does Law Protect: Israel/Lebanon/Hezbollah Conflict in 2006', *Casebook ICRC*, 2007, https://casebook.icrc.org/case-study/israellebanonhezbollah-conflict-2006
94. Ibid.
95. For the question of State responsibility, see Chapter 8.
96. Said Mahmoudi, 'The Second Lebanon War: Reflections on the 2006 Israeli Military Operations against Hezbollah', in *Law at War: The Law as It Was and the Laws as It Should Be*, edited by O. Engdahl and P. Wrange (Leiden: Brill, 2008), 179–80.
97. *Nicaragua* v. *United States of America*, Merits, Judgment, ICJ Reports, 27 June 1986, para. 191.
98. *Oil Platforms* (*Islamic Republic of Iran* v. *United States of America*), Judgment, ICJ Reports 6 November 2003, para. 64.
99. Christian J. Tams, 'The Use of Force against Terrorists', *European Journal of International Law*, vol. 20, no. 2 (2009), 379.
100. Bloom, 'The Classification of Hezbollah', 79.
101. The status of Hezbollah in the 2006 armed conflict becomes even more complicated when one considers the legal status of its captured members: are they prisoners of war? Israel has designated Hezbollah as a terrorist organisation, which would exclude the application of Article 4 of GC III. Articles 43 to 47 of AP I would not apply since Israel did not sign

AP I. Hence, if captured, Hezbollah members would be held accountable under Israeli counter-terrorism laws. Bloom has wondered whether Hezbollah members could be considered mercenaries in the 2006 armed conflict with Israel. Considering Article 47 of AP I, Bloom has quickly dismissed this label: Hezbollah members are not paid to simply execute the wishes of a foreign State. Furthermore, Iran and Syria are not providing manpower to Hezbollah. Their aid is financial and logistical. Consequently, Hezbollah members cannot qualify for mercenary status. See Bloom, 'The Classification of Hezbollah', 89–96.

102. The first report was published in October 2006, following the visit of special rapporteurs from the UN Human Rights Council and a representative of the United Nations Secretary General: 'Human Rights Council: Mission to Lebanon and Israel (7–14 September 2006), UN Doc, A/HRC/2/7, 2 October 2006. The second report was published in November 2006. The investigation was led by three lawyers nominated by the UN Human Rights Council. See Human Rights Council: Report of the Commission of Inquiry on Lebanon Pursuant to Human Rights Council Resolution S-2/I, UN Doc. A/HRC/3/2, 23 November 2006; Mahmoudi, 'The Second Lebanon War', 175–76.
103. OHCHR, 'International Legal Protection of Human Rights in Armed Conflict', 23–25.
104. For more on the Arab Spring, see Tofigh Maboudi, *The 'Fall' of the Arab Spring: Democracy's Challenges and Efforts to Reconstitute the Middle East* (Cambridge: Cambridge University Press, 2022).
105. Jamie Tarabay, 'For Many Syrians, the Story of the War Began with Graffiti in Dara'a', *CNN*, 15 March 2018.
106. Katherine March and Simon Tisdall, 'Syrian Troops Shoot Dead Protesters in Day of Turmoil', *The Guardian*, 22 April 2011.
107. Khaled Yacoub Oweis, 'Assad: Syria Won't Stop Fight against "Terrorists"', *Reuters*, 9 August 2011.
108. Liz Sly, 'In Syria, Defectors Form Dissident Army in Sign Uprising May Be Entering New Phase', *Washington Post*, 25 September 2011.
109. UN Human Rights Council, Rep. of the Independent International Commission of Inquiry on the Syrian Arabic Republic, UN. Doc. A/HRC/S-17/2/Add.1, 23 November 2011, 1.
110. S. C. Pres. Statement 2011/16 (3 August 2011).
111. Ibid.
112. See Council Regulation 442/2011 of 9 May 2011, Concerning Restrictive Measures in View of the Situation in Syria; *Official Journal of the European Union* (L121); Executive Order 13582 – Blocking Property of the Government of Syria and Prohibiting Certain Transactions with Respect to Syria, *The White House: Office of the Press Secretary*, 18 August 2011.
113. In May 2023, foreign ministers from the Arab League and state representatives voted to reinstate Syria's membership. See Al-Jazeera, 'Arab League Brings Syria Back into Its Folds after 12 Years', 7 May 2023.

114. Neil MacFarquhar and Nada Bakri, 'Isolating Syria, Arab League Imposes Broad Sanctions', *The New York Times*, 27 November 2011.
115. Mohamad Ghazi Janaby, 'The Legal Status of Hezbollah in the Syrian Conflict: An International Humanitarian Law Perspective', *Arizona Journal of International and Comparative Law*, vol. 33, no. 2 (2016), 387–90.
116. UN Human Rights Council, 'Report on the Civilians' Deaths in the Syrian Arab Republic', A/HRC/50/68, 13 June–8 July 2022.
117. AP I, art. 1(4).
118. AP II, art. 1(1).
119. AP II, art. 1(2).
120. Armenak Tokmajyan and Kheder Khaddour, 'Border Nation: The Reshaping of the Syrian-Turkish Borderlands', *Malcom H. Kerr Carnegie Middle East Center*, 30 March 2022, https://carnegie-mec.org/2022/03/30/border-nation-reshaping-of-syrian-turkish-borderlands-pub-86758
121. Peter G. Gasser, 'Internationalized Non-International Armed Conflicts: Case Studies of Afghanistan, Kampuchea, and Lebanon', *American University Law Review*, vol. 33 (1983): 145–61; Janaby, 'The Legal Status of Hezbollah', 397.
122. ICRC, 'Syria: ICRC and Syrian Arab Red Crescent Maintain Aid Effort amid Increased Fighting', 17 July 2012, https://www.icrc.org/en/doc/resources/documents/update/2012/syria-update-2012-07-17.htm
123. Ian Black and Dan Roberts, 'Hezbollah is Helping Assad Fight Syria Uprising, Says Hassan Nasrallah', *The Guardian*, 30 April 2013.
124. Ali Hashem, 'Nasrallah on Syria: "The Battle is Ours"', *Al-Monitor*, 26 May 2013.
125. Mohanad Hage Ali, 'Power Points Defining the Syria-Hezbollah Relationship', *Malcom H. Kerr Carnegie Middle East Center*, 29 March 2019, https://carnegie-mec.org/2019/03/29/power-points-defining-syria-hezbollah-relationship-pub-78730; Rebeiz, 'Deadly Strike in the Golan Heights'.
126. Janaby, 'The Legal Status of Hezbollah', 407–21.
127. GC III, art. 4(1).
128. GC III, art. 4(1); Janaby, 'The Legal Status of Hezbollah', 408.
129. Nicholas Blanford, 'The Battle for Qusayr: How the Syrian Regime and Hizb Allah Tipped the Balance', *Combating Terrorism Center*, Special Issue on Syria, vol. 6, no. 8 (2013), 18.
130. Seth G. Jones and Maxwell B. Markusen, 'The Escalating Conflict with Hezbollah in Syria', *Center for Strategic and International Studies*, 20 June 2018, https://www.csis.org/analysis/escalating-conflict-hezbollah-syria
131. France 24, 'Hezbollah Spy Released, More Prisoner Swaps Expected', 1 June 2008.
132. Janaby, 'The Legal Status of Hezbollah', 413.
133. Katharine Fortin and Ezequiel Heffes, 'Introduction: An Exploration of the Shadowland of Armed Groups and International Law', in *Armed Groups and International Law: In the Shadowland of Legality and Illegality*, edited by Katharine Fortin and Ezequiel Heffes (Cheltenham: Edward Elgar, 2023), 2.

Chapter 6

1. International Law Association, Non-State Actors, Working Session Report of 9 August 2016, Johannesburg, 2, https://www.ila-hq.org/en_GB/documents/working-session-report-johannesburg-2016-5
2. Ibid.
3. Philip Alston, 'The "Non-a-Cat" Syndrome: Can the International Human Rights Regime Accommodate Non-State Actors?' in *Non-State Actors and Human Rights*, edited by Philip Alston (Oxford: Oxford University Press, 2005), 5.
4. Ibid., 17–19.
5. Thomas Kleinlein, 'Non-State Actors from an International Constitutionalist Perspective', in *Participants in the International Legal System: Multiple Perspectives on Non-State Actors in International Law*, edited by Jean d'Aspremont (Abingdon: Taylor & Francis, 2011), 45; Beate Rudolf, 'Governance without Government: Non-State Actors and International Law', Working Paper, *American Political Science Association 2009 Annual Meeting*, Toronto, 2009, https://papers.ssrn.com/sol3/papers.cfm?abstract_id=1449182#
6. Jean d'Aspremont, 'Non-State Actors from the Perspective of Legal Positivism', 26.
7. UN Charter, art. 1 and art. 41.
8. AP II, art. 1.
9. UN Security Council, S/RES/1540 (2004), 28 April 2004.
10. UN Security Council. S/RES/2325 (2016), 15 December 2016.
11. UN Security Council. S/RES/2459 (2019), 15 March 2019.
12. Kristen Boon, 'The UN Security Council and Non-State Actors', *The American Society of International Law*, vol. 113 (2019), 201.
13. ICJ, Reparations for Injuries Suffered in the Service of the United Nations, Advisory Opinion, 11 April 1949 ICJ Rep. 174.
14. ICJ, Accordance with International Law of the Unilateral Declaration of Independence in Respect of Kosovo, Advisory Opinion, 22 July 2010 ICJ Rep. 403, 470, para. 116.
15. D'Aspremont, 'Non-State Actors from the Perspective of Legal Positivism', 27–30.
16. UN Charter, art. 2(4): 'All Members shall refrain in their international relations from the threat or use of force against the territorial integrity or political independence of any state, or in any other manner inconsistent with the Purposes of the United Nations'.
17. UN Charter, art. 40, 41: 'In order to prevent an aggravation of the situation, the Security Council may, before making the recommendations or deciding upon the measures provided for in Article 39, call upon the parties concerned to comply with such provisional measures as it deems necessary or desirable. Such provisional measures shall be without prejudice to the rights, claims, or position of the parties concerned. The Security Council shall duly take account of failure to comply with such provisional measures'. 'The Security Council may decide what measures not involving the use of

armed force are to be employed to give effect to its decisions, and it may call upon the Members of the United Nations to apply such measures. These may include complete or partial interruption of economic relations and of rail, sea, air, postal, telegraphic, radio, and other means of communication, and the severance of diplomatic relations'. Article 51: 'Nothing in the present Charter shall impair the inherent right of individual or collective self-defence if an armed attack occurs against a Member of the United Nations, until the Security Council has taken measures necessary to maintain international peace and security. Measures taken by Members in the exercise of this right of self-defence shall be immediately reported to the Security Council and shall not in any way affect the authority and responsibility of the Security Council under the present Charter to take at any time such action as it deems necessary in order to maintain or restore international peace and security'.

18. See Yaël Ronen, 'Entities That Can Be States But Do Not Claim to Be', in *Statehood and Self-Determination: Reconciling Tradition and Modernity in International Law*, edited by Duncan French (Cambridge: Cambridge University Press, 2013), 31–32, note 34.
19. Abbreviation for non-State actors.
20. Ronen, 'Entities', 33.
21. Ibid., 41.
22. In *Human Rights Obligations of Non-State* Actors, Andrew Clapham has suggested extending human rights obligations to cover human rights abuses by non-State actors. This would be beneficial in cases of torture, use of child soldiers, civilians-targeted bombings and terrorism. Andrew Clapham, *Human Rights Obligations of Non-State Actors* (Oxford: Oxford University Press, 2006), 293; quoted in Ronen, 'Entities', 43.
23. Ronen, 'Entities', 43–44.
24. Ibid., 45–46.
25. Nicholson, *Statehood and the State-Like in International Law*, 121.
26. See the definition of legal personality in Chapter 4.
27. Ronen, 'Entities', 51–57.

Chapter 7

1. Mahmoud Cherif Bassiouni, 'The New Wars and the Crisis of Compliance with the Law of Armed Conflict by Non-State Actors', *The Journal of Criminal Law and Criminology*, vol. 98, no. 3 (2008), 715.
2. Agata Kleczkowska, 'Armed Non-State Actors and Customary International Law', in *Non-State Actors and International Obligations: Creation, Evolution and Enforcement*, edited by James Summers and Alex Gough (Leiden: Brill, 2018), 66.
3. See Rajagopal Balakrishnan, *International Law from Below: Development, Social Movements and Third World Resistance* (Cambridge: Cambridge University Press, 2003); Konstantinos Mastorodimos, 'National Liberation Movements: Still a Valid Concept (with Special Reference to International Humanitarian Law', *Oregon Review of International Law*, vol. 17 (2015), 71.

4. Article 1(2) of the UN Charter stipulates that the purposes of the United Nations are: 'To develop friendly relations among nations based on respect for the principle of equal rights and self-determination, and to take other appropriate measures to strengthen universal peace'.
5. In its preamble, the Universal Declaration of Human Rights states: 'Whereas it is essential, if man is not to be compelled to have recourse, as a last resort, to rebellion against tyranny and oppression, that human rights should be protected by the rule of law'.
6. Article 1 of the ICCPR stipulates: '1. All peoples have the right of self-determination. By virtue of that right they freely determine their political status and freely pursue their economic, social and cultural development. 2. All peoples may, for their own ends, freely dispose of their natural wealth and resources without prejudice to any obligations arising out of international economic co-operation, based upon the principle of mutual benefit, and international law. In no case may a people be deprived of its own means of subsistence. 3. The States Parties to the present Covenant, including those having responsibility for the administration of Non-Self-Governing and Trust Territories, shall promote the realization of the right of self-determination, and shall respect that right, in conformity with the provisions of the Charter of the United Nations'.
7. Article 4 of the GC III stipulates that the members of organised resistance movements can benefit from the status of prisoner of war. Therefore, it recognises the legality of resistance movements. Article 43 of AP I recognises that combatants in a conflict can be organised armed forces, groups and units under the command of a party to the conflict. This applies to parties represented by 'a government or authority that is not recognised by an adverse party'. This stipulation is general and may be applied to conflicts that engage resistance or national liberational movements.
8. Antonio Cassese, 'Resistance Movements', in *Encyclopedia of Public International Law, vol. 4*, edited by Rudolf Bernhardt and Peter Macalister-Smith (Amsterdam: North Holland, 1982), 188–90.
9. Mahmoud Cherif Bassiouni, '"Terrorism": Reflections on Legitimacy and Policy Considerations', in *Values and Violence: Intangible Aspects of Terrorism*, edited by Ibrahim Karawan, Wayne McCormack and Stephen Eugene Reynolds (Dordrecht: Springer, 2008), 240.
10. Martin Wählisch, 'Liberation and Resistance Movements', *Oxford Bibliographies*, 2019, https://www.oxfordbibliographies.com/display/document/obo-9780199796953/obo-9780199796953-0186.xml
11. ICRC, 'ICRC Engagement with Non-State Armed Groups: Why, How, for What Purpose, and Other Salient Issues', Position Paper, March 2021, 2, file:///C:/Users/mgreb/Downloads/icrc_engagement_with_non-state_armed_groups_position_paper.pdf
12. AP II, art. 1(2).
13. There is no universally accepted definition of armed conflict and hostilities. The definition is often provided by negation (armed conflict cannot be disturbances or riots or a fight against colonial powers). In *Prosecutor* v.

Dusko Tadic, the ICTY provided the following definition: '[A]n armed conflict exists whenever there is a resort to armed force between States or protracted armed violence between governmental authorities and organized armed groups or between such groups within a State. International humanitarian law applies from the initiation of such armed conflicts and extends beyond the cessation of hostilities until a general conclusion of peace is reached; or, in the case of internal conflicts, a peaceful settlement is achieved. Until that moment, international humanitarian law continues to apply in the whole territory of the warring States or, in the case of internal conflicts, the whole territory under the control of a party, whether or not actual combat takes place there'. *Prosecutor* v. *Tadic*, Decision on the Defence Motion for Interlocutory Appeal on Jurisdiction, Case No. IT-94-1-AR72, A.Ch, 2 October 1995, para. 70; Charles Garraway, 'Armed Conflict and Terrorist Organisations', in *Counter-Terrorism Strategies in a Fragmented International Legal Order: Meeting the Challenges*, edited by Larissa Van Den Herik and Nico Schrijver (Cambridge: Cambridge University Press, 2013), 429–33.

14. ICTY, *The Prosecutor* v. *Fatmir Limaj*, Judgment, IT-03-66-T, 30 November 2005, para. 170.
15. ICRC, 'ICRC Engagement with Non-State Armed Groups', 4.
16. Ibid., 4.
17. United States Government, *Understanding States of Resistance: Pocket Guide* (Fort Bragg: United States Army Special Operations Command, 2019), 11.
18. *Prosecutor* v. *Tadic*, Decision on the Defence Motion for Interlocutory Appeal on Jurisdiction, Case No. IT-94-1-AR72, 96 (2 October 1995).
19. Ibid., 73; Emily Crawford, *The Treatment of Combatants and Insurgents under the Law of Armed Conflict* (Oxford: Oxford University Press, 2010), 1.
20. United States Government, *Understanding States of Resistance: Pocket Guide*, 11.
21. Aniel Caro de Beer, *Peremptory Norms of General International Law (Jus Cogens) and the Prohibition of Terrorism* (Leiden: Brill, 2019), 95.
22. UN General Assembly, A/RES/44/29 (1989), Measures to Prevent International Terrorism which endangers or takes innocent human lives or jeopardises fundamental freedoms and study of the underlying causes of those forms of terrorism and acts of violence which lie in misery, frustration, grievance and despair and which cause some people to sacrifice human lives, including their own, in an attempt to effect radical changes, 4 December 1989.
23. UN General Assembly, A/RES/46/51 (1991), Measures to Eliminate International Terrorism, 9 December 1991.
24. UN General Assembly, A/RES/60/288 (2006), The United Nations Global Counter-Terrorism Strategy, 20 September 2006.
25. UN Security Council, S/RES/1377 (2001), 12 November 2001.
26. Leopold, 'UN Cites Confusion over Maps of Shebaa Farms'.

27. Frederic C. Hof, 'Assad: The Shebaa Farms are Syrian, Whatever Hezbollah Claims', *Newlines Magazine*, 7 April 2021; Michael Young, 'Leaving Hezbollah Hanging', *Malcom H. Kerr Carnegie Middle East Center*, 13 April 2021, https://carnegie-mec.org/diwan/84303
28. Ana Arjona, Nelson Kasfir and Zachariah Mampilly (eds), *Rebel Governance in Civil War* (New York: Cambridge University Press, 2015), 2.
29. Dietrich Schindler, 'The Different Types of Armed Conflicts According to the Geneva Conventions and Protocols', *Hague Academy of International Law*, vol. 163, no. 2 (1979), 147; René-Jean Wilhelm, 'Problèmes relatifs à la protection de la personne humaine par le droit international dans les conflits armés ne présentant pas un caractère international', *Le Recueil des Cours de l'Académie de Droit International de La Haye*, vol. 137 (1972), 347–48.
30. René Provost, *Rebel Courts: The Administration of Justice by Armed Insurgents* (Oxford: Oxford University Press, 2021), 7.
31. Natasha Ezrow, *Global Politics and Violent Non-State Actors* (Los Angeles: Sage, 2017), 94. The concept of organised crime was coined in the United States. The term started to be used in Europe in the 1960s and 1970s. It was recognised internationally with the adoption of the UN Convention against Transnational Organized Crime (Palermo Convention) in 2000. Klaus von Lampe, *Organized Crime: Analyzing Illegal Activities, Criminal Structures, and Extra-Legal Governance* (Los Angeles: Sage, 2015), 15. For Ezrow, organised criminal groups are composed of three or more persons who plan and execute serious crimes for material gain. In contrast to sporadic crime, organised crime is well planned prior to execution and often evades detection. Sporadic crime does not involve a network of actors and complexity. Some organised crimes include smuggling, robbery, piracy, money-laundering and trafficking of drugs, weapons and humans. Members of this group can be violent, especially when challenged by the State (133).
32. Ibid., 87.
33. Ibid., 90.
34. David H. Ukco, *The Insurgent's Dilemma: A Struggle to Prevail* (Oxford: Oxford University Press, 2022), 2.
35. Ibid., 4.
36. Ibid.
37. Hans-Peter Grasser, 'International Humanitarian Law: An Introduction', *Henry Dunant Institute* (1993), 65, https://www.icrcndresourcecentre.org/wp-content/uploads/2016/03/EnglishTotal.pdf
38. Clapham, *Human Rights Obligations*, 273. As seen in Chapter 4, this was the case with the PLO when its Chairman Yassir Arafat proclaimed the independence of the Palestinian State in 1988. Youssef M. Ibrahim, 'PLO Proclaims Palestine to Be an Independent State; Hints at Recognising Israel', *The New York Times*, 15 November 1988.
39. Annyssa Bellal, 'What Are 'Armed Non-State Actors'? A Legal and Semantic Approach', in *International Humanitarian Law and Non-State Actors*, edited by Ezequiel Heffes, Marcos D. Kotlik and Manuel J. Ventura (The Hague: T. M. C. Asser Press, 2020), 37.
40. France 24, 'Beirut Street Clashes Turn Deadly', 9 May 2005.

41. Arnold K. Amet, 'Terrorism and International Law: Cure the Underlying Problem, Not Just the Symptom', *Annual Survey of International and Comparative Law*, vol. 19, no. 1 (2013), 17.
42. Larissa van den Herik and Nico Schrijver, 'The Fragmented International Legal Response to Terrorism', in *Counter-Terrorism Strategies in a Fragmented International Legal Order: Meeting the Challenges,* edited by Larissa van den Herik and Nico Schrijver (Cambridge: Cambridge University Press, 2013), 4; see Peter McPhee, *Robespierre: A Revolutionary Life* (New Haven: Yale University Press, 2012); Marco Pinfari, *Terrorists as Monsters: The Unmanageable Other from the French Revolution to the Islamic State* (New York: Oxford University Press, 2019).
43. de Beer, *Peremptory Norms*, 13.
44. Ibid., 13.
45. UN Office of Counter-Terrorism, *International Legal Instruments*, https://www.un.org/counterterrorism/international-legal-instruments
46. UN Convention on Offences and Certain Other Acts Committed on Board Aircraft, Tokyo, 14 September 1963.
47. Dan Porat, 'The Hijacking of El Al Flight 426: The Advent of Air Terrorism', *Journal of Contemporary History*, vol. 57, no. 4 (2022): 1072–88.
48. UN Convention for the Suppression of Unlawful Seizure of Aircraft, The Hague, 16 December 1970.
49. UN Convention for the Suppression of Unlawful Acts against the Safety of Civil Aviation (with Final Act of the International Conference on Air Law Held under the Auspices of the International Civil Aviation Organisation at Montreal in September 1971), Montreal, 23 September 1971.
50. UN General Assembly, GA/RES/3166 (1973), Convention on the Prevention and Punishment of Crimes Against Internationally Protected Persons, Including Diplomatic Agents, New York, 14 December 1973.
51. UN General Assembly, International Convention against Taking of Hostages, New York, 17 December 1979.
52. UN Supplementary Protocol for the Suppression of Unlawful Acts against the Safety of Fixed Platforms Located on the Continental Shelf, Rome, 10 March 1988.
53. UN Convention on the Suppression of Unlawful Acts Relating to International Civil Aviation, Beijing, 10 September 2010.
54. UN Protocol Supplementary to the Convention for the Suppression of Unlawful Seizure of Aircraft, Beijing, 10 September 2010.
55. UN Convention for the Suppression of Unlawful Acts against the Safety of Maritime Navigation, Rome, 10 March 1988.
56. UN Protocol to the Convention for the Suppression of Unlawful Acts against the Safety of Maritime Navigation, London, 14 October 2005.
57. UN Convention on the Physical Protection of Nuclear Material, Vienna, 26 October 1979.
58. UN Amendment to the Convention on the Physical Protection of Nuclear Material, Vienna, 8 July 2005.
59. UN International Convention for the Suppression of Terrorist Bombings, New York, 12 January 1998.

60. UN International Convention for the Suppression of the Financing of Terrorism, New York, 10 January 2000.
61. UN International Convention for the Suppression of Acts of Nuclear Terrorism, New York, 14 September 2005.
62. UN General Assembly, A/RES/49/60 (1995), Measures to Eliminate International Terrorism, 17 February 1995.
63. UN General Assembly, A/RES/51/2010 (1997), Measures to Eliminate International Terrorism, 16 January 1997.
64. UN General Assembly, A/RES/72/284 (2018), The United Nations Global Counter-Terrorism Strategy, 2 July 2018.
65. UN Security Council, S/RES/2133 (2014), 27 January 2014.
66. UN Security Council, S/RES/2170 (2014), 15 August 2014; UN Security Council, S/RES/2368 (2017) 20 July 2017.
67. UN Security Council, S/RES/2242 (2015), 13 October 2015.
68. UN Security Council, S/RES/2249 (2015), 11 November 2015; UN Security Council, S/RES/2253 (2015), 17 December 2015; UN Security Council, S/RES/2255 (2015), 12 December 2015; UN Security Council, S/RES/2322 (2016), 12 December 2016; UN Security Council, S/RES/2395 (2017), 21 December 2017; UN Security Council, S/RES/2396 (2017), 22 December 2017.
69. UN Security Council, S/RES/2427 (2018), 9 July 2018.
70. UN Security Council, S/RES/1371 (2001), 28 September 2001; de Beer, *Peremptory Norms*, 27.
71. UN Security Council, S/RES/1377 (2001), 12 November 2001.
72. Ibid.
73. Van den Herik and Schrijver, 'The Fragmented International Legal Response', 13; Eric Rosand, 'Resolution 1373 and the CTC: The Security Council's Capacity Building', in *International Cooperation in Counter-Terrorism: The United Nations and Regional Organisations in the Fight Against Terrorism*, edited by Giuseppe Nesi, 1st edition (Aldershot: Ashgate, 2006), 81.
74. League of Arab States, The Arab Convention for the Suppression of Terrorism, Article 2, Cairo, April 1998. Translated from Arabic by the United Nations English Translation Service, 29 May 2000.
75. Organisation of Islamic Cooperation, Convention of the Organisation of the Islamic Conference on Combating International Terrorism, Article 1(2), Ouagadougou, 1 July 1999.
76. The Organisation of African Unity Convention on the Prevention and Combating Terrorism, Article 1(3), Algiers, 14 July 1999.
77. The Organisation of American States, The Inter-American Convention Against Terrorism, Bridgetown 3 July 2002.
78. Council of Europe, European Convention on the Suppression of Terrorism, Strasbourg, 27 January 1977.
79. Council of Europe, European Convention on Extradition, Paris, 13 November 1957.
80. Council of Europe, Additional Protocol to the European Convention on Extradition, Strasbourg, 15 October 1975.

81. Council of Europe, Protocol Amending the European Convention on the Suppression of Terrorism, Strasbourg, 15 May 2003.
82. Council of Europe, Convention on the Prevention of Terrorism, Warsaw, 16 May 2005.
83. Council of Europe, Additional Protocol to the Council of Europe Convention on the Prevention of Terrorism, Riga, 22 October 2015.
84. Council of Europe, Convention on Laundering, Search, Seizure and Confiscation of the Proceeds from Crime and on the Financing of Terrorism, Warsaw, 16 May 2005.
85. There is an assumption that all States are opposed to terrorism with no exception, which would make the prohibition of terrorism a peremptory norm of general international law (*jus cogens*). A *jus cogens* is defined as 'a norm accepted and recognised by the international community of states as a norm from which no derogation is permitted'; de Beer, *Peremptory Norms*, 2.
86. de Beer, *Peremptory Norms*, 45.
87. In *Bosnia and Herzegovina* v. *Serbia and Montenegro*, the ICJ stated that *jus cogens* norms are peremptory norms because they are moral and humanitarian principles; Application of the Convention on the Prevention and Punishment of the Crime of Genocide (*Bosnia and Herzegovina* v. *Serbia and Montenegro*), Judgment, ICJ Reports 2007, p. 43, para. 161. In *Democratic Republic of Congo* v. *Rwanda*, the Court re-affirmed that 'the principles underlying the [Genocide] Convention are principles which are recognised by civilized nations as binding on States, even without any conventional obligation', and that these principles are certainly *jus cogens* norms; Armed Activities on the Territory of the Congo (New Application: 2002) (*Democratic Republic of the Congo* v. *Rwanda*), Jurisdiction and Admissibility, Judgment, ICJ Reports 2006, p. 6, para. 64; de Beer, *Peremptory Norms*, 80.
88. de Beer, *Peremptory Norms*, 87–88.
89. UN Security Council, SC/7143 (2001), 12 September 2001.
90. de Beer, *Peremptory Norms*, 17.
91. There were multiple attempts to define terrorism. In 2000, the Sixth Committee was tasked to draft a comprehensive convention on international terrorism. Article 2 of the draft stipulates: '1. Any person commits an offence within the meaning of this Convention if that person, by any means, unlawfully and intentionally, does an act intended to cause: (a) Death or serious bodily injury to any person; or (b) Serious damage to a State or government facility, a public transportation system, communication system or infrastructure facility with the intent to cause extensive destruction of such a place, facility or system, or where such destruction results or is likely to result in major economic loss; when the purpose of such act, by its nature or context, is to intimidate a population, or to compel a government or an international organisation to do or abstain from doing any act. 2. Any person also commits an offence if that person attempts to commit an offence or participates as an accomplice in

an offence as set forth in paragraph 1. 3. Any person also commits an offence if that person: (a) Organizes, directs or instigates others to commit an offence as set forth in paragraph 1 or 2; or (b) Aids, abets, facilitates or counsels the commission of such an offence; or (c) In any other way contributes to the commission of one or more offences referred to in paragraphs 1, 2 or 3 (a) by a group of persons acting with a common purpose; such contribution shall be intentional and either be made with the aim of furthering the general criminal activity or purpose of the group or be made in the knowledge of the intention of the group to commit the offence or offences concerned'. However, the draft was never finalised. Members of the Committee could not agree on a final version of the definition and whether to include or exclude the right to self-determination. UN General Assembly, A/C.6/55/1 (2000), Draft Comprehensive Convention on International Terrorism, Working Document Submitted by India, New York, 28 August 2000, art. 2. In 2004, Resolution 1566 of the Security Council offered an indirect definition of terrorism in Resolution as 'criminal acts, including against civilians, committed with the intent to cause death or serious bodily injury, or taking of hostages, with the purpose to provoke a state of terror in the general public or in a group of persons or particular persons, intimidate a population or compel a government or an international organisation to do or to abstain from doing any act [. . .] constitute offences within the scope of an as defined in the international conventions and protocols relating to terrorism'. UN Security Council, S/RES/1566 (2004), 8 October 2004, para. 3.

92. Van den Herik and Schrijver, 'The Fragmented International Legal Response', 1–25.
93. 18 U.S.C. § **2331 (2009).**
94. Public Law 107-56, H.R.3162 – The Uniting and Strengthening of America by Providing Appropriate Tools Required to Intercept and Obstruct Terrorism (USA Patriot Act) of 2001, 107th Congress (2001), 26 October 2001.
95. Canada, Criminal Code 1985, Part II.1, Terrorism.
96. The Commonwealth of Australia, Criminal Code Act 1995, Part 5.3 – Terrorism.
97. The United Kingdom, Terrorism Act 2000.
98. La République Française, Code Pénal, Titre II, Articles 421-1 to 422-7.
99. The Lebanese Republic, Criminal Code, art. 314. Translated into English for the Special Tribunal of Lebanon, 2015; see Nidal Nabil Jurdi, 'The Crime of Terrorism in Lebanon and International Law', in *The Special Tribunal for Lebanon: Law and Practice*, edited by Amal Alamuddin (Oxford: Oxford University Press, 2014), 75.
100. Israeli Minister of Defence, *Fighting Terror in the Legal Arena*, 2018, https://english.mod.gov.il/About/Innovative_Strength/Pages/Fighting_Terror_in_the_Legal_Arena.aspx
101. Council on Foreign Relations, 'Israel's New Counter-Terrorism Law and Terrorism in Cyberspace', 22 August 2016, https://www.cfr.org/blog/israels-new-counter-terrorism-law-and-terrorism-cyberspace

102. Christopher Blacksley, *Terror and Anti-Terrorism: A Normative and Practical Assessment* (Leiden: Brill, 2006), 19.
103. The US Department of State, Bureau of Counterterrorism, 'Foreign Terrorist Organisations: Hizballah', 8 October 1997.
104. US Department of the Treasury, Office of Foreign Assets Control, Notice of OFAC Sanctions Actions, Federal Register, vol. 84, no. 245, 20 December 2019; Department of Justice, Office of Public Affairs, 'OFAC-Designated Hezbollah Financier and Eight Associates Charged with Multiple Crimes Arising out of Scheme to Evade Terrorism-Related Sanctions', 18 April 2023.
105. The United Kingdom Government, Treasury, 'Suspected Hizballah Financier Sanctioned under Counter-Terrorism Regulations', 18 April 2023; Daniel Boffey, 'UK Imposes Sanctions on Art Collector Accused of Financing Hezbollah', *The Guardian*, 18 April 2023.
106. US Department of the Treasury (Press Release), 'Treasury Sanctions Oil Shipping Network Supporting IRGC-QF and Hizballah', 3 November 2022, https://home.treasury.gov/news/press-releases/jy1076
107. Public Law 114-102, H.R.2297 – Hizballah International Financing Prevention Act of 2015, 114th Congress (2015–16), 18 December 2015.
108. Nicolas Dot-Pouillard, 'Les armes du Hezbollah: Terrorisme, droit à la résistance et principe de légalité', *Revue Confluences Méditerranée*, vol. 3, no. 102 (2017), 93.
109. Public Law 115-272, S.1595 – Hizballah International Financing Prevention Amendments Act of 2018, 115th Congress (2017–18), 25 October 2018.
110. Indictment, *United States of America* v. *Alexei Saab* (19 Cir, SDNY, 1/19/19); Department of Justice, US Attorney's Office, Southern District of New York, 'New Jersey Man Convicted of Receiving Military-Type Training from Hizballah, Marriage Fraud and Making False Statements', 11 May 2022.
111. *Kaplan* v. *Hezbollah*, 19-cv-3187 (BMC) (ST) (EDNY), 16 September 2022.
112. Regulations Amending the Regulations Establishing a List of Entities, Criminal Code, SOR/2002-454, 10 December 2002; Canada Gazette, Part II, vol. 136, no. 17, 13 December 2002.
113. Government of Canada, 'Hizballah', *Currently Listed Entities*, 21 November 2018.
114. Australian Government, 'Hizballah', *Australian National Security*, 10 December 2021.
115. The United Kingdom Government, 'Hizballah', *Policy Paper: Proscribed Terrorist Groups or Organisations*, 26 November 2021.
116. Georges Marion and Pascale Robert-Diard, 'M. Jospin qualifie de "terroristes" les attaques du Hezbollah contre Israël', *Le Monde*, 26 February 2000.
117. Reuters, 'Paris accuse le Hezbollah d'avoir rompu un accord', 23 May 2013; Dot-Pouillard, 'Les armes du Hezbollah', 95.
118. John Irish, 'France Wants Hezbollah Armed Wing on EU Terror List by End-June', *Reuters*, 23 May 2013.

119. 2013/C 355 E/01, 5 December 2013, Official Journal of the European Union, European Parliament, Written Questions with Answer, Written Questions by Members of the European Parliament and their answers given by a European Union institution.
120. Council Implementing Regulation (EU) 2022/147 of 3 February 2022 implementing Article 2(3) of Regulation (EC) No. 2580/2001 on specific restrictive measures directed against certain persons and entities with a view to combating terrorism, and repealing Implementing Regulation (EU) 2021/1188, Official Journal of the European Union, vol. 65, 4 February 2022.
121. Dot-Pouillard, 'Les armes du Hezbollah', 96.
122. H. R. No. 558 (2021–22), 117th Congress, Urging the European Union to designate Hizballah in its entirety as a terrorist organisation, 20 September 2022.
123. Reuters, 'Arab League Labels Hezbollah a Terrorist Organisation', 11 March 2016.
124. Al-Jazeera, 'GCC Declares Lebanon's Hezbollah a "Terrorist" Group', 2 March 2016.
125. Beatrice Farhat and Adam Lucente, 'What's behind Arab League Decision to Drop Hezbollah Terror Label?', *Al-Monitor*, 1 July 2024.
126. See Chapter 3 on the General Amnesty Law in Lebanon of 1991.
127. UN Security Council, S/RES/1559 (2004), 2 September 2004.
128. UN Security Council, S/RES/1701 (2006), 11 August 2006.
129. Louis Casiano, 'UN Envoy Thanks Hezbollah Terror Group, Draws Rebuke from Israeli Officials: "Is This Real?"', *FoxNews*, 17 January 2023.
130. Reuters, 'Lebanon's Siniora Asks UN to Set Up Hariri Court', 14 May 2007.
131. UN Security Council, S/RES/1757 (2007), 30 May 2007.
132. Special Tribunal for Lebanon, 14th Annual Report (2022–23), 4, https://www.stl-tsl.org/sites/default/files/documents/annual-reports/STL_Annual_Report_2022-2023.pdf
133. Anton du Plessis, 'A Snapshot of International Criminal Justice Cooperation against Terrorism Since 9/11', in *Counter-Terrorism Strategies in a Fragmented International Legal Order: Meeting the Challenges*, edited by Larissa van den Herik and Nico Schrijver (Cambridge: Cambridge University Press, 2013), 34.
134. Daniel A. Bellemare, 'Bringing Terrorists before International Justice: A View from the Frontlines', *Criminal Law Forum*, vol. 23 (2012), 425.
135. STL allows trials *in absentia* in compliance with the Lebanese Criminal Code.
136. *The Prosecutor vs. Salim Jamil Ayyash*, STL-11-01/S/TC, The Trial Chamber, 11 December 202; Special Tribunal for Lebanon, 13th Annual Report (2021–22), 5, https://www.stl-tsl.org/sites/default/files/documents/annual-reports/STL_13th_Annual_Report.pdf
137. *The Prosecutor* v. *Hassan Habib Merhi, Hussein Hassan Oneissi*, STL-11-01/A-2/AC, The Appeals Chamber, 10 March 2022.

138. *The Prosecutor* v. *Hassan Habib Merhi, Hussein Hassan Oneissi*, STL-11-01/S-2/AC, The Appeals Chamber, Sentencing Judgment, 16 June 2022, para. 45.
139. UN Special Tribunal for Lebanon (The Pre-Trial Judge), Order on Preliminary Questions Addressed to the Judges of the Appeals Chamber Pursuant to Rule 68, paragraph (G), of the Rules of Procedure and Evidence (STL-11-01/I), 21 January 2011, § 2; Matthew Gillet and Matthias Schuster, 'Fast-Track Justice: The Special Tribunal for Lebanon Defines Terrorism', *Journal of International Criminal Justice*, vol. 9, no. 5 (2011), 990.
140. Ibid., 992.
141. Ibid., 993.
142. Article 2 stipulates: 'The following shall be applicable to the prosecution and punishment of the crimes referred to in article 1, subject to the provisions of this Statute: (a) The provisions of the Lebanese Criminal Code relating to the prosecution and punishment of acts of terrorism, crimes and offences against life and personal integrity, illicit associations and failure to report crimes and offences, including the rules regarding the material elements of a crime, criminal participation and conspiracy; and (b) Articles 6 and 7 of the Lebanese law of 11 January 1958 on Increasing the penalties for sedition, civil war and interfaith struggle'. Art 2, STL, UN, Security Council, S/RES/1757 (2007).
143. Article 314 stipulates: 'Terrorist acts are all acts intended to cause a state of terror and committed by means liable to create a public danger such as explosive devices, inflammable materials, toxic or corrosive products and infectious or microbial agents'. The Lebanese Republic, Criminal Code, translated into English for the Special Tribunal of Lebanon, 2015.
144. UN Special Tribunal for Lebanon (Appeals Chamber), Interlocutory Decision on the Applicable Law: Terrorism, Conspiracy, Homicide, Perpetration, Cumulative Charging (STL-11-01/I), 16 February 2011, § 85.
145. Ben Saul, 'Legislating from a Radical Hague: The United Nations Special Tribunal for Lebanon Invents an International Crime of Transnational Terrorism', *Leiden Journal of International Law*, vol. 24 (2011), 677.
146. Gillet and Schuster, 'Fast-Track Justice', 1012.
147. UN Security Council, S/RES/1559 (2004), 2 September 2004.
148. Aurélie Daher, *Hezbollah: Mobilization and Power*, translated by H. W. Randolph (Oxford: Oxford University Press, 2019), 259–65.
149. France 24, 'Beirut Street Clashes Turn Deadly', 9 May 2005.
150. Sara Ghsemilee, 'Hezbollah Will "Cut off Hands" of Those Targeting Hariri Suspects', *Al-Arabiya News*, 2 July 2011.
151. *The Prosecutor vs. Salim Jamil Ayyash*, STL-11-01/S/TC, The Trial Chamber, 11 December 2020. It is important to note that Salim Jamil Ayyash was also prosecuted for his involvement in three other attacks against Marwan Hamade, George Hawi and Elias El-Murr. Investigations found that these attacks were all related to the 14 February 2005 attack and therefore fell under the STL jurisdiction. On 13 July 2021, Trial Chamber

II ordered the continued temporary stay in the proceedings until further notice from the United Nations Security Council would be received.

152. Olga Kavran, 'The Special Tribunal for Lebanon and Its Outreach Programme', *Journal of International Criminal Justice*, vol. 20 (2022): 84–88.
153. Special Tribunal for Lebanon, 14th Annual Report (2022–23), 6.
154. Blacksley, *Terror and Anti-Terrorism*, 19.
155. Paul Staniland, 'States, Insurgents, and Wartime Political Orders', *Perspectives on Politics*, vol. 10, no. 2 (2012), 243–44.
156. Jeremy M. Weinstein, *Inside Rebellion: The Politics of Insurgent Violent* (Cambridge: Cambridge University Press, 2006), 17–18.
157. Mahmoud Cherif Bassiouni, 'The Subjects of International Criminal Law: Ratione Personae', in *International Criminal Law*, vol. 1 (Leiden: Brill, 2013), 41.

Chapter 8

1. Levy Firestone Muse, 'A Foreseeable Genocide: The Role of the French Government in Connection with Genocide against the Tutsi in Rwanda', 19 April 2021, https://www.gov.rw/fileadmin/user_upload/gov_user_upload/2021.04.19_MUSE_REPORT.pdf A separate report ordered by the French President Emmanuel Macron arrived at the same conclusion. Commission de Recherche sur les Archives Françaises Relatives au Rwanda et au Génocide des Tutsi, 'La France, le Rwanda et le génocide des Tutsi (1990–94): Rapport remis au Président de la République le 26 mars 2021', https://medias.vie-publique.fr/data_storage_s3/rapport/pdf/279186.pdf President Emmanuel Macron issued an apology shortly after. BBC, 'Macron Asks Rwanda to Forgive France over 1994 Genocide Role', 27 May 2021.
2. Oona A. Hathaway, Alexandra Francis, Alyssa Yamamoto, Srinath Reddy Kethireddy and Aaron Haviland, 'State Responsibility for US Support of the Saudi-led Coalition in Yemen', *Just Security*, 25 April 2018.
3. James Crawford, 'Articles on Responsibility of States for Internationally Wrongful Acts', *United Nations Audiovisual Library of International Law*, 2012.
4. Keith John Michael Smith, *A Modern Treatise on the Law of Criminal Complicity* (Oxford: Clarendon Press, 1991), 1–2.
5. Miles Jackson, *Complicity in International Law* (Oxford: Oxford University Press, 2015), 11.
6. Article 34 of the Vienna Convention on the Law of Treaties stipulates: 'A treaty does not create either obligations or rights for a third State without its consent'. Article 35 adds: 'An obligation arises for a third State from a provision of a treaty if the parties to the treaty intend the provision to be the means of establishing the obligation and the third State expressly accepts that obligation in writing'.
7. Jackson, *Complicity in International Law*, 11.
8. Ibid., 18.

9. Albin Eser, 'Individual Criminal Responsibility: Mental Elements: Mistake of Facts and Mistake of Law', in *The Rome Statute of the International Criminal Court: A Commentary, Vol. 1*, edited by Antonio Cassese, Paola Gaeta and John Jones (Oxford: Oxford University Press, 2002), 781.
10. Ibid., 782.
11. Jackson, *Complicity in International Law*, 18.
12. UN General Assembly Resolution 56/83 of 12 December 2001, corrected by document A/56/49 (Vol. I), Corr.4; International Law Commission, 'Responsibility of States for Internationally Wrongful Acts', 2001, vol. II (Part Two).
13. International Law Commission. 'Draft on Responsibility of States for Internationally Wrongful Acts, with Commentaries', 2001, vol. II (Part Two, as corrected).
14. André Nollkaemper and Dov Jacobs, 'Shared Responsibility in International Law: A Conceptual Framework', *Michigan Journal of International Law*, vol. 34, no. 2 (2013), 386; cited in Jackson, *Complicity in International Law*, 20.
15. Jackson, *Complicity in International Law*, 28.
16. UN Charter, San Francisco, 1945; Jackson, *Complicity in International Law*, 126.
17. UN General Assembly, Res 2625 (XXV), Declaration on Principles of International Law concerning Friendly Relations and Cooperation among States in Accordance with the Charter of the United Nations, 24 October 1970; Jackson, *Complicity in International Law*, 128.
18. Armed Activities on the Territory of the Congo (*Democratic Republic of the Congo* v. *Uganda*), Judgment, ICJ Reports 2005, 168, para. 162; Jackson, *Complicity in International Law*, 128.
19. The Rome Statute of the International Criminal Court, Rome, 17 July 1998, art. 25 (3).
20. This position seems to be supported by the ICTY in *Prosecutor* v. *Dusko Tadic* where it stipulates Article 7(1) and where the word 'committed' 'covers first and foremost the physical perpetration of a crime by the offender himself'. *Prosecutor* v. *Tadic*, Case No. IT-94-1-A, Judgment, Appeals Chamber, 15 July 1999, para. 188.
21. Kai Ambos, 'Article 25: Individual Criminal Responsibility', in *Commentary on the Rome Statute of the International Criminal Court, Observers' Notes, Article by Article*, edited by Otto Triffterer, 2nd edition (München: Beck/Hart, 2008), 749. For instance, in *Prosecutor* v. *Dusko Tadic*, the court held that Article 7(1) of the Rome Statute covers the co-perpetuation of crimes. It states: 'Most of the time these crimes do not result from the criminal propensity of single individuals but constitute manifestations of collective criminality: the crimes are often carried out by groups of individuals acting in pursuance of a common criminal design. Although only some members of the group may physically perpetrate the criminal act (murder, extermination, wanton destruction of cities, towns or villages, etc.), the participation and contribution of the other members of the group

is often vital in facilitating the commission of the offence in question. It follows that the moral gravity of such participation is often no less – or indeed no different – from that of those actually carrying out the acts in question'. *Prosecutor* v. *Tadic,* Case No. IT-94-1-A, Judgment, Appeals Chamber, 15 July 1999, para. 191. For Ambos, the court distinguishes between three categories of collective criminal responsibility: the first one is the most basic where all participants act with a common intention and design. The second one is the systematic form which requires planning for the execution of a common purpose. This was the case of concentration camps where the crimes committed required military and administrative planning. The third one is the 'extended joint enterprise where one of the co-perpetrators actually engages in acts going beyond the common plan but his or her acts still constitute a "natural and foreseeable consequence" of the realization of the plan'. In short, co-perpetrators have a common plan and purpose.

22. Ambos, 'Article 25', 754.
23. In the *Akayesu* judgment, the ICTR held: 'By ordering the commission of one of the crimes referred to in Articles 2 to 4 of the Statute, a person also incurs individual criminal responsibility. Ordering implies a superior-subordinate relationship between the person giving the order and the one executing it. In other words, the person in a position of authority uses it to convince another to commit an offence'. *Prosecutor* v. *Akayesu*, Case No. ICTR-96-4-T, Judgment, Trial Chamber, 2 Sep. 1998, para. 483. I
24. In *Prosecutor* v. *Dusko Tadic*, the ICTY defined these criteria and decided that contribution must be direct and substantial to the commission of the crime: '[T]he substantial contribution requirement calls for a contribution that in fact has an effect on the commission of the crime. This is supported by the foregoing Nürnberg cases where, in virtually every situation, the criminal act most probably would not have occurred in the same way had not someone acted in the role that the accused in fact assumed'. *Prosecutor* v. *Tadic*, Case No. IT-94-1-T, Trial Chamber, 7 May 1997, para. 688.
25. Ambos, 'Article 25', 759.
26. Ibid., 760; International Convention for the Suppression of Terrorist Bombings, UN Doc. A/RES/52/164 (1998), Annex (37 I.L.M. 249 (1998).
27. Ambos, 'Article 25', 761; Zurab Sanikize, 'The Level of "Contribution" Required under Article 25(3)(D) of the Rome Statute of the International Criminal Court', *Revue Internationale de Droit Pénal*, vol. 83, no. 1 (2012), 223.
28. Article 3 of the Convention on the Prevention and Punishment of the Crime of Genocide stipulates: 'The following acts shall be punishable: (a) Genocide; (b) Conspiracy to commit genocide; (c) Direct and public incitement to commit genocide; (d) Attempt to commit genocide; (e) Complicity in genocide'.
29. Ambos, 'Article 25', 766.
30. Kai Ambos, 'General Principles of Criminal Law in the Rome Statute', *Criminal Law Forum*, vol. 10 (1999), 11.

31. Jackson, *Complicity in International Law*, 34–35.
32. AP I, art. 85 (4)(b).
33. AP I, art. 86.
34. Jackson, *Complicity in International Law*, 40.
35. Application of the Convention on the Prevention and Punishment of the Crime of Genocide (*Bosnia and Herzegovina* v. *Serbia and Montenegro*), Judgment, ICJ Reports 2007, p. 43, para. 438.
36. As seen in Chapter 4 with the concept of State-like entity.
37. UN General Assembly, Res 56/83 of 12 December 2001, corrected by document A/56/49 (Vol. I) Corr.4; International Law Commission, 'Responsibility of States for Internationally Wrongful Acts', 2001, vol. II (Part Two). It is interesting that Lebanon Article 4's includes 'any other functions' as State representative. In its comments, Lebanon argued that 'any other functions' are 'incompatible with the principle of the sovereignty of States with regard to the identification of the person or body that may be assigned to undertake an act'. UN, General Assembly, A/68/69 (2013), 27 March 2013, Responsibility of States for internationally wrongful acts, Comments and information received from Governments, Report of the Secretary-General.
38. International Law Commission, 'Draft on Responsibility of States for Internationally Wrongful Acts, with commentaries', 2001, vol. II (Part Two, as corrected).
39. *Nicaragua* v. *United States of America*, Merits, Judgment, ICJ. Reports, 27 June 1986, para. 115.
40. *Nicaragua* v. *United States of America*, para. 15. It is worth mentioning that, so as to engage State responsibility, the State must have knowledge of the actions of non-State actors. In Case Concerning United States Diplomatic and Consular Staff in Tehran *(US v Iran)*, the ICJ established that the Iranian authorities '(a) were fully aware of their obligations under the conventions in force to take appropriate steps to protect the premises of the United States Embassy and its diplomatic and consular staff from any attack and from any infringement of their inviolability, and to ensure the security of such other persons as might be present on the said premises ; (b) were fully aware, as a result of the appeals for help made by the United States Embassy, of the urgent need for action on their part ; (c) had the means at their disposal to perform their obligations ; (d) completely failed to comply with these obligations'. Judgment, ICJ Reports 1980, p. 3, 24 May 1980.
41. *Prosecutor* v. *Tadic*, Case No. IT-94-1-A, ICTY Appeals Chamber, 15 July 1999, para. 137; Tams, 'The Use of Force, 367.
42. It is worth mentioning that there has been a call to walk away from the effective control test as required in *Nicaragua* v. *United States of America*, especially that State practice suggests as much. In fact, many States are quick to claim self-defence when violence emanates from a non-State actor on the territory of another State, thus immediately attributing the act of violence to the host State and triggering the right to self-defence. Tams, 'The Use of Force', 384.

43. Majid Rafizadeh, 'In First, Hezbollah Confirms All Financial Support Comes from Iran', *Al-Arabiya News*, 25 June 2016.
44. Yaroslav Shiryaev, 'The Right of Armed Self-Defense in International Law and Self-Defense Arguments Used in the Second Lebanon War', *Acta Societatis Martensis*, vol. 3 (2007/8), 93.
45. *Nicaragua* v. *United States of America*, para. 195; Jackson, *Complicity in International Law*, 180.
46. For a detailed analysis of the crime of aggression in international law and its historical evolution, see Antonio Cassese, 'On Some Problematic Aspects of the Crime of Aggression', *Leiden Journal of International Law*, vol. 20, no. 4 (2007): 841–49; Goran Bandov and Dorotea Ogorec, 'Crime of Aggression in International Law and International Relations', *Journal of Liberty and International Affairs*, vol. 6, no. 1 (2020): 48–69.
47. *Democratic Republic of the Congo* v. *Uganda*, para. 147; Jackson, *Complicity in International Law*, 181.
48. UN Charter, art. 51.
49. Jackson, *Complicity in International Law*, 182.
50. UN Security Council, S/Res/1368 (2001), 12 September 2001; Jackson, *Complicity in International Law*, 184.
51. *Nicaragua* v. *United States of America*, para. 191.
52. *Oil Platforms* (*Islamic Republic of Iran* v. *United States of America*), Judgment, ICJ Reports 6 November 2003, para. 64.
53. Jackson, *Complicity in International Law*, 188.
54. UN General Assembly, Res 56/83 of 12 December 2001, corrected by document A/56/49 (Vol. I) Corr. 4; International Law Commission. 'Responsibility of States for Internationally Wrongful Acts', 2001, vol. II (Part Two).
55. *Bosnia and Herzegovina* v. *Serbia and Montenegro*, para. 418.
56. International Law Commission, 'Report on the Work of Its Fifty-Third Session' (23 April–1 June and 2 July–10 August 2001), General Assembly, Official Records, Fifty-Fifth Session, Supplement No. 10 (1/56/10), https://casebook.icrc.org/case-study/international-law-commission-articles-state-responsibility
57. Antonio Cassese, 'On the Use of Criminal Law Notions in Determining State Responsibility for Genocide', *Journal of International Criminal Justice*, vol. 5, no. 4 (2007), 877.
58. Jackson, *Complicity in International Law*, 206.
59. Ibid., 208.
60. Ibid., 209.
61. The Declaration on Principles of International Law Concerning Friendly Relations and Co-Operation among States in Accordance with the Charter of the United Nations, GA, Res 2625 (XXV), 1970.
62. UN General Assembly, Res 40/61, 9 December 1985, 302.
63. *Bosnia and Herzegovina* v. *Serbia and Montenegro*, para. 432.
64. Jackson, *Complicity in International Law*, 210.
65. Akhbar Khan and Han Zhaoying, 'Iran-Hezbollah Alliance Reconsidered: What Contributes to the Survival of State-Proxy Alliance', *Journal of Asian Security and International Affairs*, vol. 7, no. 1 (2020), 109.

66. UN Charter, art. 2.
67. UN General Assembly, Res of 3314 (XXIX) of 14 December 1974.
68. **Elizabeth Wilmshurst**, 'Definition of Aggression: General Assembly Resolution 3314 (XXIX)', *Audiovisual Library of International Law*, 14 December 1974.
69. UN General Assembly, Res of 3314 (XXIX) of 14 December 1974.
70. Swiss Info, 'Swiss Stick to Policies of the Gulf War', 21 February 2003.
71. Sarah El-Deeb, 'Lebanon Files Urgent Complaint to UN against Israel Flights', *AP*, 12 January 2021; Middle East Monitor, 'Lebanon Files Complaint with UN over Israel's Use of Its Airspace to Strike Syria', 20 August 2021.
72. Maxim Moskalkov, 'Belarus Finds Itself as Accomplice in Russia's War against Ukraine', *Voice of America*, 1 September 2022.
73. Jackson, *Complicity in International Law*, 141.
74. UN Security Council, S/RES/1929 (2010), 9 June 2010.
75. UN Security Council, S/RES/2231 (2015), 20 July 2015.
76. It is beyond the scope of this chapter to examine the sanctions on Iran. For more detail, see Enrico Carisch and Loraine Rickard-Martin, *United Nations Sanctions on Iran and North Korea: An Implementation Manual* (New York: International Peace Institute, 2014); Mazahir Bootwala, 'The Iran Problem: An Evaluation of US Sanctions and Global Reactions', *Georgetown Journal of International Affairs*, vol. 21 (2020): 136–41.
77. René Värk, 'State Responsibility for Private Armed Groups in the Context of Terrorism', *Juridica International*, vol. 11 (2006), 192.
78. Jean d'Aspremont, André Nollkaemper, Ilias Plakokefalos and Cedric Ryngaert, 'Sharing Responsibility between Non-State Actors and States in International Law: Introduction', *Netherlands International Law Review*, vol. 62 (2015), 50.

Chapter 9

1. Richard MacKenzie-Gray Scott, *State Responsibility for Non-State Actors: Past, Present and Prospects for the Future* (Oxford: Bloomsbury, 2022), 31.

Works Cited

Books and Book Chapters

Ajami, Fouad. *The Vanished Imam: Musa al-Sadr and the Shia of Lebanon*. 1st edition. Ithaca: Cornell University Press, 1986.

Aksenova, Marina. 'The Role of International Criminal Tribunals in Shaping the Historical Accounts of Genocide'. In *Law and Memory: Towards Legal Governance of History*. Edited by Uladzislau Belavusau and Aleksandra Gliszczyńska-Grabias, 48–69. Cambridge: Cambridge University Press, 2017.

Alagha, Joseph. *Hezbollah's Documents: From the 1985 Open Letter to the 2009 Manifesto*. Amsterdam: Pallas Publication; Amsterdam University Press, 2011.

Al-Dawoody, Ahmad. *The Islamic Law of War: Justifications and Regulations*. New York: Palgrave Macmillan, 2011.

Alston, Philip. 'The "Not-a-Cat" Syndrome: Can the International Human Rights Regime Accommodate Non-State Actors?' In *Non-State Actors and Human Rights*. Edited by Philip Alston, 3–37. Oxford: Oxford University Press, 2005.

Ambos, Kai. 'Article 25: Individual Criminal Responsibility'. In *Commentary on the Rome Statute of the International Criminal Court, Observers' Notes, Article by Article*. Edited by Otto Triffterer, 743–70. 2nd edition. München: Beck/Hart, 2008.

Anderson, Benedict. *Imagined Communities: Reflections on the Origin and Spread of Nationalism*. Revised edition. London: Verso, 2006.

Arjona, Ana, Nelson Kasfir and Zachariah Mampilly (eds). *Rebel Governance in Civil War*. New York: Cambridge University Press, 2015.

Ashplant, T. G., Graham Dawson and Michael Roper. 'The Politics of War Memory and Commemoration'. In *The Politics of War Memory and Commemoration*. Edited by T. G. Ashplant, Graham Dawson and Michael Roper, 1–73. London: Routledge, 2000.

Arcidiacono, Bruno. 'Contra Pluralitatem Principatuum: Trois critiques du système dit Westphalien: Formulées avant la Paix de Westphalie'. In *The*

Roots of International Law/Les Fondements du Droit International. Edited Pierre-Marie Dupuy and Vincent Chetail, 465–85. Leiden: Brill, 2014.

Balakrishnan, Rajagopal. *International Law from Below: Development, Social Movements and Third World Resistance.* Cambridge: Cambridge University Press, 2003.

Bassiouni, Mahmoud Cherif. '"Terrorism": Reflections on Legitimacy and Policy Considerations'. In *Values and Violence: Intangible Aspects of Terrorism.* Edited by Ibrahim Karawan, Wayne McCormack and Stephen Eugene Reynolds, 233–56. Dordrecht: Springer, 2008.

—. 'The Subjects of International Criminal Law: Ratione Personae'. In *International Criminal Law*, vol. 1, 41–70. Leiden: Brill, 2013.

Bederman, David, and Chimene Keitner. *International Law Frameworks (Concepts and Insights).* 4th edition. St Paul, MN: Foundation Press, 2016.

Belavusau, Uladzislau, and Aleksandra Gliszczyńska-Grabias. 'Memory Laws: Mapping a New Subject in Comparative Law and Transitional Justice'. In *Law and Memory: Towards Legal Governance of History.* Edited by Uladzislau Belavusau and Aleksandra Gliszczyńska-Grabias, 1–26. Cambridge: Cambridge University Press, 2017.

Bellal, Annyssa. 'What Are "Armed Non-State Actors"? A Legal and Semantic Approach'. In *International Humanitarian Law and Non-State Actors.* Edited by Ezequiel Heffes, Marcos D. Kotlik and Manuel J. Ventura, 21–46. The Hague: T. M. C. Asser Press, 2020.

Berdine, Michael. *Redrawing the Middle East: Sir Mark Sykes, Imperialism and the Sykes-Picot Agreement.* London: Bloomsbury, 2018.

Berger, Maurits. 'Islamic Views on International Law'. In *Culture and International Law (From Peace to Justice Series).* Edited by Paul Meerts, 105–17. The Hague: Hague Academy Press, 2008.

Blacksley, Christopher. *Terror and Anti-Terrorism: A Normative and Practical Assessment.* Leiden: Brill, 2006.

Bray, Gerald (ed.). 'The Declaration of Breda, 1660'. In *Documents of the English Reformation.* Cambridge: The Lutterworth Press; James Clarke & Co Ltd, 1994.

Byron, Leo C. *From Tourist to Hostage: A Traveler's Tale of Terrorism.* Hatfield: Penn Valley Printing, 1988.

Carty, Anthony. *The Decay of International Law? A Reappraisal of the Limits of Legal Imagination in International Affairs.* Manchester: Manchester University Press, 1986.

Cassese, Antonio. 'Resistance Movements'. In *Encyclopaedia of Public International Law, vol. 4.* Edited by Rudolf Bernhardt and Peter Macalister-Smith, 188–90. Amsterdam: North Holland, 1982.

Cassese, Antonio, and Paola Gaeta. *Cassese's International Criminal Law.* Oxford: Oxford University Press, 2013.

Clapham, Andrew. *Human Rights Obligations of Non-State Actors.* Oxford: Oxford University Press, 2006.

Close, Josepha. *Amnesty, Serious Crimes and International Law: Global Perspectives in Theory and Practice*. Abingdon: Routledge, 2019.

Comaty, Lyna. *Post-Conflict Transition in Lebanon: The Disappeared of the Civil War*. New York: Routledge, 2021.

Crawford, Emily. *The Treatment of Combatants and Insurgents under the Law of Armed Conflict*. Oxford: Oxford University Press, 2010.

Crawford, Emily, and Alison Pert. *International Humanitarian Law*. 2nd edition. Cambridge: Cambridge University Press, 2020.

—. 'Historical Development of International Humanitarian Law'. In *International Humanitarian Law*, 2nd edition, 4–29. Cambridge: Cambridge University Press, 2020.

Crawford, James R. *The Creation of States in International Law*. 2nd edition. Oxford: Oxford University Press, 2007.

—. 'Sovereignty as a Legal Value'. In *The Cambridge Companion to International Law*. Edited by James Crawford and Martti Koskenniemi, 117–34. Cambridge: Cambridge University Press, 2012.

Daher, Aurélie. *Hezbollah: Mobilization and Power*. Translated by H. W. Randolph. Oxford: Oxford University Press, 2019.

d'Aspremont, Jean. 'Non-State Actors from the Perspective of Legal Positivism'. In *Participants in the International Legal System: Multiple Perspectives on Non-State Actors in International Law*. Edited by Jean d'Aspremont, 23–40. Abingdon: Taylor & Francis, 2011.

David, Eric. 'Brèves remarques sur les origines du droit international'. In *The Roots of International Law/Les Fondements du Droit International*. Edited by Pierre-Marie Dupuy and Vincent Chetail, 437–47. Leiden: Brill, 2014.

de Beer, Aniel Caro. *Peremptory Norms of General International Law (Jus Cogens) and the Prohibition of Terrorism*. Leiden: Brill, 2019.

Deeb, Marius. *Syria, Iran, and Hezbollah: The Unholy Alliance and Its War on Lebanon*. Palo Alto: Hoover Institution Press, 2013.

de Larramendi, Miguel. 'Mauritania's Challenges'. In *Political Regimes in the Arab World: Society and the Exercise of Power*. 1st edition. Edited by Ferran Izquierdo Brichs, 122–25. Abingdon: Routledge, 2013.

del Sarto, Raffael A. *Fragmented Borders, Interdependence and External Relations: The Israel-Palestine-European Union Triangle*. London: Palgrave Macmillan, 2015.

du Plessis, Anton. 'A Snapshot of International Criminal Justice Cooperation against Terrorism Since 9/11'. In *Counter-Terrorism Strategies in a Fragmented International Legal Order: Meeting the Challenges*. Edited by Larissa van den Herik and Nico Schrijver, 29–67. Cambridge: Cambridge University Press, 2013.

Dupuy, Pierre-Marie. 'Quelques réflexions sur les origines historiques de l'ordre juridique international'. In *The Roots of International Law/Les Fondements du Droit International*. Edited by Pierre-Marie Dupuy and Vincent Chetail, 389–403. Leiden: Brill, 2014.

El-Barghouti, Tamim. *The Umma and the Dawla: The Nation-State and the Arab Middle East*. London: Pluto Press, 2008.

El-Harak, Mazhar. 'The Legal Framework of Associations in Lebanon'. In *International Governance for NGOs in Lebanon*, 13–28. Beirut: Ministry of Social Affairs, 2004.

Eser, Albin. 'Individual Criminal Responsibility: Mental Elements: Mistake of Facts and Mistake of Law'. In *The Rome Statute of the International Criminal Court: A Commentary, Vol. 1*. Edited by Antonio Cassese, Paola Gaeta and John Jones, 767–822. Oxford: Oxford University Press, 2002.

Ezrow, Natasha. *Global Politics and Violent Non-State Actors*. Los Angeles: Sage, 2017.

Farha, Mark. 'From Anti-Imperial Dissent to National Consent: The First World War and the Formation of a Trans-Sectarian National Consciousness in Lebanon'. In *The First World War and Its Aftermath: The Shaping of the Middle East*. Edited by T. G. Fraser, 91–110. London: Gingko Library, 2015.

Feltman, Jeffrey. 'Hezbollah: Revolutionary Iran's Most Successful Export'. In *The Ripple Effect of Iran's Revolution across the Middle East*. Edited by Suzanne Maloney, 143–55. Washington DC: Brookings Institution Press, 2020.

Fisk, Robert. *Pity the Nation: Lebanon at War*. Oxford: Oxford University Press, 2001.

Fortin, Katharine, and Ezequiel Heffes. 'Introduction: An Exploration of the Shadowland of Armed Groups and International Law'. In *Armed Groups and International Law: In the Shadowland of Legality and Illegality*. Edited by Katharine Fortin and Ezequiel Heffes, 1–14. Cheltenham: Edward Elgar, 2023.

Frank, Benis M. *US Marines in Lebanon, 1982–1984*. Washington DC: History and Museum Division Headquarters, US Marine Corps, 1987.

French, Duncan. 'Introduction'. In *Statehood and Self-Determination: Reconciling Tradition and Modernity in International* Law. Edited by Duncan French, 1–20. Cambridge: Cambridge University Press, 2013.

Frisch, Andrea. 'Learning to Forget'. In *Forgetting Differences: Tragedy, Historiography, and the French Wars of Religion*, 1–25. Edinburgh: Edinburgh University Press, 2015.

Garraway, Charles. 'Armed Conflict and Terrorist Organisations'. In *Counter-Terrorism Strategies in a Fragmented International Legal Order: Meeting the Challenges*. Edited by Larissa van den Herik and Nico Schrijver, 425–53. Cambridge: Cambridge University Press, 2013.

Geraghty, Timothy J. (Ret. Col. USMC). 'Suicide Bombings and Aftermath'. In *Peacekeepers at War: Beirut 1983: The Marine Commander Tells His Story*, 91–123. Washington DC: Potomac Books; an imprint of the University of Nebraska Press, 2009.

Grant, Tom. 'How to Recognise a State (and Not): Some Practical Considerations'. In *Sovereignty, Statehood and State Responsibility: Essays in Honor of James Crawford*. Edited by Christine Chinkin and Freya Baetens, 192–208. Cambridge: Cambridge University Press, 2015.

Haggenmacher, Peter. *Grotius et la doctrine de la guerre juste*. Paris: Presses Universitaires de France, 1983.

Halbwachs, Maurice. *On Collective Memory*. Edited, translated and with an introduction by Lewis A. Coser. Chicago: The University of Chicago Press, 1992.

Hamzeh, Ahmad. *In the Path of Hizbullah*. Syracuse: Syracuse University Press, 2004.

Henckaerts, Jean-Marie, and Louise Doswald-Beck (eds). *Customary International Humanitarian Law, Vol. I: Rules*. Cambridge: Cambridge University Press, 2005.

Hokayem, Antoine. *La Genèse de la Constitution Libanaise de 1926: Le contexte du Mandat Français, les projets préliminaires, les auteurs, le texte final. Beyrouth: Éditions Universitaires du Liban, 1996.*

Hourani, Albert. *Syria and Lebanon: A Political Essay*. London: Oxford University Press, 1946.

Hunt, Nigel. *Memory, War and Trauma*. Cambridge: Cambridge University Press, 2010.

Jaber, Hala. *Hezbollah: Born with a Vengeance*. New York: Columbia University Press, 1997.

Jackson, Miles. *Complicity in International Law*. Oxford: Oxford University Press, 2015.

Jeffery, Renée. *Amnesties, Accountability, and Human Rights*. Philadelphia: University of Pennsylvania Press, 2014.

Jurdi, Nidal Nabil. 'The Crime of Terrorism in Lebanon and International Law'. In *The Special Tribunal for Lebanon: Law and Practice*. Edited by Amal Alamuddin, 73–87. Oxford: Oxford University Press, 2014.

Kammerhofer, Jörg. 'Non-State Actors from the Perspective of the Pure Theory of Law'. In *Participants in the International Legal System: Multiple Perspectives on Non-State Actors in International Law*. Edited by Jean d'Aspremont, 54–63. Abingdon: Taylor & Francis, 2011.

Kelsen, Hans. *Pure Theory of Law*. Berkley: University of California Press, 1967.

Kesselring, Rita. *Bodies of Truth: Law, Memory, and Emancipation in Post-Apartheid South Africa*. Palo Alto: Stanford University Press, 2016.

Kipnis, Yigal. *The Golan Heights: Political History, Settlement and Geography since 1949*. 1st edition. Abingdon: Routledge, 2013.

Kleczkowska, Agata. 'Armed Non-State Actors and Customary International Law'. In *Non-State Actors and International Obligations: Creation, Evolution and Enforcement*. Edited by James Summers and Alex Gough, 60–85. Leiden: Brill, 2018.

Kleinlein, Thomas. 'Non-State Actors from an International Constitutionalist Perspective'. In *Participants in the International Legal System: Multiple Perspectives on Non-State Actors in International Law*. Edited by Jean d'Aspremont, 41–53. Abingdon: Taylor & Francis, 2011.

McPhee, Peter. *Robespierre: A Revolutionary Life.* New Haven: Yale University Press, 2012.

Knop, Karen. 'Statehood: Territory, People, Government'. In *The Cambridge Companion to International Law.* Edited by James Crawford and Martti Koskenniemi, 95–117. Cambridge: Cambridge University Press, 2012.

Kolb, Robert. 'Considérations sur le droit international public des anciennes cultures extra-Européennes'. In *The Roots of International Law/ Les Fondements du Droit International.* Edited by Pierre-Marie Dupuy and Vincent Chetail, 673–709. Leiden: Brill, 2014.

Koposov, Nikolay. *Memory Laws, Memory Wars: The Politics of the Past in Europe and Russia.* Cambridge: Cambridge University Press, 2017.

Laron, Guy. *Six Day War: The Breaking of the Middle East.* New Haven: Yale University Press, 2017.

Loja, Melissa. *International Agreements between Non-State Actors as a Source of International Law.* Oxford: Hart, 2022.

Lowe, Vaughan. *International Law: A Very Short Introduction.* Oxford: Oxford University Press, 2015.

Maboudi, Tofigh. *The 'Fall' of the Arab Spring: Democracy's Challenges and Efforts to Reconstitute the Middle East.* Cambridge: Cambridge University Press, 2022.

McDowell, Sara, and Màire Braniff. *Commemoration as Conflict: Space, Memory and Identity in Peace Processes.* London: Palgrave Macmillan, 2014.

MacKenzie-Gray Scott, Richard. *State Responsibility for Non-State Actors: Past, Present and Prospects for the Future.* Oxford: Bloomsbury, 2022.

Mahmoudi, Said. 'The Second Lebanon War: Reflections on the 2006 Israeli Military Operations against Hezbollah'. In *Law at War: The Law as It Was and the Laws as It Should Be.* Edited by O. Engdahl and P. Wrange, 187–202. Leiden: Brill, 2008.

Makary, Marc. *The Lebanese Constitution of May 23rd, 1926, and the Constitutional Laws of the 3rd French Republic: A Comparative Approach.* Unpubl. Thesis, Library of the Saint Joseph University School of Law and Political Sciences, Beirut, 2006.

Malanczuk, Peter. 'Multinational Enterprises and Treaty Making'. In *Multilateral Treaty-Making: The Current Status of Challenges to and Reforms Needed in the International Legislative Process.* Edited by Vera Gowlland-Debbas, Hassiba Hadj-Sahraoui and Nobuo Hayashi, 45–72. Leiden: Brill, 2000.

Martin, Ian. 'Justice and Reconciliation: Responsibilities and Dilemmas of Peacemakers and Peacebuilders'. In *The Legacy of Abuses: Confronting the Past, Facing the Future*, edited by Alice H. Hankin, 81–91. Washington DC: The Aspen Institute, 2002.

Merari, Ariel. 'The Readiness to Kill and Die: Suicidal Terrorism in the Middle East'. In *Origins of Terrorism.* Edited by Walter Reich, 192–207. New York: Cambridge University Press, 1990.

Miaille, Michel. *Une introduction critique au droit.* Paris: F. Maspero, 1976.

Nicholson, Rowan. *Statehood and the State-Like in International Law.* Oxford: Oxford University Press, 2019.

Noortmann, Math. 'Towards an Interdisciplinary Approach to Non-State Participation in the Formation of Global Law and Order'. In *Participants in the International Legal System: Multiple Perspectives on Non-State Actors in International Law.* Edited by Jean d'Aspremont, 76–81. Abingdon: Taylor & Francis, 2011.

Norton, Augustus R. *Hezbollah: A Short History.* Princeton: Princeton University Press, 2007.

—. *Amal and the Shia: Struggle for the Soul of Lebanon.* Austin: University of Texas Press, 1987.

Nowak, Manfred, and Elizabeth McArthur. *The United Nations Convention against Torture: A Commentary.* Oxford: Oxford University Press, 2008.

O'Malley, Alanna. *The Diplomacy of Decolonisation: America, Britain and the United Nations during the Congo Crisis, 1960–1964.* 1st edition. Manchester: Manchester University Press, 2018.

Passemiers, Lazlo. *Decolonisation and Regional Geopolitics: South Africa and the 'Congo Crisis', 1960–1965.* 1st edition. Abingdon: Routledge, 2019.

Pinfari, Marco. *Terrorists as Monsters: The Unmanageable Other from the French Revolution to the Islamic State.* New York: Oxford University Press, 2019.

Provost, René. *Rebel Courts: The Administration of Justice by Armed Insurgents.* Oxford: Oxford University Press, 2021.

Quigley, John B. *The Case for Palestine: An International Law Perspective.* 2nd edition. Durham, NC: Duke University Press, 2005.

Rabinovich, Itamar. 'Postscript: The Lebanese Crisis in 1983'. In *The War for Lebanon, 1970–1983*, 174–82. Ithaca: Cornell University Press, 1984.

Rebeiz, Mireille. *Gendering Civil War: Francophone Women's Writing in Lebanon.* Edinburgh: Edinburgh University Press, 2022.

Ronen, Yaël. 'Entities that can be states but do not claim to be'. In *Statehood and Self-Determination: Reconciling Tradition and Modernity in International Law.* Edited by Duncan French, 23–59. Cambridge: Cambridge University Press, 2013.

Rosand, Eric. 'Resolution 1373 and the CTC: The Security Council's Capacity Building'. In *International Cooperation in Counter-Terrorism: The United Nations and Regional Organisations in the Fight Against Terrorism.* Edited by Giuseppe Nesi, 81–88. 1st edition. Aldershot: Ashgate, 2006.

Rustum Shehadeh, Lamia. *Women and War in Lebanon.* Gainesville: University Press of Florida, 1999.

Seibert-Fohr, Anja. *Prosecuting Serious Human Rights Violations.* Oxford: Oxford University Press, 2009.

Sloyan, Patrick J. 'Burying the Marines'. In *When Reagan Sent in the Marines: The Invasion of Lebanon*, 135–51. New York: Thomas Dunne Books, 2019.

Smith, Keith John Michael. *A Modern Treatise on the Law of Criminal Complicity.* Oxford: Clarendon Press, 1991.

Tal, David. 'The 1956 Sinai War: A Watershed in the History of the Arab-Israeli Conflict'. In *Reassessing Suez 1956: New Perspectives on the Crisis and its Aftermath*. Edited by Simon C. Smith, 132–45. London: Routledge, 2016.

United States Government. *Understanding States of Resistance: A Pocket Guide*. Fort Bragg: United States Army Special Operations Command, 2019.

Ukco, David H. *The Insurgent's Dilemma: A Struggle to Prevail*. Oxford: Oxford University Press, 2022.

van den Herik, Larissa, and Nico Schrijver. 'The Fragmented International Legal Response to Terrorism'. In *Counter-Terrorism Strategies in a Fragmented International Legal Order: Meeting the Challenges*. Edited by Larissa van den Herik and Nico Schrijver, 1–26. Cambridge: Cambridge University Press, 2013.

Vidmar, Jure. *Democratic Statehood in International Law: The Emergence of New States in Post-Cold War Practice*. Portland: Bloomsbury, 2013.

—. 'Unilateral Declarations of Independence in International Law'. In *Statehood and Self-Determination: Reconciling Tradition and Modernity in International Law*. Edited by Duncan French, 60–78. Cambridge, Cambridge University Press, 2013.

Volk, Lucia. *Memorials and Martyrs in Modern Lebanon*. Bloomington: Indiana University Press, 2010.

von Lampe, Klaus. *Organized Crime: Analyzing Illegal Activities, Criminal Structures, and Extra-Legal Governance*. Los Angeles: Sage, 2015.

Weinstein, Jeremy M. *Inside Rebellion: The Politics of Insurgent Violent*. Cambridge: Cambridge University Press, 2006.

Whaley, Joachim. *Germany and the Holy Roman Empire, Vol. 1: Maximilian I to the Peace of Westphalia, 1493–1648*. Oxford : Oxford University Press, 2011.

Wyler, Eric. *Théorie et pratique de la reconnaissance d'état: Une approche épistémologique du droit international*. Bruxelles: Éditions Bruylant, 2013.

Wynter, Kevin. *Critical Race Theory and Jordan Peele's* Get Out. New York: Bloomsbury Academic, 2022.

Yassine-Hamdan, Nahla, and Frederic Pearson. *Arab Approaches to Conflict Resolution: Mediation, Negotiation and Settlement of Political Disputes*. 1st edition. Oxfordshire: Routledge, 2017.

Zahler, Kathy A. 'The Assad Family Dictatorship'. In *The Assads' Syria*, 48–87. 2nd edition. Minneapolis: Twenty-First Century Books, 2010.

Cases and Advisory Opinions

*Permanent Court of International Justice *** no longer existing*

Austro-German Customs Union, PCIJ ser. A/B no. 41 (1932), 57–58.

International Court of Justice

Advisory Opinion, Reparation for Injuries Suffered in the Service of the United Nations, 11 April 1949, ICJ Reports 1949, 174.

Advisory Opinion on Interpretation of the Agreement of 25 March 1951 between the WHO and Egypt, 28 May 1980, ICJ Reports 1980, 73.

Reparations for Injuries Suffered in the Service of the United Nations, Advisory Opinion, 11 April 1949, ICJ Reports 174.

Advisory Opinion on Reservations to the Convention on the Prevention and Punishment of the Crime of Genocide, 28 May 1951, ICJ Reports 15.

Case Concerning United States Diplomatic and Consular Staff in Tehran *(US v Iran)*, Judgment, ICJ Reports 1980, 3, 24 May 1980.

Nicaragua v. *United States of America*, Merits, Judgment, ICJ Reports, 27 June 1986.

Oil Platforms (Islamic Republic of Iran v. *United States of America*), Judgment, ICJ Reports, 6 November 2003.

Legal Consequences of the Construction of a Wall in the Occupied Palestinian Territory, Advisory Opinion 2004.

Armed Activities on the Territory of the Congo (*Democratic Republic of the Congo* v. *Uganda*), Judgment, ICJ Reports 2005, 168.

Armed Activities on the Territory of the Congo (New Application 2002) (*Democratic Republic of the Congo* v. *Rwanda*), Jurisdiction and Admissibility, Judgment, ICJ Reports 2006, 6.

Application of the Convention on the Prevention and Punishment of the Crime of Genocide (*Bosnia and Herzegovina* v. *Serbia and Montenegro*), Judgment, ICJ Reports 2007, 43.

Accordance with International Law of the Unilateral Declaration of Independence in Respect of Kosovo, Advisory Opinion, 22 July 2010, ICJ Reports 403, 470.

International Criminal Tribunal for the Former Yugoslavia

Prosecutor v. *Tadic*, Case No. IT-94-1-AR72, Decision on the Defence Motion on Jurisdiction in the Trial Chamber of the International Tribunal, 127 (2 October 1995) (Appeal on Jurisdiction).

Prosecutor v. *Tadic*, Case No. IT-94-1-T, Trial Chamber, 7 May 1997.

Prosecutor v. *Tadic*, Case No. IT-94-1-A, ICTY Appeals Chamber, 15 July 1999.

Prosecutor v. *Anto Furundzija*, ICTY, 10 December 1998.

Prosecutor v. *Fatmir Limaj*, Judgment, IT-03- 66-T, 30 November 2005.

International Criminal Tribunal for Rwanda

Prosecutor v. *Akayesu*, Case No. ICTR-96-4-T, Judgment, Trial Chamber, 2 September 1998.

The Special Tribunal for Lebanon

Order on Preliminary Questions Addressed to the Judges of the Appeals Chamber Pursuant to Rule 68, paragraph (G), of the Rules of Procedure and Evidence (The Pre-Trial Judge) (STL-11-01/I), 21 January 2011.
Interlocutory Decision on the Applicable Law: Terrorism, Conspiracy, Homicide, Perpetration, Cumulative Charging (Appeals Chamber) (STL-11-01/I), 16 February 2011.
The Prosecutor vs. Salim Jamil Ayyash, STL-11-01/S/TC, The Trial Chamber, 11 December 2020.
The Prosecutor v. *Hassan Habib Merhi, Hussein Hassan Oneissi*, STL-11-01/A-2/AC, The Appeals Chamber, 10 March 2022.
The Prosecutor v. *Hassan Habib Merhi, Hussein Hassan Oneissi*, STL-11-01/S-2/AC, The Appeals Chamber, Sentencing Judgment, 16 June 2022.

Domestic Legal Documents (Court Cases, Legislations, Public Notices)

Australia

The Commonwealth of Australia, Criminal Code Act 1995, Part 5.3 – Terrorism.
Australian Government, 'Hizballah', in *Australian National Security*, 10 December 2021.

Canada

Canada, Criminal Code 1985, Part II.1, Terrorism.
Regulations Amending the Regulations Establishing a List of Entities, Criminal Code, SOR/2002-454 10 December 2002, Canada Gazette, Part II, vol. 136, no. 17, 13 December 2002.
Government of Canada, 'Hizballah', in *Currently Listed Entities*, 21 November 2018.

Germany

Deutsche Continental Gas-Gesellschaft v. *Polish State*, Germano-Polish Mixed Arbitral Tribunal, 1 August 1929, *Annual Digest of Public International Law Cases: Being a Selection from the Decisions of International and National Courts and Tribunals Given during the Years 1929 and 1930*. Edited by H. Lauterpacht. Cambridge: Grotius, 1981.

France

Loi du 1er Juillet 1901 relative au contrat d'association.
The Constitution of the French Fifth Republic of 4 October 1958.

La République Française, Code Pénal, Titre II, Articles 421-1 to 422-7.
Loi n. 2001-70 du 29 Janvier 2001 relative à la reconnaissance du génocide arménien de 1915.
Loi n. 2005-158 du 23 février 2005 portant reconnaissance de la Nation et contribution nationale en faveur des Français rapatriés.
Loi n. 2001-434 du 21 mai 2011 tendant à la reconnaissance de la traite et de l'esclavage en tant que crime contre l'humanité.
Conseil Constitutionnel, Décision no. 2012-647 DC of 28 February 2012.

Lebanon

Law of Associations, 1909.
The Lebanese Constitution, 1926.
The Lebanese Republic, Criminal Code.
Decision of French Colonial Powers No. 60, Official Gazette No. 3273, 29 April 1936.
Law of Finances and Credits, 1963.
The Cairo Agreement, 2 November 1969, *United Nations Relief and Works Agency for Palestine Refugees in the Near East.*
Lebanese Municipality Law, No. 118 of 30/6/1977 with amendments.
The Taif Agreement, Taif, October 1989.
Law No. 84, 26/08/1991, General Amnesty Law of 1991.
Lebanese Government, Decree n. 15215, 27 September 2005.
Ziade, Caroline. 'Identical Letters dated 13 July 2006 from the Chargé d'affaires a.i. of the Permanent Mission of Lebanon to the United Nations addressed to the Secretary-General and the President of the Security Council'. *United Nations Digital Library*, 13 July 2006.
The Lebanese Republic, Office of the Prime Minister. Ministerial Statement of 9 November 2009.

Singapore

Civil Aeronautics Administration v. *Singapore Airlines*, 14 January 2004. *International Law Reports*, vol. 133 (2008): 371–88.

The United Kingdom

Balfour Declaration, 2 November 1917. *Jewish Virtual Library. A Project of AICE.*
The United Kingdom, Terrorism Act 2000.
The United Kingdom Government. 'Hizballah'. In *Policy Paper: Proscribed Terrorist Groups or Organisations*, 26 November 2021.
The United Kingdom Government, Treasury. 'Suspected Hizballah Financier Sanctioned Under Counter-Terrorism Regulations', 18 April 2023.

United States of America

The US Declaration of Independence, Philadelphia, 1776.
The US Constitution, Philadelphia, 1787.
H. R. No. 390 (1996) 104th Cong., 2d Session. Concerning the Prohibition on the Use of United States Passports for Travel to Lebanon (1996) (enacted).
The US Department of State, Bureau of Counterterrorism, 'Foreign Terrorist Organisations – Hizballah,' 8 October 1997.
Public Law 107-56, H. R.3162 – The Uniting and Strengthening America by Providing Appropriate Tools Required to Intercept and Obstruct Terrorism (USA Patriot Act) of 2001, 107th Congress (2001), 26 October 2001.
18 U. S. C. § 2331 (2009).
H. R. No. 112-35 (2011), *Hezbollah in Latin America – Implications for US Homeland Security, before the Subcommittee on Counterterrorism and Intelligence of the Committee of Homeland Security* (statements by Patrick Meehan, a Representative in Congress from the State of Pennsylvania and Jackie Speier, a Representative in Congress from the State of California).
Executive Order 13582 – Blocking Property of the Government of Syria and Prohibiting Certain Transactions with Respect to Syria. *The White House. Office of the Press Secretary*, 18 August 2011.
Public Law 114-102, H. R. 2297 – Hizballah International Financing Prevention Act of 2015, 114th Congress (2015–16), 18 December 2015.
Public Law 115-272, S.1595 – Hizballah International Financing Prevention Amendments Act of 2018, 115th Congress (2017–18), 25 October 2018.
Indictment, *United States of America* v. *Alexei Saab* (19 Cir, SDNY, 1/19/19).
US Department of the Treasury, Office of Foreign Assets Control. Notice of OFAC Sanctions Actions. Federal Register, vol. 84, no. 245, 20 December 2019.
Bartlett, et al. v. *Société Générale de Banque au Liban SAL, et al.*, EDNY, 13 December 2020.
H. R. No. 3235 (2021) 117th Cong. To Restrict Executive Agencies from Acting in Contravention of Executive Order 13950.
Department of Justice, US Attorney's Office, Southern District of New York. 'New Jersey Man Convicted of Receiving Military – Type Training from Hizballah, Marriage Fraud, and Making False Statements,' 11 May 2022.
Kaplan v. *Hezbollah*, 19-cv-3187 (BMC) (ST) (EDNY), 16 September 2022.
H. R. No. 558 (2021–22) 117th Cong. Urging the European Union to Designate Hizballah in Its Entirety as a Terrorist Organisation, 20 September 2022.
Department of Justice, Office of Public Affairs. 'OFAC-Designated Hezbollah Financier and Eight Associates Charged with Multiple Crimes Arising Out of Scheme to Evade Terrorism-Related Sanctions'. 18 April 2023.

Films and Documentaries

Al-Issawi, Omar, dir. *Harb Lubnan* [*The War of Lebanon*]. 2004; Beirut: Arab Film Distribution, DVD.

Lappé, Anthony, and Tony Khoury, dir. *Lebanon Wins the World Cup*. 2015; Beirut: Still See a Spark Production, Online.

Weaver, Abi, and Danille Rugo. *About a War*. 2019; Lebanon and UK: Iterations Film, Online.

Journal Articles

Abboud, Samer. 'The Siege of Nahr Al-Bared and the Palestinian Refugees in Lebanon'. *Arab Studies Quarterly*, vol. 31, no. 1/2 (2009): 31–48.

Abdul-Hussain, Hussain. 'Hezbollah: A State within a State'. *Current Trends in Islamist Ideology*, vol. 8 (2009): 68–81.

Acquaviva, Guido. 'Subjects of International Law: A Power-Based Analysis'. *Vanderbilt Journal of Transnational Law*, vol. 38, no. 2 (2005): 345–96.

Akhavan, Payam. 'The Crime of Genocide in the ICTR Jurisprudence'. *Journal of International Criminal Justice* 3, no. 4 (2005): 989–1006.

Ali, Rafid Fadhil. 'New Hezbollah Manifesto Emphasizes Political Role in a United Lebanon'. *Terrorism Monitor*, vol. 7, no. 38 (2009): 3–4.

Ambos, Kai. 'General Principles of Criminal Law in the Rome Statute'. *Criminal Law Forum*, vol. 10 (1999): 1–32.

Amet, Arnold K. 'Terrorism and International Law: Cure the Underlying Problem, Not Just the Symptom'. *Annual Survey of International and Comparative Law*, vol. 19, no. 1 (2013): 17–43.

Anfinson, Aaron. 'The Treachery of Images: Visualizing "Statehood" as a Tactic for the Legitimization of Non-State Actors'. *Terrorism and Political Violence*, vol. 23, no. 4 (2021): 720–42.

Arkin, William M. 'Divine Victory to Whom? Airpower in the 2006 Israel-Hezbollah War'. *Strategic Studies Quarterly*, vol.1, no. 2 (2007): 98–141.

Azani, Eitan. 'The Hybrid Terrorist Organisation: Hezbollah as a Case Study'. *Studies in Conflict and Terrorism*, vol. 36 (2013): 899–916.

Bachmann, Klaus, Igor Lyubashenko, Christian Garuka, Grazyna Baranowska and Vjeran Pavlakovic. 'The Puzzle of Punitive Memory Laws: New Insights into the Origins and Scope of Punitive Memory Laws'. *East European Politics and Societies and Cultures*, vol. 35, no. 4 (2020): 1–17.

Bandov, Goran, and Dorotea Ogorec. 'Crime of Aggression in International Law and International Relations'. *Journal of Liberty and International Affairs*, vol. 6, no. 1 (2020): 48–69.

Bassiouni, Mahmoud Cherif. 'The New Wars and the Crisis of Compliance with the Law of Armed Conflict by Non-State Actors'. *The Journal of Criminal Law and Criminology*, vol. 98, no. 3 (2008): 711–810.

Barak, Oren. '"Don't Mention the War?" The Politics of Remembrance and Forgetfulness in Postwar Lebanon'. *Middle East Journal*, vol. 61, no. 1 (2007): 49–70.

Bayramzadeh, Kamal. 'Non-State Actors and the Security of Small States: The Case of Hezbollah in Lebanon'. *Journal of South Asian and Middle Eastern Studies*, vol. 41, no. 1 (2017): 54–69.

Bellemare, Daniel A. 'Bringing Terrorists Before International Justice: A View from the Frontlines'. *Criminal Law Forum*, vol. 23 (2012): 425–35.

Berman, F. D. 'Statement of Mr. FD Berman'. *British Yearbook of International Law*, vol. 55 (7 December 1984): 446.

Blaik Hourani, Rida. 'A Call for Unitary History Textbook Design in Post-Conflict Era: The Case of Lebanon'. *The History Teacher*, vol. 50, no. 2 (2017): 255–84.

Blandford, Nicholas. 'The Battle for Qusayr: How the Syrian Regime and Hizb Allah Tipped the Balance'. *Combating Terrorism Center, Syria Special Issue*. vol. 6, no. 8 (2013): 18–32.

—. 'The United States-Lebanese Armed Forces Partnership: Challenges, Risks, and Rewards'. *Atlantic Council* (2018): 1–15.

Bloom, Catherine. 'The Classification of Hezbollah in Both International and Non-International Armed Conflicts'. *Annual Survey of International and Comparative Law*, vol. 14, no. 1 (2008): 61–97.

Boon, Kristen. 'The UN Security Council and Non-State Actors'. *The American Society of International Law*, vol. 113 (2019): 209–12.

Bootwala, Mazahir. 'The Iran Problem: An Evaluation of US Sanctions and Global Reactions'. *Georgetown Journal of International Affairs*, vol. 21 (2020): 136–41.

Börzel, Tanja A., and Thomas Risse. 'Dysfunctional State Institutions, Trust, and Governance in Areas of Limited Statehood'. *Regulation and Governance*, vol. 10 (2016): 149–60.

Cassel, Douglass. 'Lessons from the Americas: Guidelines for International Response to Amnesties for Atrocities'. *Law and Contemporary Problems*, vol. 59, no. 4 (1996): 197–230.

Cassese, Antonio. 'Genocide and the International Community: The Case of Sabra and Shatila'. *New Directions in Human Rights*. Edited by Ellen Lutz, Hurst Hannum and Kathryn Burke, 97–106. Philadelphia: University of Pennsylvania Press, 1989.

—. 'On Some Problematic Aspects of the Crime of Aggression'. *Leiden Journal of International Law*, vol. 20, no. 4 (2007): 841–49.

—. 'On the Use of Criminal Law Notions in Determining State Responsibility for Genocide'. *Journal of International Criminal Justice*, vol. 5, no. 4 (2007): 875–88.

Cutler, A. Claire. 'Critical Reflections on the Westphalian Assumptions of International Law and Organisation: A Crisis of Legitimacy'. *Review of International Studies*, vol. 27, no. 2 (April 2001): 133–50.

Daniels, Lesley-Ann. 'How and When Amnesty during Conflicts Affects Conflict Termination'. *Journal of Conflict Resolution*, vol. 64, no. 9 (2020): 1612–37.

Dassa Kaye, Dalia. 'The Israeli Decision to Withdraw from Southern Lebanon: Political Leadership and Security Policy'. *Political Science Quarterly*, vol. 117, no. 4 (2002–3): 561–85.

d'Aspremont, Jean, André Nollkaemper, Ilias Plakokefalos and Cedric Ryngaert. 'Sharing Responsibility between Non-State Actors and States in International Law: Introduction'. *Netherlands International Law Review*, vol. 62 (2015): 49–67.

DeVore, Marc R., and Armin B. Stähli. 'Explaining Hezbollah's Effectiveness: Internal and External Determinants of the Rise of Violent Non-State Actors'. *Terrorism and Political Violence*, vol. 27, no. 2 (2015): 331–57.

Dot-Pouillard, Nicole. 'Les armes du Hezbollah: Terrorisme, droit à la résistance et principe de légalité'. *Revue Confluences Méditerranée*, vol. 3, no. 102 (2017): 89–102.

Fachiri, Alexander P. 'The Austro-German Customs Union Case'. *British Yearbook of International Law*, vol. 13 (1932): 68–75.

Flanigan, Shawn Teresa, and Mounah Abdel-Samad. 'Hezbollah's Social Jihad: Nonprofits as Resistance Organisations'. *Middle East Policy*, vol. 16 (2009): 122–37.

Fregonese, Sara. 'Beyond the "Weak State": Hybrid Sovereignties in Beirut'. *Environment and Planning D: Society and Space*, vol. 30 (2012): 655–74.

Gasser, Peter G. 'Internationalized Non-International Armed Conflicts: Case Studies of Afghanistan, Kampuchea, and Lebanon'. *American University Law Review*, vol. 33 (1983): 145–61.

Geahchan, Sandra. 'Beyond the Failure of Justice: Lebanon's General Amnesty Law of 1991 and Access to Redress for Victims of the 1975–1990 Civil War'. *SOAS Law Journal* 6, no. 1 (2019): 17–86.

Gillet, Matthew, and Matthias Schuster. 'Fast-Track Justice: The Special Tribunal for Lebanon Defines Terrorism'. *Journal of International Criminal Justice*, vol. 9, no. 5 (2011): 989–1020.

Gutman, Yifat. 'Memory Laws: An Escalation in Minority Exclusion or a Testimony to the Limits of State Power'. *Law and Society Review*, vol. 50, no. 3 (2016): 575–607.

Harik, Judith P. 'Change and Continuity among the Lebanese Druze Community: The Civil Administration of the Mountains, 1983–1990'. *Middle Eastern Studies*, vol. 29, no. 3 (1993): 377–98.

Hassan, Fareed Mohd, Mohd Izzat Amysar Mohd Arif, Hisham Hanapi, Muhammad Syahlan bin Shafie. 'The Concept of State under International Law and Islamic Law Perspective'. *The International Journal of Business Management and Technology*, vol. 3, no. 1 (2019): 61–72.

Hohfeld, W. N., and Wesley Newcomb. 'Some Fundamental Legal Conceptions as Applied in Judicial Reasoning [Part 1]'. *The Yale Law Journal*, vol. 23, no. 1 (1913): 16–59.

Hohfeld, W. N. 'Some Fundamental Legal Conceptions as Applied in Judicial Reasoning [Part 2]'. *The Yale Law Journal*, vol. 26, no. 8 (1917): 710–70.

Huber, Daniela, and Eckart Woertz. 'Resilience, Conflict and Areas of Limited Statehood in Iraq, Lebanon and Syria'. *Democratization*, vol. 28, no. 7 (2021): 1261–79.

Huber, Max Huber. 'Award Speech in *Island of Palmas*'. Award of 4 April 1928, *Reports of International Arbitral Awards*, vol. 2 (1928): 829–71.

Janaby, Mohamad Ghazi. 'The Legal Status of Hezbollah in the Syrian Conflict: An International Humanitarian Law Perspective'. *Arizona Journal of International and Comparative Law*, vol. 33, no. 2 (2016), 383–422.

Johnson, Todd M., and Gina A. Zurlo. 'Ongoing Exodus: Tracking the Emigration of Christians from the Middle East'. *Harvard Journal of Middle Eastern Politics and Policy*, vol. 3 (2013–14): 39–49.

Jones, Zelena. 'Culture's Ties to the Land: The Belize-Guatemala Border Conflict's Implications for the Maya Communities in Light of the UN Declaration'. *Wisconsin International Law Journal*, vol. 29, no. 4 (2012): 773–806.

Kattan, Victor. 'From Beirut to Brussels: Universal Jurisdiction, Statelessness and the Sabra and Chatila Massacres'. *Yearbook of Islamic and Middle Eastern Law*, vol. 11 (2004–5): 33–82.

Kavran, Olga. 'The Special Tribunal for Lebanon and Its Outreach Programme'. *Journal of International Criminal Justice*, vol. 20 (2022): 81–96.

Khan, Akhbar, and Han Zhaoying. 'Iran-Hezbollah Alliance Reconsidered: What Contributes to the Survival of State-Proxy Alliance'. *Journal of Asian Security and International Affairs*, vol. 7, no. 1 (2020): 101–23.

Khatib, Lina. 'How Hezbollah Holds Sway Over the Lebanese State'. Research Paper in *Middle East and North Africa Program* (2021): 1–36.

Kosirnik, René. 'Les Protocoles de 1977: Une étape cruciale dans le développement du droit international humanitaire'. *Revue Internationale de la Croix Rouge* 827 (1997): 517–41.

Krasner, Stephen D., and Thomas Risse. 'External Actors, State-Building, and Service Provision in Areas of Limited Statehood: Introduction'. *Governance: An International Journal of Policy, Administration, and Institutions*, vol. 27, no. 4 (2014): 545–67.

Kurtulus, Ersun N. '"The Cedar Revolution": Lebanese Independence and the Question of Collective Self-Determination'. *Journal of Middle Eastern Studies*, vol. 36, no. 2 (August 2009): 195–214.

LaPlante, Lisa J. 'Outlawing Amnesty: The Return of Criminal Justice in Transitional Justice Schemes'. *Virginia Journal of International Law*, vol. 49, no. 4 (2009): 915–24.

Liang, Yuen-li. 'Notes on Legal Questions Concerning the United Nations Reparation for Injuries Suffered in the Service of the United Nations'. *American Journal of International Law*, vol. 43, no. 3 (1949): 460–78.

Loytomaki, Stiina. 'Law and Memory: The Politics of Victimhood'. *Griffith Law Review*, vol. 21, no. 1 (2012): 1–22.

Makary, Marc. 'Notification or Registration? Guarantees of Freedom of Association in Non-Democratic Environments: Case Studies of Lebanon and Jordan'. *The International Journal of Not-for-Profit Law*, vol. 10, no. 1 (2007), [n. p.].

Maktabi, Rania. 'The Lebanese Census of 1932 Revisited: Who are the Lebanese?' *British Journal of Middle Eastern Studies*, vol. 26, no. 2 (1999): 219–41.

Mansour, Imad. 'The State of Hezbollah? Sovereignty as a Potentiality in Global South Contexts'. *Oxford Research Encyclopedias: Politics* (2017): 1–25.

Marquis-Bissonnette, Camille. 'L'article 6(5) PAII : Quelle pertinence à l'ère du contre-terrorisme?' *Revue Québécoise de droit international*, vol. 30, no. 2 (2017): 151–69.

Mastorodimos, Konstantinos. 'National Liberation Movements: Still a Valid Concept (with Special Reference to International Humanitarian Law'. *Oregon Review of International Law*, vol. 17 (2015): 71–110.

Meier, Daniel. 'Hizbullah's Shaping Lebanon Statehood'. *Small Wars and Insurgencies*, vol. 29, no. 3 (2018): 515–36.

Nasar Chattha, Asma. 'Perspective of the Islamic Law of War on the Armed Non-State Actor's Militancy'. *Journal of Islamic Thought and Civilization*, vol. 11, no. 2 (2021): 345–60.

Nasr, Philomene. 'Dirassat Hawla Kanun al-Afu al-Aam an al-Jaraeim al-Mortakaba kabla Tareekh 28 Azar 1991 [Study of the Amnesty Law of the Crimes Committed before 28 March 1991]'. *Revue Juridique de l'USEK* 2 (1993): 63–89.

Nollkaemper, André, and Dov Jacobs. 'Shared Responsibility in International Law: A Conceptual Framework'. *Michigan Journal of International Law*, vol. 34, no. 2 (2013): 359–438.

Nora, Pierre. 'Between Memory and History: *Les Lieux de Mémoire*'. *Representations*, vol. 26 (1989): 7–24.

Norton, August Richard. 'Hizballah and the Israeli Withdrawal from Southern Lebanon'. *Journal of Palestine Studies*, vol. 30, no. 1 (2000): 22–35.

Ojah Egbai, Uti, and Jonathan O. Chimakonam. 'Protecting the Rights of Victims in Transitional Justice: An Interrogation of Amnesty'. *African Human Rights Law Journal*, vol. 19, no. 2 (2019): 608–23.

Olivier, Lalieu. 'L'invention du 'devoir de mémoire''. *Vingtième Siècle, Revue d'Histoire*, vol. 69 (2001) : 83–94.

Orakhelashvili, Alexander. 'Statehood, Recognition and the United Nations System: A Unilateral Declaration of Independence in Kosovo'. *Max Planck Yearbook of United Nations Law*, vol. 12 (2008): 1–44.

Palabi, Mustafa Serdar. 'The Emergence of the Idea of "International Law" in the Ottoman Empire before the Treaty of Paris'. *Middle Eastern Studies*, vol. 50, no. 2 (2014): 233–51.

Porat, Dan. 'The Hijacking of El Al Flight 426: The Advent of Air Terrorism'. *Journal of Contemporary History*, vol. 57, no. 4 (2022): 1072–88.

Rebeiz, Mireille. 'The Israel-Lebanon Maritime Border Agreement: Does Lebanon Implicitly Recognise the State of Israel?' *Dickinson Law Review*, vol. 128 (2023): 197–231.

Reder, Emeraude. 'Désinvestir la mémoire: Le cas d'étude du musée Beit Beirut'. *Confluences Méditerranée*, vol. 112 (2020): 193–206.

Rémond, René. 'L'Histoire et la Loi'. *Études*, vol. 4046 (2006): 763–73.

Rudolf, Beate. 'Governance without Government: Non-State Actors and International Law'. Working Paper, *American Political Science Association 2009 Annual Meeting*, Toronto, 2009.

Sanikize, Zurab. 'The Level of "Contribution" Required under Article 25(3) (D) of the Rome Statute of the International Criminal Court'. *Revue Internationale de Droit Pénal*, vol. 83, no. 1 (2012): 221–32.

Saul, Ben. 'Legislating from a Radical Hague: The United Nations Special Tribunal for Lebanon Invents an International Crime of Transnational Terrorism'. *Leiden Journal of International Law*, vol. 24 (2011): 677–700.

Schabas, William A. 'Retroactive Application of the Genocide Convention'. *University of St Thomas Journal of Law and Public Policy*, vol. 4, no. 2 (2010): 36–59.

Scharf, Michael. 'The Letter of the Law: The Scope of the International Legal Obligation to Prosecute Human Rights Crimes'. *Law and Contemporary Problems*, vol. 59 (1996): 41–62.

—. 'Earned Sovereignty: Juridical Underpinnings'. *Denver Journal of International Law and Policy*, vol. 31, no. 3 (2003): 373–85.

Schindler, Dietrich. 'The Different Types of Armed Conflicts According to the Geneva Conventions and Protocols'. *Hague Academy of International Law*, vol. 163, no. 2 (1979): 121–63.

Sheikh al-Zuhili, Wahbeh. 'Islam and International Law'. *International Review of the Red Cross*, vol. 87, no. 858 (2005): 269–82.

Shiryaev, Yaroslav. 'The Right of Armed Self-Defense in International Law and Self-Defense Arguments Used in the Second Lebanon War'. *Acta Societatis Martensis*, vol. 3 (2007/8): 80–97.

Staniland, Paul. 'States, Insurgents, and Wartime Political Orders'. *Perspectives on Politics*, vol. 10, no. 2 (2012): 243–64.

Tamimova, May. 'The Black Saturday Massacre of 1975: The Discomfort of Assembling the Lebanese Civil War Narrative'. *Contemporary Levant*, vol. 3, no. 2 (2018): 123–36.

Tams, Christian J. 'The Use of Force against Terrorists'. *European Journal of International Law*, vol. 20, no. 2 (2009): 359–98.

Värk, René. 'State Responsibility for Private Armed Groups in the Context of Terrorism'. *Juridica International*, vol. 11 (2006): 184–93.

Visoka, Gëzim. 'Statehood and Recognition in World Politics: Towards a Critical Research Agenda'. *Cooperation and Conflicts*, vol. 57, no. 2 (2021): 1–19.

Weinberg, Leonard, and Ami Pedahzur. 'Suicide Terrorism'. *Religion Compass*, vol. 4, no. 4 (2010): 234–44.

Westbrook, David A. 'Islamic International Law and Public International Law: Separate Expressions of World Order'. *Virginia Journal of International Law*, vol. 33 (1993): 819–97.

Wilhelm, René-Jean. 'Problèmes relatifs à la protection de la personne humaine par le droit international dans les conflits armés ne présentant pas un caractère international'. *Le Recueil des Cours de l'Académie de Droit International de La Haye*, vol. 137 (1972): 311–417.

Williams, Paul R., Abigail Avoryie and Carlie Armstrong. 'Earned Sovereignty Revisited: Creating a Strategic Framework for Managing Self-Determination Based Conflicts'. *ISLA Journal of International and Comparative Law*, vol. 21, no. 2 (2015): 1–27.

Yannis, Alexandros. 'The Concept of Suspended Sovereignty in International Law and Its Implications in International Politics'. *European Journal of International Law*, vol. 13, no. 5 (2002): 1037–52.

Newspaper Articles and Press Releases

By General Staff

Al-Jazeera. 'GCC Declares Lebanon's Hezbollah a "Terrorist' Group"'. 2 March 2016.

—. 'Arab League Brings Syria Back into Its Folds after 12 Years'. 7 May 2023.

—. 'Iran Warns Israel of "Obliterating War" If It Attacks Lebanon'. 29 June 2024.

Al-Monitor. 'Aoun Sees Role for Hezbollah until Threats to Lebanon Cease-Fire'. 21 September 2017.

BBC. 'Mustafa Badreddine Street Sparks Outrage in Lebanon'. 19 September 2018.

—. 'Macron Asks Rwanda to Forgive France over 1994 Genocide Role'. 27 May 2021.

—. 'Israel-Hezbollah Conflict in Maps: Ceasefire in Effect in Lebanon'. 27 November 2024.

CNN. 'Israel, Hezbollah Swap Prisoners'. 29 January 2004.

France24. 'Beirut Street Clashes Turn Deadly'. 9 May 2005.

—. 'Hezbollah Spy Released, More Prisoner Swaps Expected'. 1 June 2008.

Government Offices of Sweden. 'Sweden Recognises Palestine and Increases Aid'. 30 October 2014.

L'Orient-Le Jour. 'Les Commissions Apportent des Amendements Mineurs au Projet d'Amnistie Générale'. 23 August 1991.

—. 'Législatives au Liban: Retour sur les scrutins de 2005 et 2009'. 4 May 2018.

L'Orient Today. 'Israel to Keep Troops at Five "Strategic Points" in Lebanon beyond Tuesday'. 17 February 2025.
Middle East Monitor. 'Lebanon Files Complaint with UN Over Israel's Use of Its Airspace to Strike Syria'. 20 August 2021.
Reuters. 'Lebanon's Siniora Asks UN to Set Up Hariri Court'. 14 May 2007.
—. 'Paris accuse le Hezbollah d'avoir rompu un accord'. 23 May 2013.
—. 'Arab League Labels Hezbollah a Terrorist Organisation'. 11 March 2016.
Statement of the Foreign Minister of Japan on the Independence on the Republic of South Sudan, 9 July 2011.
Swiss Info. 'Swiss Stick to Policies of the Gulf War'. 21 February 2003.
Tasnim News Agency. 'Iran's Velayati Hails Election of Aoun as Lebanon's President'. 31 October 2016.
Tehran Times. 'Iran Congratulates Lebanon on Anniv. of Victory against Israel'. 26 May 2021.
The Arab Weekly. 'Controversy Unabated in Lebanon over Statue of Suleimani'. 12 January 2021.
The New York Times. '117 Bodies Found in Lebanese Village Recaptured from Christians'. 17 February 1984.
—. 'Lebanese Government Resigns amid Protests'. 28 February 2005.
—. 'Pro-Syrian Protests Gather in Beirut'. 8 March 2005.
The Washington Post. 'Amal Forces Push Hezbollah'. 27 November 1988.
UN News, 'General Assembly Grants Palestine Non-Member Observer State Status at the United Nations'. 29 November 2012.
US Department of State Statement. On US Relations with South Sudan. Bilateral Relations Fact Sheet. Bureau of African Affairs. 21 January 2022.
US Department of the Treasury, Press Release. 'Treasury Targets Corruption in Lebanon'. 6 November 2020.
—. 'Treasury Sanctions Oil Shipping Network Supporting IRGC-QF and Hizballah'. 3 November 2022.

By Individual Authors

Abouzeid, Rania. 'How Corruption Ruined Lebanon'. *The New York Times*, 28 October 2021.
Abouzeid, Rania, and Megan K. Stack. 'Lebanese Official Hurt in Motorcade Bombing'. *Los Angeles Times*, 13 July 2005.
Ahmado, Nisan. 'US Sanctions on Syria Leave Hezbollah More Isolated in Lebanon'. *Voxnews*, 19 July 2020.
Antonios, Zeina. 'Montagne druzo-chrétienne : Quel État ne nous force pas à partir une deuxième fois'. *L'Orient – Le Jour*, 3 August 2018.
Bassam, Laila, and Erika Solomon. 'Suicide Bombings Kill 23 Near Iran Embassy in Beirut'. *Reuters*, 19 November 2013.
Bergman, Ronen. 'Mossad Sheds New Light on Argentina Terrorist Attacks in 1990s'. *The New York Times*, 22 July 2022.

Bergman, Ronen, Aaron Boxerman, Adam Rasgon and Thomas Fuller. 'Israel Prepares for Expected Attacks by Iran and Hezbollah'. *The New York Times*, 8 August 2024.
Black, Ian, and Dan Roberts. 'Hezbollah is Helping Assad Fight Syria Uprising, Says Hassan Nasrallah'. *The Guardian*, 30 April 2013.
Boffey, Daniel. 'UK Imposes Sanctions on Art Collector Accused of Financing Hezbollah'. *The Guardian*, 18 April 2023.
Borgmann, Monika, and Lokman Slim. 'Le nouvel échec de la loi d'amnistie, signe d'un essoufflement du système Libanais'. *L'Orient-Le Jour*, 6 June 2020.
Botelho, Greg. 'Since His Hostage Years, Terry Anderson Relishes "Very, Very Good Life"'. *CNN*, 9 February 2016.
Boustany, Nora. 'Hezbollah, Syrian Forces Clash in Beirut Suburbs'. *The Washington Post*, 14 May 1988.
—. 'Amal Forces Push Hezbollah'. *The Washington Post*, 27 November 1988.
— 'Aoun Leaves Lebanon to Live in Exile'. *The Washington Post*, 30 August 1991.
Casiano, Louis. 'UN Envoy Thanks Hezbollah Terror Group, Draws Rebuke from Israeli Officials "Is This Real?"' *Foxnews*, 17 January 2023.
Chehayeb, Kareem. 'Hezbollah-Brokered Iranian Fuel Arrives in Crisis-Hit Lebanon'. *Al-Jazeera*, 16 September 2021.
Chulov, Martin. 'Lebanon's Unity Government Collapses'. *The Guardian*, 12 January 2011.
Dadouch, Sarah, and Nader Durgham. 'Hezbollah and Allies Lose Majority in Lebanon's Parliamentary Elections'. *The Washington Post*, 17 May 2022.
Dakroub, Hussein. 'Three-Month Battle Ends as Army Takes over Refugee Camp'. *The Guardian*, 3 September 2007.
de Baecque, Antoine. 'Il s'est fait traiter'. *Libération*, 15 March 2006.
de Onis, Juan. '22 Palestinians Killed in Beirut'. *The New York Times*, 14 April 1975.
E-l Deeb, Sarah. 'Lebanon Files Urgent Complaint to UN against Israel Flights'. *AP*, 12 January 2021.
El-Hage, Anne-Marie. 'Adoptés du Liban: Une association dénonce un véritable trafic d'enfants durant plus de 40 ans'. *L'Orient Le Jour* [Beirut], 22 June 2019.
Evans, Dominic. 'Hezbollah Rejects Call by UN's Ban to Disarm'. *Reuters,* 14 January 2012.
Farhat, Beatrice and Adam Lucente. 'What's behind Arab League Decision to Drop Hezbollah Terror Label?' *Al-Monitor*, 1 July 2024.
Fetini, Alyssa. 'A Brief History of Hizballah'. *Time*, 8 June 2009.
Frommer, Frederic J. 'Steve Kerr's Life Was Shaken by Gun Violence When It Took His Father'. *The Washington Post*, 25 May 2022.
Fox, Margalit. 'First Lebanon Hostage, David Dodge, Dies at 86'. *The New York Times*, 30 January 2009.

Gan, Nectar. 'Who Was Qassem Suleimani, The Iranian Commander Killed by a US Airstrike'. *CNN*, 3 January 2020.

Ghsemilee, Sara. 'Hezbollah Will "Cut off Hands" of Those Targeting Hariri Suspects'. *AlArabiyaNews*, 2 July 2011.

Goldman, Adam, and Ellen Nakashima. 'CIA and Mossad Killed Senior Hezbollah Figure in Car Bombing'. *The Washington Post*, 30 January 2015.

Halabi, Fares. 'From "Overthrowing the Regime" to "All Means All": An Analysis of the Lebanonisation of Arab Spring Rhetoric'. *Arab Reform Initiative*, 18 December 2019.

Hashem, Ali. 'Nasrallah on Syria: "The Battle is Ours"'. *Al-Monitor*, 26 May 2013.

Hayek, Caroline. 'Faire reconnaître le viol de guerre est très important pour les survivants'. *L'Orient Le Jour*, 8 March 2019.

Hof, Frederic C. 'Assad: The Shebaa Farms Are Syrian, Whatever Hezbollah Claims'. *Newlines Magazine*, 7 April 2021.

Hubbard, Ben, and Hwaida Saad. 'With Fuel from Iran, Hezbollah Steps in Where Lebanon Has Failed'. *The New York Times*. 16 September 2021, updated 15 October 2021.

Hudson, John, Yasmeen Abutaleb and Shane Harris. 'Israel's Talk on Expanding War to Lebanon Alarms US'. *The Washington Post*, 7 January 2024.

Ibrahim, Youssef M. 'PLO Proclaims Palestine to Be an Independent State; Hints at Recognising Israel'. *The New York Times*, 15 November 1988.

Irish, John. 'France Wants Hezbollah Armed Wing on EU Terror List by End-June'. *Reuters*, 23 May 2013.

Joffe, Lawrence. 'George Hawi'. *The Guardian*, 21 June 2005.

Kim, Juliana. 'The State Department Will Begin Spelling Turkey as Türkiye'. *NPR*, 8 January 2023.

Klarsfeld, Arno. 'L'histoire n'appartient pas aux historiens'. *Le Monde*, 27 January 2006.

Knox, Brady. 'Lebanon's Once-Thriving Christian Population Dwindling as Country Approaches Collapse'. *Washington Examiner*, 11 February 2023

Kourdi, Eyad. 'Syria Formally Recognises Independence of 2 Pro-Russian Separatist-Held Regions in Ukraine's Donbas'. *CNN*, 29 June 2022.

Ladki, Nadim. 'Hezbollah Cuts Islamist Rhetoric in New Manifesto'. *Reuters*, 30 November 2009.

Leopold, Evelyn. 'UN Cites Confusion over Maps of Shebaa Farms'. *Reuters*, 19 January 2007.

Lippman, Thomas W. 'Palestinians Lose Another Lebanese Refuge'. *The Washington Post*, 18 May 1977.

Lyon, Alistair. 'Disarm Hezbollah, UN Chief Tells Lebanon'. *Reuters*, 13 January 2012.

MacAskill, Ewen, Patrick Wintour, Nicholas Watt and Tania Branigan. 'West Flounders as Old Divisions Resurface'. *The Guardian*, 17 July 2006.

MacFarquhar, Neil, and Nada Bakri. 'Isolating Syria, Arab League Imposes Broad Sanctions'. *The New York Times*, 27 November 2011.
McGreal, Chris. 'Capture of Soldiers Was "Act of War" Says Israel'. *The Guardian*, 12 July 2006.
March, Katherine, and Simon Tisdall. 'Syrian Troops Shoot Dead Protesters in Day of Turmoil'. *The Guardian*, 22 April 2011.
Marion, George, and Pascale Robert-Diard. 'M. Jospin qualifie de "terroristes" les attaques du Hezbollah contre Israël'. *Le Monde*, 26 February 2000.
Markham, James M. 'US Ambassador and Aid Kidnapped and Murdered in Beirut Combat Sector'. *The New York Times*, 17 June 1976.
Mineo, Liz. 'A Day of Reckoning'. *The Harvard Gazette*, 8 October 2020.
Moskalkov, Maxim. 'Belarus Finds Itself as Accomplice in Russia's War against Ukraine'. *Voice of America*, 1 September 2022.
Mroue, Bassam, and Fay Abuelgasim. 'Lebanese Environmental Group Accused of Being Hezbollah Arm'. *The Washington Post*, 23 January 2023.
Myre, Greg, and Steven Erlanger. 'Israeli Forces Enter Lebanon after 2 Soldiers Are Seized'. *The New York Times*, 12 July 2006.
Nahas, Charbel. 'Study Warns of "Drastic Change in Lebanon's demographic fabric"'. *L'Orient Le Jour*, 11 January 2024.
Nenov, Stoyan. 'Israel Blames Iran for Bulgaria Bus Bomb that Killed Six'. *Reuters*, 18 July 2012.
Nora, Pierre. 'Lois mémorielles: Pour en finir avec ce sport législatif purement français'. *Le Monde*, 27 December 2011.
Noun, Fady. 'La réconciliation de la montagne, un Souvenir teinté d'amertume'. *L'Orient – Le Jour*, 13 November 2018.
Pawlak, Justyna, and Adrian Croft. 'EU adds Hezbollah's Military Wing to Terrorism List'. *Reuters*, 22 July 2013.
Porter, Lizzie. 'A Legacy of Torture: Inside of Lebanon's Khiam Jail'. *Al-Jazeera*, 14 August 2017.
Rafizadeh, Majid. 'In First, Hezbollah Confirms All Financial Support Comes from Iran'. *Al-Arabiya News*, 25 June 2016.
Ravid, Barak. 'Israel Told US Hezbollah Will Pay "Disproportionate Price" If Attack Hits Civilians'. *Axios*, 7 August 2024.
Rebeiz, Mireille. 'What We Choose to Remember Depends on Who Is Calling the Shots'. *PennLive*, 18 October 2021.
—. 'Veterans Like Jeff Have Stories to Tell: Americans Need to Hear Them'. *PennLive*, 2 November 2022.
—. 'Beirut Barracks Bombing of 1983: Is Justice Possible after 40 Years'. *PennLive*, 14 March 2023.
—. 'Death of Marine Commander Scarred by 1983 Beirut Bombing Serves as Reminder of Risks US Troops Stationed in the Middle East Still Face,' *The Conversation*, 22 April 2024.
—. 'Deadly Strike in the Golan Heights Risks Opening New Front in Long-Disputed Territory'. *The Conversation*, 30 July 2024.

Richburg, Keith B. 'Belgian Court Dismisses Sharon War Crimes Case'. *The Washington Post*, 27 June 2002.
Rose, Sunniva. 'Qassem Suleimani Statue Receives Warm Welcome in Suburb of Beirut'. *The National News*, 27 January 2021.
Segal, Jerome. '"Land of Three Faiths": The Little Known History of the Palestinian Declaration of Independence'. *Haaretz*, 15 November 2017.
Schneider, Howard. 'Blast Kills Ex-Commander Tied to Lebanon Massacre'. *The Washington Post*, 25 January 2002.
Shadid, Anthony, and Nora Boustany. 'Blast Kills Anti-Syrian Journalist in Lebanon'. *The Washington Post*, 3 June 2005.
Slackman, Michael. 'Car Bomb Kills Anti-Syrian Lawmaker in Beirut,' *The New York Times*, 12 December 2005.
Sly, Liz. 'In Syria, Defectors Form Dissident Army in Sign Uprising May Be Entering New Phase'. *Washington Post*, 25 September 2011.
Smith, Craig S. 'Critic of Syria Loses a Hand and a Foot, But Not Heart'. *The New York Times*, 15 April 2006.
Tarabay, Jamie. 'For Many Syrians, the Story of the War Began with Graffiti in Dara'a'. *CNN*, 15 March 2018.
Torbati, Yeganch. 'US Imposes Sanctions on Hezbollah Officials for Syria Support'. *Reuters*, 21 July 2015.
Waddell, Kaveh. 'The Desperate Search for Lebanon's Mass Graves'. *The Atlantic*, 22 April 2018.
Whitaker, Brian. 'By Unpopular Demand'. *The Guardian*, 6 September 2004.
Yacoub Oweis, Khaled. 'Assad: Syria Won't Stop Fight against "Terrorists"'. *Reuters*, 9 August 2011.
Zaatari, Mohammed. 'Has Lebanon Recognised Israel by Striking a Maritime Border Deal?' *Al-Jazeera*, 27 October 2022.

Online Sources

By Organisation

Council on Foreign Relations. 'Israel's New Counter-Terrorism Law and Terrorism in Cyberspace'. 22 August 2016. https://www.cfr.org/blog/israels-new-counter-terrorism-law-and-terrorism-cyberspace (accessed 1 May 2023).
ICRC. 'In Lebanon, Addressing Question of Missing Persons Remains a Humanitarian Priority for ICRC'. 28 August 2020. https://www.icrc.org/en/document/lebanon-addressing-question-missing-persons-remains-humanitarian-priority-icrc
—. 'ICRC Launches the Missing Persons Lebanon Community and Calls for the Swift Operationalization of the National Commission for the Missing and Forcibly Disappeared'. 30 August 2021. https://www.icrc.org/en/document/icrc-launches-missing-persons-lebanon-community-and-calls-swift-operationalization-national (accessed 28 August 2020).

Israeli Minister of Defense. ‘Fighting Terror in the Legal Arena’. 2018. https://english.mod.gov.il/About/Innovative_Strength/Pages/Fighting_Terror_in_the_Legal_Arena.aspx (accessed 1 May 2023).

LBCI. ‘A Look into Illicit Enrichment at Ministry of Displaced’. 7 December 2020. https://www.lbcgroup.tv/news/d/corruption-lbci-reports/563786/a-look-into-illicit-enrichment-at-ministry-of-disp/en (accessed 1 September 2023).

Legal Action WorldWide and UN Women. ‘Gendered Crimes during the Lebanese Civil War. Apr 13, 1975–Oct 13, 1990’. https://storymaps.arcgis.com/stories/70164462cc66465db317c63516e21168 (accessed 6 January 2022).

The International Center for Not-For-Profit Law. ‘Legislation for Non-Profit Organisations: Recognition and Protection of NGOs in International Law’. *The International Journal of Not-For-Profit Law*, vol. 2, no. 2 (1999). https://www.icnl.org/resources/research/ijnl/international-developments (accessed 22 June 2022).

The United Nations. ‘The Question of Palestine’. https://www.un.org/unispal/history/ (accessed 22 June 2022).

The United Nations. Office of Counter-Terrorism. International Legal Instruments. https://www.un.org/counterterrorism/international-legal-instruments (accessed 25 April 2023).

The World Bank Data. ‘Population, Total: Small States’. https://data.worldbank.org/indicator/SP.POP.TOTL?locations=S1-NR

—. ‘Lebanon: Poverty More than Triples over the Last Decade Reaching 44% under a Protracted Crisis’. 23 May 2024. https://www.worldbank.org/en/news/press-release/2024/05/23/lebanon-poverty-more-than-triples-over-the-last-decade-reaching-44-under-a-protracted-crisis (accessed 9 August 2024).

The World Trade Organisation. ‘Taiwan’. https://www.wto.org/english/thewto_e/whatis_e/tif_e/org6_e.htm (accessed 16 June 2022).

By Individual Authors

Badran, Tony, and Emanuelle Ottolenghi. ‘Hezbollah’s al-Qard al-Hasan and Lebanon’s Banking Sector’. *Foundation for Defense of Democracies*, 11 May 2021. https://www.fdd.org/analysis/2021/05/11/hezbollahs-al-qard-al-hasan-and-lebanons-banking-sector/ (accessed 12 October 2023).

Beate, Rudolf. ‘Governance without Government: Non-State Actors and International Law’. Working Paper, *American Political Science Association 2009 Annual Meeting*, Toronto, 2009. https://papers.ssrn.com/sol3/papers.cfm?abstract_id=1449182# (accessed 17 April 2023).

Blandford, Nicholas. ‘Twenty-Eight Years Ago Hezbollah’s Leader Was Assassinated, and Israel Paid a Price’. *Atlantic Council*, 6 January 2020. https://www.atlanticcouncil.org/blogs/iransource/twenty-eight-years-ago-hezbollahs-leader-was-assassinated-and-israel-paid-a-price/ (accessed 2 November 2022).

Carisch, Enrico, and Loraine Rickard-Martin. 'United Nations Sanctions on Iran and North Korea: An Implementation Manual'. *International Peace Institute*, 2014. https://www.ipinst.org/2014/04/united-nations-sanctions-on-iran-and-north-korea-an-implementation-manual (accessed 14 August 2024).

Crawford, James. 'Articles on Responsibility of States for Internationally Wrongful Acts'. *United Nations Audiovisual Library of International Law*, 2012. https://legal.un.org/avl/pdf/ha/rsiwa/rsiwa_e.pdf (accessed 6 April 2023).

Deeb, Lara. 'Hizballah: A Primer'. *Middle East Research and Information Project*, 31 July 2006. https://merip.org/2006/07/hizballah-a-primer/ (accessed 2 November 2022).

Grasser, Hans-Peter. 'International Humanitarian Law. An Introduction'. *Henry Dunant Institute* (1993): 1–92. https://www.icrcndresourcecentre.org/wp-content/uploads/2016/03/EnglishTotal.pdf (accessed 22 April 2023).

Hage Ali, Mohanad. 'Power Points Defining the Syria-Hezbollah Relationship'. *Malcom H. Kerr Carnegie Middle East Center*, 29 March 2019. https://carnegie-mec.org/2019/03/29/power-points-defining-syria-hezbollah-relationship-pub-78730 (accessed 1 October 2022).

Hathaway, Ooana A., Alexandra Francis, Alyssa Yamamoto, Srinath Reddy Kethireddy and Aaron Haviland. 'State Responsibility for US Support of the Saudi-led Coalition in Yemen'. *Just Security*, 25 April 2018. https://www.justsecurity.org/55367/state-responsibility-u-s-support-saudi-led-coalition-yemen/ (accessed 1 April 2023).

Henley, Alexander D. M. 'Religious Authority and Sectarianism in Lebanon'. *Carnegie Endowment for International Peace*, 16 December 2016. https://carnegieendowment.org/2016/12/16/religious-authority-and-sectarianism-in-lebanon-pub-66487#:~:text=The%20Lebanese%20state%20recognises%20eighteen,sects%3B%20and%20the%20Jewish%20community (accessed 2 November 2022).

Humud, Carla E. 'Lebanon'. *Congressional Research Service* (2017): 1–36. https://www.hsdl.org/?view&did=805912 (accessed 7 September 2022).

Jones, Seth G., and Maxwell B. Markusen. 'The Escalating Conflict with Hezbollah in Syria'. *Center for Strategic and International Studies*, 20 June 2018. https://www.csis.org/analysis/escalating-conflict-hezbollah-syria (accessed 4 October 2022).

Khatib, Lina. 'The Political and Security Fallout of the Battle in Arsal'. *Malcom H. Kerr Carnegie Middle East Center*, 14 August 2014. https://carnegie-mec.org/2014/08/16/political-and-security-fallout-of-battle-in-arsal-pub-56408 (accessed 7 September 2022).

Nerguizian, Aram. 'The Lebanese Armed Forces and Hezbollah: Military Dualism in Post-War Lebanon'. *Malcom H. Kerr Carnegie Middle East Center*, 30 October 2018. https://carnegie-mec.org/2018/10/30/lebanese-armed-forces-and-hezbollah-military-dualism-in-post-war-lebanon-pub-77598 (accessed 18 August 2022).

Ortega, Aurora. 'Hezbollah in Colombia: Past and Present Modus Operandi and the Need for Greater Scrutiny'. *The Washington Institute for Near East Policy*, 28 March 2022. https://www.washingtoninstitute.org/policy-analysis/hezbollah-colombia-past-and-present-modus-operandi-and-need-greater-scrutiny (accessed 4 January 2023).

Pan, Esther. 'Lebanon: Elections Results'. *Council on Foreign Relations*, 21 June 2005. https://www.cfr.org/backgrounder/lebanon-election-results (accessed 14 August 2022).

Ray, Rashawan, and Alexandra Gibbons. 'Why Are States Banning Critical Race Theory'. *Brookings*, November 2021. https://www.brookings.edu/blog/fixgov/2021/07/02/why-are-states-banning-critical-race-theory/ (accessed 17 January 2023).

Riedel, Bruce. 'Beirut 1958: How America's Wars in the Middle East Began'. *Brookings*, 29 October 2019. https://www.brookings.edu/blog/order-from-chaos/2019/10/29/beirut-1958-americas-origin-story-in-the-middle-east/ (accessed 20 November 2022).

Stork, Joe. 'The War of the Camps, the War of the Hostages'. *Middle East Research and Information Project: Critical Coverage of the Middle East since 1971*, June 1985. https://merip.org/1985/06/the-war-of-the-camps-the-war-of-the-hostages/ (accessed 5 November 2022).

Tokmajyan, Armenak, and Kheder Khaddour. 'Border Nation: The Reshaping of the Syrian-Turkish Borderlands'. *Malcom H. Kerr Carnegie Middle East Center*, 30 March 2022. https://carnegie-mec.org/2022/03/30/border-nation-reshaping-of-syrian-turkish-borderlands-pub-86758 (accessed 1 October 2022).

Verbruggen, Yola. 'The Israel-Hamas Conflict'. *International Bar Association*, 30 November 2023. https://www.ibanet.org/The-Israel-Hamas-conflict (accessed 30 January 2024).

Wählisch, Martin. 'Liberation and Resistance Movements'. *Oxford Bibliographies*, 2019. https://www.oxfordbibliographies.com/display/document/obo-9780199796953/obo-9780199796953-0186.xml (accessed 18 April 2023).

Wilmshurst, Elizabeth. 'Definition of Aggression: General Assembly Resolution 3314 (XXIX)'. *Audiovisual Library of International Law*, 14 December 1974. https://legal.un.org/avl/ha/da/da.html (accessed 11 April 2023).

Young, Michael. 'Leaving Hezbollah Hanging,' *Malcom H. Kerr Carnegie Middle East Center*, 13 April 2021. https://carnegie-mec.org/diwan/84303 (accessed 17 August 2022).

Reports

Amnesty International. 'Extrajudicial Executions, Lebanon: Over 30 People Captured and Executed by Syrian Forces'. 21 October 1990. https://www.amnesty.org/en/documents/mde18/001/1991/en/ (accessed 16 November 2022).

—. 'Israel/Lebanon: Unlawful Killings during Operation "Grapes of Wrath"'. 23 July 1996, https://www.amnesty.org/en/documents/mde15/042/1996/en/. (accessed 17 January 2023).
—. 'Report on Lebanon: Human Rights Developments and Violations'. 8 October 1997. https://www.amnesty.org/en/documents/mde18/019/1997/en/ (accessed 14 August 2024).
—. 'Lebanon Protests Explained'. 22 September 2020. https://www.amnesty.org/en/latest/news/2019/11/lebanon-protests-explained/ (accessed 20 August 2022).
Central Intelligence Agency. 'Heroes: William Buckley'. https://www.cia.gov/legacy/honoring-heroes/heroes/william-f-buckley/ (accessed 5 November 2022).
European Education and Culture Executive Agency. 'Europe for Citizens Programme in 2014–2020'. https://www.eacea.ec.europa.eu/grants/2014-2020/europe-citizens_en#:~:text=The%20aim%20of%20the%20Europe,and%20engagement%20at%20EU%20level (accessed 6 January 2023).
Issam Fares Institute for Public Policy and International Affairs. 'Report of the Focus Group with Stakeholders in the Middle East'. Menara Working Document, 6 May 2019. file:///C:/Users/mgreb/Downloads/menara_wd_6.pdf (accessed 21 August 2022).
Human Rights Watch (HRW). 'Israel/Lebanon – "Operation Grapes of Wrath" – The Civilian Victims', vol. 9, no. 8 (1997). https://www.hrw.org/legacy/summaries/s.israel-lebanon979.html (accessed 17 January 2023).
—. 'World Report: Syria and Syrian-Controlled Lebanon – 1992'. https://www.hrw.org/reports/1992/WR92/MEW2-03.htm (accessed 22 December 2021).
—. 'How Does Law Protect. Israel/Lebanon/Hezbollah Conflict in 2006'. *Casebook ICRC*, 2007. https://casebook.icrc.org/case-study/israellebanonhezbollah-conflict-2006 (accessed 9 September 2022).
International Center for Transitional Justice. 'Lebanon's Legacy of Political Violence: A Mapping of Serious Violations of International Human Rights and Humanitarian Law in Lebanon, 1975–2008' (September 2013): 1–135. https://www.ictj.org/publication/lebanon-legacy-political-violence
—. 'Lebanon: Failing to Deal with the Past: What Cost to Lebanon?' (January 2014): 1–47. https://www.ictj.org/publication/failing-deal-past-what-cost-lebanon (accessed 4 November 2022).
—. 'How People Talk about the Lebanon Wars: A Study of the Perceptions and Expectations of Residents in Greater Beirut' (October 2014): 1–54.
International Committee of the Red Cross. 'Syria: ICRC and Syrian Arab Red Crescent Maintain Aid Effort amid Increased Fighting'. 17 July 2012. https://www.icrc.org/en/doc/resources/documents/update/2012/syria-update-2012-07-17.htm (accessed 1 October 2022).
—. Advisory Service on International Humanitarian Law. 'Amnesties and International Humanitarian Law: Purpose and Scope'. *International Review of the Red Cross: Memory and War*, vol. 101, no. 1 (2019):

357–63. https://international-review.icrc.org/sites/default/files/reviews-pdf/2019-12/irrc_101_910_18.pdf (accessed 28 December 2021).
—. 'Treaties, States Parties and Commentaries'. https://ihl-databases.icrc.org/applic/ihl/ihl.nsf/vwTreatiesByCountrySelected.xsp?xp_countrySelected=LB (accessed 4 January 2022).
—. 'ICRC Engagement with Non-State Armed Groups: Why, How, for What Purpose, and Other Salient Issues'. Position Paper, 2 March 2021. file:///C:/Users/mgreb/Downloads/icrc_engagement_with_non-state_armed_groups_position_paper.pdf (accessed 6 August 2024).
International Law Association. Non-State Actors, Working Session Report of 9 August 2016, Johannesburg. https://www.ila-hq.org/en_GB/documents/working-session-report-johannesburg-2016-5 (accessed 18 April 2023).
International Law Commission. 'Responsibility of States for Internationally Wrongful Acts', vol. II (Part Two), 2001.
—. 'Report on the Work of Its Fifty-Third Session' (23 April–1 June and 2 July–10 August 2001). General Assembly, Official Records, Fifty-Fifth Session, Supplement No. 10 (1/56/10). https://casebook.icrc.org/case-study/international-law-commission-articles-state-responsibility (accessed 7 April 2023).
La Commission de Recherche sur les Archives Françaises Relatives au Rwanda et au Génocide des Tutsi: La France, le Rwanda et le génocide des Tutsi (1990–1994). Rapport remis au Président de la République le 26 mars 2021. https://medias.vie-publique.fr/data_storage_s3/rapport/pdf/279186.pdf (accessed 1 April 2023).
Levy Firestone Muse. A Foreseeable Genocide: The Role of the French Government in Connection with Genocide against the Tutsi in Rwanda, 19 April 2021. https://www.gov.rw/fileadmin/user_upload/gov_user_upload/2021.04.19_MUSE_REPORT.pdf (accessed 1 April 2023).
Special Tribunal for Lebanon. 13th Annual Report (2021–22): 1–28. https://www.stl-tsl.org/sites/default/files/documents/annual-reports/STL_13th_Annual_Report.pdf (accessed 3 May 2023).
—. 14th Annual Report (2022–23): 1–18. https://www.stl-tsl.org/sites/default/files/documents/annual-reports/STL_Annual_Report_2022-2023.pdf (accessed 3 May 2023).
United States Department of State. Office of International Religious Freedom. 'International Religious Freedom Report for 2019: Lebanon' (2019): 1–15. https://www.state.gov/reports/2019-report-on-international-religious-freedom/lebanon/ (accessed 2 November 2022).
Wairimu Nderitu, Alice. 'Combatting Holocaust and Genocide Denial, Protecting Survivors, Preserving Memories, and Promoting Prevention: Policy Paper'. *The UN Office on Genocide Prevention in Collaboration with the Jacob Blaustein Institute for the Advancement of Human Rights* (June 2022): 1–11. https://www.un.org/en/genocideprevention/documents/publications-and-resources/22-00041_OSAPG_PolicyPaper_Final.pdf (accessed 7 January 2023).

Treaties and Agreements

International Treaties (in Chronological Order)

Treaty of Westphalia, Münster, 24 October 1648.
Treaty of Paris, Paris, 30 March 1856.
Montevideo Convention on the Rights and Duties of States, Montevideo, 26 December 1933.
Charter of the United Nations, San Francisco, 26 June 1945.
Universal Declaration of Human Rights, Paris, 10 December 1948.
Convention on the Prevention and Punishment of the Crime of Genocide, Paris, 9 December 1948.
Convention (I) for the Amelioration of the Condition of the Wounded and Sick in Armed Forces in the Field, Geneva, 12 August 1949.
Convention (II) for the Amelioration of the Condition of Wounded, Sick and Shipwrecked Members of Armed Forces at Sea, Geneva, 12 August 1949.
Convention (III) Relative to the Treatment of Prisoners of War, Geneva, 12 August 1949.
Convention (IV) Relative to the Protection of Civilian Persons in Time of War, Geneva, 12 August 1949.
Convention on Offences and Certain Other Acts Committed on Board Aircraft, Tokyo, 14 September 1963.
The International Covenant on Civil and Political Rights, New York, 16 December 1966.
The International Covenant on Economic, Social and Cultural Rights, New York, 16 December 1966.
Convention on the Non-Applicability of Statutory Limitations to War Crimes and Crimes against Humanity, New York, 26 November 1968.
Vienna Convention on the Law of Treaties, Vienna, 23 May 1969.
Declaration on Principles of International Law concerning Friendly Relations and Cooperation among States in Accordance with the Charter of the United Nations, New York, 24 October 1970.
Convention for the Suppression of Unlawful Seizure of Aircraft, The Hague, 16 December 1970.
Convention for the Suppression of Unlawful Acts against the Safety of Civil Aviation (with Final Act of the International Conference on Air Law held under the auspices of the International Civil Aviation Organisation at Montreal in September 1971), Montreal, 23 September 1971.
Convention on the Prevention and Punishment of Crimes against Internationally Protected Persons, Including Diplomatic Agents, New York, 14 December 1973.
Protocol Additional to the Geneva Conventions of 12 August 1949, and Relating to the Protection of Victims of International Armed Conflicts (Protocol I), Geneva, 8 June 1977.
Protocol Additional to the Geneva Conventions of 12 August 1949, and Relating to the Protection of Victims of Non-International Armed Conflicts (Protocol II), Geneva, 8 June 1977.

Convention on the Physical Protection of Nuclear Material, Vienna, 26 October 1979.
International Convention against Taking of Hostages, New York, 17 December 1979.
Convention against Torture and Other Cruel, Inhuman or Degrading Treatment or Punishment, New York, 10 December 1984.
Convention for the Suppression of Unlawful Acts against the Safety of Maritime Navigation, Rome, 10 March 1988.
Supplementary Protocol for the Suppression of Unlawful Acts Against the Safety of Fixed Platforms Located on the Continental Shelf, Rome, 10 March 1988.
Declaration on the Protection of all Persons from Enforced Disappearance, New York, 18 December 1992.
International Convention for the Suppression of Terrorist Bombings, New York, 12 January 1998.
Rome Statute of the International Criminal Court, Rome, 17 July 1998.
International Convention for the Suppression of the Financing of Terrorism, New York, 10 January 2000.
The Organisation of American States, The Inter-American Convention Against Terrorism, Bridgetown, 3 July 2002.
Amendment to the Convention on the Physical Protection of Nuclear Material, Vienna, 8 July 2005.
International Convention for the Suppression of Acts of Nuclear Terrorism, New York, 14 September 2005.
Protocol to the Convention for the Suppression of Unlawful Acts against the Safety of Maritime Navigation, London, 14 October 2005.
Protocol Additional to the Geneva Conventions of 12 August 1949, and Relating to the Adoption of an Additional Distinctive Emblem (Protocol III), Geneva, 8 December 2005.
International Convention for the Protection of All Persons from Enforced Disappearance, New York, 20 December 2006.
Convention on the Suppression of Unlawful Acts Relating to International Civil Aviation, Beijing, 10 September 2010.
Protocol Supplementary to the Convention for the Suppression of Unlawful Seizure of Aircraft, Beijing, 10 September 2010.

Regional Treaties and Agreements

Treaty of Peace between The Republic of China and Japan (Treaty of Taipei), Taipei, 28 April 1952.
The Universal Islamic Declaration of Human Rights, adopted by the Islamic Council of Europe on 19 September 1981. University of Minnesota, Human Rights Library.
The Inter-American Convention on Forced Disappearance of Persons, Belem do Para, 9 June 1994.

League of Arab States, The Arab Convention for the Suppression of Terrorism, Article 2, Cairo, April 1998. Translated from Arabic by the United Nations English Translation Service, 29 May 2000.

Organisation of Islamic Cooperation, Convention of the Organisation of the Islamic Conference on Combatting International Terrorism, Article 1(2), Ouagadougou, 1 July 1999.

The Organisation of African Unity Convention on the Prevention and Combating of Terrorism, Article 1(3), Algiers, 14 July 1999.

The Arab Charter of Human Rights, 2004. Original text is available in Arabic. The Translation was provided by the League of Arab States to the United Nations Office of the High Commissioner of Human Rights.

Israel-Lebanon Maritime Border Agreement, 12 October 2022, *Haaretz*, 12 October 2022.

European Union Legal Documents

Council of Europe, European Convention on Extradition, Paris, 13 November 1957.

Council of Europe, Additional Protocol to the European Convention on Extradition, Strasbourg, 15 October 1975.

Council of Europe, European Convention on the Suppression of Terrorism, Strasbourg, 27 January 1977.

Sidiropoulos and Others v. *Greece*, Judgment No. 57/1997/841/1047, ECtHR, 10 July 1998.

Council of Europe, Protocol Amending the European Convention on the Suppression of Terrorism, Strasbourg, 15 May 2003.

Council of Europe, Convention on the Prevention of Terrorism, Warsaw, 16 May 2005.

Council of Europe, Convention on Laundering, Search, Seizure and Confiscation of the Proceeds from Crime and on the Financing of Terrorism, Warsaw, 16 May 2005.

Decision No 1904/2006/EC of the European Parliament and of the Council of 12 December 2006 establishing for the period 2007 to 2013 the programme Europe for Citizens to promote active European citizenship, L378/32, 2006.

Council Regulation 442/2011 of 9 May 2011, Concerning Restrictive Measures in View of the Situation in Syria. *Official Journal of the European Union* (L121).

Cyprus v. *Turkey*, Application No. 25781/91, ECtHR, 10 May 2011, repr. 120 *International Law Reports*.

2013/C 355 E/01, 5 December 2013, Official Journal of the European Union, European Parliament, Written Questions with Answer, Written Questions by Members of the European Parliament and Their Answers Given by a European Union Institution.

Council of Europe, Additional Protocol to the Council of Europe Convention on the Prevention of Terrorism, Riga, 22 October 2015.

Council Implementing Regulation (EU) 2022/147 of 3 February 2022 implementing Article 2(3) of Regulation (EC) No. 2580/2001 on specific restrictive measures directed against certain persons and entities with a view to combating terrorism, and repealing Implementing Regulation (EU) 2021/1188, *Official Journal of the European Union*, vol. 65, 4 February 2022, 23.

EU, 2023/2742(RSP), 12 July 2023.

United Nations Documents

General Assembly

Gen. Ass. Res. 3314 (XXIX) of 14 December 1974.

A/RES/37/123 (1982), The Situation in the Middle East, 16 December 1982.

Gen. Ass. Res. 40/61 of 9 December 1985.

A/RES/43/160 [A] (1988), Observer Status of National Liberal Movements Recognised by the Organisation of African Unity and/or the League of Arab States, 9 December 1988.

A/RES/44/29 (1989), Measures to Prevent International Terrorism which endangers or takes innocent human lives or jeopardises fundamental freedoms and study of the underlying causes of those forms of terrorism and acts of violence which lie in misery, frustration, grievance and despair and which cause some people to sacrifice human lives, including their own, in an attempt to effect radical changes, 4 December 1989.

A/RES/46/51 (1991), Measures to Eliminate International Terrorism, 9 December 1991.

A/RES/49/60 (1995), Measures to Eliminate International Terrorism, 17 February 1995.

A/RES/51/2010 (1997), Measures to Eliminate International Terrorism, 16 January 1997.

A/C.6/55/1 (2000), Draft Comprehensive Convention on International Terrorism, Working Document Submitted by India, New York, 28 August 2000.

Gen. Ass. Res 56/83 of 12 December 2001, corrected by document A/56/49 (Vol. I) Corr.4.

A/RES/60/288 (2006), The United Nations Global Counter-Terrorism Strategy, 20 September 2006.

A/68/69 (2013), 27 March 2013, Responsibility of States for Internationally Wrongful Acts, Comments and information received from Governments, Report of the Secretary-General.

A/RES/72/284 (2018), The United Nations Global Counter-Terrorism Strategy, 2 July 2018.

A/ES-10/L.30/Rev.1 (2024) Illegal Israeli actions in Occupied East Jerusalem and the rest of the Occupied Palestinian Territory, 10 May 2024.

Security Council (in Chronological Order)

SC/7143 (2001), 12 September 2001.
S/Res/1368 (2001), 12 September 2001.
S/RES/1371 (2001), 28 September 2001.
S/RES/1377 (2001), 12 November 2001.
S/RES/1540 (2004), 28 April 2004.
Report of the Secretary-General, 'The Rule of Law and Transitional Justice in Conflict and Post-Conflict Societies', 23 August 2004, S/2004/616.
S/RES/1559 (2004), 2 September 2004.
S/RES/1566 (2004), 8 October 2004.
S/RES/1583 (2005), 28 January 2005.
S/RES/1701 (2006), 11 August 2006.
S/RES/1757 (2007), 30 May 2007.
S/2008/392 (2008), 10 June 2008. Letter dated 22 May 2008 from the Permanent Observer of the League of Arab States to the United Nations addressed to the President of the Security Council.
UN Security Council, S/RES/1929 (2010), 9 June 2010.
SC Pres. Statement 2011/16, 3 August 2011.
S/RES/2133 (2014), 27 January 2014.
S/RES/2170 (2014), 15 August 2014.
UN Security Council, S/RES/2231 (2015), 20 July 2015.
S/RES/2242 (2015), 13 October 2015.
S/RES/2249 (2015), 11 November 2015.
S/RES/2255 (2015), 12 December 2015.
S/RES/2253 (2015), 17 December 2015.
S/RES/2322 (2016), 12 December 2016.
S/RES/2325 (2016), 15 December 2016.
S/RES/2368 (2017), 20 July 2017.
S/RES/2395 (2017), 21 December 2017.
S/RES/2396 (2017), 22 December 2017.
S/RES/2427 (2018), 9 July 2018.
S/RES/2459 (2019), 15 March 2019.
S/RES/15670 (2024), 18 April 2024.

Reports and Decisions

Office of the United Nations High Commissioner on Human Rights

OHCHR. A/HRC/RES/S-2/1, 11 August 2006.
OHCHR. 'Rule-of-Law Tools for Post-Conflict States: Amnesties'. *United Nations Publication* (2009), 1–56.
OHCHR. 'International Legal Protection of Human Rights in Armed Conflict'. New York and Geneva, 2011.
OHCHR. 'UN Experts Call for International Investigation into 2020 Beirut Explosion'. August 2022.

United Nations Council of Human Rights

Human Rights Council. 'Mission to Lebanon and Israel (7–14 September 2006)'. UN Doc. Mission to Lebanon and Israel. A/HRC/2/7, 2 October 2006.

Human Rights Council. 'Report of the Commission of Inquiry on Lebanon Pursuant to Human Rights Council Resolution S-2/I, UN Doc. A/HRC/3/2', 23 November 2006.

Human Rights Council. 'Rep. of the Independent International Commission of Inquiry on the Syrian Arabic Republic', UN Doc. A/HRC/S-17/2/Add.1, 23 November 2011.

Human Rights Council. 'Report on the Civilians Deaths in the Syrian Arab Republic'. A/HRC/50/68, 13 June–8 July 2022.

United Nations Committee on Human Rights

Human Rights Committee. CCPR/C/77/D/886/1999. *Schedko* v. *Belarus* (886/1999), 28 April 2003.

Human Rights Committee. 'Report of the intersessional open-ended working group to elaborate a draft legally binding normative instrument for the protection of all persons from enforced disappearance', 23 February 2004, E/CN.4/2004/59.

Other

United Nations Conference on International Organisation, Amendments and Observations on the Dumbarton Oaks Proposal, 4 May 1945, UNIO, Doc. 2, G/7.

UN Sub-Commission on the Prevention of Discrimination and Protection of Minorities, 'Study on Amnesty Laws and Their Role in the Safeguard and Promotion of Human Rights', in *Preliminary Report by Special Rapporteur Mr Louis Joinet*, 21 June 1985, UN Doc E/CN.4/Sub.2/1985/16.

UN Peacemaker. 'Taif Accords', 22 October 1989.

Mr X v. *Australia*, The Committee Against Torture, 30 April 2009 CAT/C/42/D/324/2007.

The UN Refugee Agency (UNHCR). *Lebanon at a Glance*, 2024. https://www.unhcr.org/lb/at-a-glance (accessed 9 August 2024).

Index